P9-CMO-272

7-01

Chicago Public Library

REFERENCE

Form 178 rev. 1-94

SOUTH CHICAGO BRANCH
9055 S. HOUSTON AVE.
CHICAGO, ILLINOIS 60617

BODY BY DESIGN

*From the
Digestive
System to
the Skeleton*

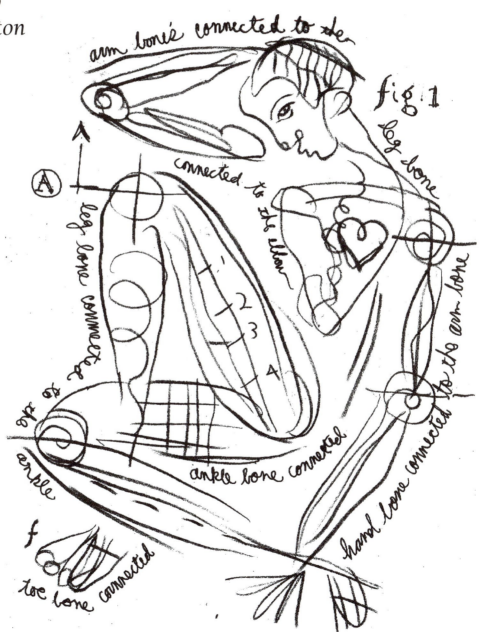

BODY BY DESIGN

*From the
Digestive
System to
the Skeleton*

volume

2

**nervous system
reproductive system
respiratory system
skeletal system
urinary system
special senses**

Rob Nagel • **Betz Des Chenes, Editor**

AN IMPRINT OF THE GALE GROUP

DETROIT · SAN FRANCISCO · LONDON
BOSTON · WOODBRIDGE, CT

Body by Design
From the Digestive System to the Skeleton

Rob Nagel

STAFF

Elizabeth A. Des Chenes, *U•X•L Senior Editor*
Thomas L. Romig, *U•X•L Publisher*

Margaret A. Chamberlain, *Permissions Specialist (Pictures)*

Rita Wimberley, *Senior Buyer*
Evi Seoud, *Assistant Production Manager*
Dorothy Maki, *Manufacturing Manager*
Mary Beth Trimper, *Production Director*

Michelle Di Mercurio, *Senior Art Director*
Cynthia Baldwin, *Product Design Manager*

GGS Information Services, Inc., *Typesetting*

Cover illustration by Kevin Ewing Illustrations.

Library of Congress Cataloging-in-Publication Data.
Nagel, Rob.
     Body by Design: from the digestive system to the skeleton/Rob Nagel.
          p. cm.
     Includes bibliographical references and index.
Contents: v. 1. The cardiovascular system. The digestive system.
The endocrine system. The integumentary system. The lymphatic
system. The muscular system. v.2. The nervous system. The
reproductive system. The respiratory system. The skeletal system.
The urinary system. The special senses.
     ISBN 0-7876-3897-8 (set). -ISBN 0-7876-3898-6 (v.1). -ISBN 0-7876-3899-4 (v.2.)
     1. Human physiology Juvenile literature. [1. Body. Human. 1.
Human physiology. 3. Human anatomy.] I. Title.
QP36.N33 1999
612-dc21   99-14642

This publication is a creative work fully protected by all applicable copyright laws, as well as by misappropriation, trade secret, unfair competition, and other applicable laws. The editors of this work have added value to the underlying factual material herein through one or more of the following: unique and original selection, coordination, expression, arrangement, and classification of the information. All rights to this publication will be vigorously defended.

Copyright © 2000 U•X•L, an imprint of the Gale Group
All rights reserved, including the right of reproduction in whole or in part in any form.

Printed in United States of America
10 9 8 7 6 5 4 3 2

R01918 40800

To the memory of
Michael D. Merker
(1961–1999)

SOUTH CHICAGO BRANCH
9055 S. HOUSTON AVE.
CHICAGO, ILLINOIS 60617

Contents

Reader's Guide

Body by Design: From the Digestive System to the Skeleton presents the anatomy (structure) and physiology (function) of the human body in twelve chapters spread over two volumes. Each chapter is devoted to one of the eleven organ systems that make up the body. The last chapter focuses on the special senses, which allow humans to connect with the real world.

Each chapter begins with a paragraph overview of that particular organ system (or the special senses) and its function or role in the body. The remaining information in the chapter is broken into four sections, each labeled by a particular subhead:

- The material under the subhead **Design** comprises the anatomy section of each chapter. It is a detailed presentation of the organs and any associated structures that compose that particular organ system or the special senses. Weight, size, color, position, and composition of the organs and their structures are given, where applicable, in this section.

- The material under the subhead **Workings** comprises the physiology section of each chapter. It is a step-by-step exploration of the functions of the organs and any associated structures that compose that particular organ system or the special senses. The mechanics of muscle contraction, the transmission of nerve impulses, the actions of swallowing and breathing, and numerous other physiological processes are all examined in depth in this section.

- The material under the subhead **Ailments** is a presentation of some of the many diseases and disorders that can target the organs or associated structures in that particular organ system or the special senses. Most of the ailments presented are well known, but a few are not. For each ailment, the number of people generally affected, causes, symptoms, and treatments are all covered.

- The material under the subhead **Taking care** is a presentation of ways an individual can keep a particular system healthy. Because of the connectedness of the organ systems, forming the human body as a whole, steps to keep a system healthy are often steps to keep the body healthy. Many of these steps are general (some would say common sense) approaches.

Each chapter also contains illustrations or photos (many in color) of the particular organs and any associated structures. Where applicable, photos depicting specific ailments have also been included. Historical discoveries, recent medical advances, short biographies of scientists, and other interesting facts relating to that particular system are presented in sidebar boxes sprinkled throughout each chapter.

A "Words to Know" box included at the beginning of each chapter provides pronunciations and definitions of words and terms used in that chapter. Another "Words to Know" box later in each chapter is devoted to system ailments. At the end of each chapter, under the heading "For More Information," appears a list of books and annotated web sites that provide students with further information about that particular system.

Each volume of *Body by Design* includes an overview essay, "How Systems and Other Structures Form the Living Body," followed by a comprehensive glossary collected from all the "Words to Know" boxes in the twelve chapters.

Each volume ends with a general bibliography section. The offerings in this section, twenty books and fifteen annotated web sites, are not system specific, but explore the human body as a whole. A cumulative index providing access to all major terms and topics covered throughout *Body by Design* concludes each volume.

Related Reference Sources

Body by Design is only one component of the three-part U•X•L Complete Health Resource. Other titles in this library include:

- *Sick! Diseases and Disorders, Injuries and Infections:* This four-volume set contains 140 alphabetically arranged entries on diseases, disorders, and injuries, including information on their causes, symptoms, diagnoses, tests and treatments, and prognoses. Each entry, four to seven pages long, includes sidebars on related people and topics, as well as a list of sources for further research. Each volume contains a 16-page color insert. *Sick* also features more than 240 black-and-white photographs and a cumulative subject index.

- *Healthy Living:* This three-volume set examines fitness, nutrition, and other lifestyle issues across fifteen subject chapters. Topics covered include hygiene, mental health, preventive care, alternative medicine, and careers in health care. Sidebar boxes within entries provide information on related issues, while over 150 black-and-white illustrations help illuminate the text. *Healthy Living* also features a cumulative index.

Acknowledgments

A note of appreciation is extended to the *Body by Design* advisors, who provided invaluable suggestions when this work was in its formative stages:

Carole Branson
Seminar Science Teacher
Wilson Middle School
San Diego, California

Bonnie L. Raasch
Media Specialist
Vernon Middle School
Marion, Iowa

Doris J. Ranke
Science Teacher
West Bloomfield High School
West Bloomfield, Michigan

I would like to express my deep appreciation to occupational therapist Diane Collins for her close reading of the material and her insightful comments and suggestions.

Thanks are also extended to Tom Romig, U•X•L Publisher, for giving me words of encouragement at a crucial point during the project. Finally, my debts on this project are great, but none is greater than to my editor, Elizabeth Des Chenes. Without her unflagging support and guidance, this work would not have come to fruition. It has been a collaborative effort, and I proudly share the cover with her.

Comments and Suggestions

We welcome your comments on *Body by Design: From the Digestive System to the Skeleton.* Please write: Editors, *Body by Design,* U•X•L, 27500 Drake Rd., Farmington Hills, Michigan, 48331–3535; call toll free: 1–800–877–4253; fax: 248–414–5043; or send e-mail via http://www.galegroup.com.

Please Read: Important Information

Body by Design is a medical reference product designed to inform and educate readers about the human body. U•X•L believes this product to be comprehensive, but not necessarily definitive. While U•X•L has made substantial efforts to provide information that is accurate and up to date, U•X•L makes no representations or warranties of any kind, including without limitation, warranties of merchantability or fitness for a particular purpose, nor does it guarantee the accuracy, comprehensiveness, or timeliness of the information contained in this product.

Readers should be aware that the universe of medical knowledge is constantly growing and changing, and that differences of medical opinion exist among authorities. They are also advised to seek professional diagnosis and treatment for any medical condition, and to discuss information obtained from this book with their health care provider.

Overview: How Systems and Other Structures Form the Living Body

The human body is composed of eleven organ systems. An organ is any part of the body formed of two or more tissues that performs a specialized function. Examples of organs are the brain, heart, kidneys, liver, lungs, and stomach. An organ system is a group of organs whose combined workings contribute to a particular function for the body as a whole.

All systems have important functions they alone perform. The cardiovascular system—composed of the heart, blood, and blood vessels—transports nutrients, dissolved gases, and hormones to cells throughout the body. No other system in the body carries out this vital work.

But the cardiovascular system, like all other systems, cannot function alone. Indeed, to perform its work, it must interact with other systems. The red blood cells in the blood it transports are formed in the red bone marrow of certain bones (skeletal system). The nutrients it carries come from the breakdown of food by the organs of the digestive system. Oxygen and carbon dioxide, the dissolved gases that pass between the blood and cells of the body, are exchanged with the surrounding air through the work of the lungs and the passageways that carry air to them (respiratory system). Hormones, chemical messengers that maintain and regulate basic bodily functions, are produced by the glands of the endocrine system.

Although all organ systems are connected, certain systems combine with certain others to produce specific actions. The cardiovascular and lymphatic systems transport fluids through the body and provide defense against diseases and foreign substances. The nervous and endocrine systems regulate and coordinate the body's internal operations. The integumentary, muscular, and skeletal systems provide body support and movement. The digestive, respiratory, and urinary systems interact with the outside environment, exchanging material.

Overview

The human body is a well-designed and well-built machine. When its perfectly fitting parts are operating normally, the body runs smoothly and efficiently. When any part breaks down, however, so does the body. Indeed, the loss of just one system would result in death. All organ systems are necessary for survival. Thus, it is of vital importance to keep the body systems healthy, since all the systems work together.

Words to Know

Accommodation (ah-kah-mah-DAY-shun): Process of changing the shape of the lens of the eye to keep an image focused on the retina.

Acetylcholine (ah-see-til-KOE-leen): Neurotransmitter chemical released at the neuromuscular junction by motor nerves that translates messages from the brain to muscle fibers.

Acne (AK-nee): Disorder in which hair follicles of the skin become clogged and infected, often forming pimples as a result.

Acromegaly (ak-ro-MEG-ah-lee): Disorder in which the anterior pituitary overproduces growth hormone, resulting in abnormal enlargement of the extremities—nose, jaw, fingers, and toes; in children, the disorder produces gigantism.

Addison's disease (ADD-i-sonz): Disorder in which the adrenal cortex underproduces cortisol and aldosterone, resulting in the disruption of numerous bodily functions.

Adenosine triphosphate (ah-DEN-o-seen try-FOS-fate): High-energy molecule found in every cell in the body.

Adrenal cortex (ah-DREE-nul KOR-tex): Outer layer of the adrenal glands, which secretes cortisol and aldosterone.

Adrenal glands (ah-DREE-nul): Glands located on top of each kidney consisting of an outer layer (adrenal cortex) and an inner layer (adrenal medulla).

Adrenal medulla (ah-DREE-nul muh-DUH-luh): Inner layer of the adrenal glands, which secretes epinephrine and norepinephrine.

Adrenocorticotropic hormone (ah-dree-no-kor-ti-koh-TROH-pik): Hormone secreted by the anterior pituitary that stimulates the adrenal cortex to secrete cortisol.

Aerobic metabolism (air-ROH-bic muh-TAB-uh-lizm): Chemical reactions that require oxygen in order to create adenosine triphosphate.

Agglutination (ah-glue-ti-NA-shun): Clumping of blood cells brought about by the mixing of blood types.

AIDS: Acquired immune deficiency syndrome, a disorder caused by a virus (HIV) that infects helper T cells and weakens immune responses.

Aldosterone (al-DOS-te-rone): Hormone secreted by the adrenal cortex that controls the salt and water balance in the body.

Alimentary canal (al-i-MEN-tah-ree ka-NAL): Also known as the digestive tract, the series of muscular structures through which food passes while being converted to nutrients and waste products; includes the oral cavity, pharynx, esophagus, stomach, large intestine, and small intestine.

Allergen (AL-er-jen): Substance that causes an allergy.

Allergy (AL-er-jee): An abnormal immune reaction to an otherwise harmless substance.

Alveoli (al-VEE-oh-lie): Air sacs of the lungs.

Alzheimer's disease (ALTS-hi-merz): Disease of the nervous system marked by a deterioration of memory, thinking, and reasoning.

Amylase (am-i-LACE): Any of various digestive enzymes that convert starches to sugars.

Amyotrophic lateral sclerosis (a-me-o-TROW-fik LA-ter-al skle-ROW-sis): Also known as Lou Gehrig's disease, a disease that breaks down motor neurons, resulting in the loss of the ability to move any of the muscles in the body.

Androgens (AN-dro-jens): Hormones that control male secondary sex characteristics.

Anemia (ah-NEE-me-yah): Diseased condition in which there is a deficiency of red blood cells or hemoglobin.

Anorexia nervosa (an-ah-REK-see-ah ner-VO-sa): Eating disorder usually occurring in young women that is characterized by an abnormal fear of becoming obese, a persistent aversion to food, and severe weight loss.

Antagonist (an-TAG-o-nist): Muscle that acts in opposition to a prime mover.

Antibody (AN-ti-bod-ee): Specialized substance produced by the body that can provide immunity against a specific antigen.

Antibody-mediated immunity (AN-ti-bod-ee MEE-dee-a-ted i-MYOO-ni-tee): Immune response involving B cells and their production of antibodies.

Antidiuretic hormone (an-tee-die-yu-REH-tik HOR-mone): Hormone produced by the hypothalamus and stored in the posterior pituitary that increases the absorption of water by the kidneys.

Antigen (AN-ti-jen): Any substance that, when introduced to the body, is recognized as foreign and activates an immune response.

Aorta (ay-OR-ta): Main artery of the body.

Apocrine sweat glands (AP-oh-krin): Sweat glands located primarily in the armpit and genital areas.

Appendicitis (ah-pen-di-SIGH-tis): Inflammation of the appendix.

Appendix (ah-PEN-dix): Small, apparently useless organ extending from the cecum.

Aqueous humor (AYE-kwee-us HYOO-mer): Tissue fluid filling the cavity of the eye between the cornea and the lens.

Arachnoid (ah-RAK-noid): Weblike middle layer of the three meninges covering the brain and spinal cord.

Arrector pili muscle (ah-REK-tor PIE-lie): Smooth muscle attached to a hair follicle that, when stimulated, pulls on the follicle, causing the hair shaft to stand upright.

Arteriole (ar-TEER-e-ohl): Small artery.

Arteriosclerosis (ar-tir-ee-o-skle-ROW-sis): Diseased condition in which the walls of arteries become thickened and hard, interfering with the circulation of blood.

Artery (AR-te-ree): Vessel that carries blood away from the heart.

Asthma (AZ-ma): Respiratory disease often caused by an allergy that is marked by tightness in the chest and difficulty in breathing.

Astigmatism (ah-STIG-mah-tiz-um): Incorrect shaping of the cornea that results in an incorrect focusing of light on the retina.

Atherosclerosis (ath-a-row-skle-ROW-sis): Diseased condition in which fatty material accumulates on the interior walls of arteries, making them narrower.

Athlete's foot: Common fungus infection in which the skin between the toes becomes itchy and sore, cracking and peeling away.

Atria (AY-tree-a): Upper chambers of the heart that receive blood from the veins.

Atrioventricular (AV) node (a-tree-oh-ven-TRICK-u-lar): Node of specialized tissue lying near the bottom of the right atrium that fires an electrical impulse across the ventricles, causing them to contract.

Atrioventricular (AV) valves: Valves located between the atria and ventricles.

Autoimmune disease (au-toe-i-MYOON): Condition in which the body produces antibodies that attack and destroy the body's own tissues.

Autonomic nervous system (aw-toh-NOM-ik NERV-us SIS-tem): Part of the peripheral nervous system that controls involuntary actions, such as the heartbeat, gland secretions, and digestion.

Axon (AK-son): Taillike projection extending out a neuron that carries impulses away from the cell body.

B

B cell: Also called B lymphocyte, a type of lymphocyte that originates from the bone marrow and that changes into antibody-producing plasma cells.

Basal cell carcinoma (BAY-sal CELL car-si-NO-ma): Skin cancer that affects the basal cells in the epidermis.

Basal ganglia (BAY-zul GANG-lee-ah): Paired masses of gray matter within the white matter of the cerebrum that help coordinate subconscious skeletal muscular movement.

Bile: Greenish yellow liquid produced by the liver that neutralizes acids and emulsifies fats in the duodenum.

Biliary atresia (BILL-ee-a-ree ah-TREE-zee-ah): Condition in which ducts to transport bile from the liver to the duodenum fail to develop in a fetus.

Binocular vision (by-NOK-yoo-lur VI-zhun): Ability of the brain to create one image from the slightly different images received from each eye.

Blood pressure: Pressure or force the blood exerts against the inner walls of the blood vessels.

Bolus (BO-lus): Rounded mass of food prepared by the mouth for swallowing.

Botulism (BOCH-a-liz-em): Form of food poisoning in which a bacterial toxin prevents the release of acetylcholine at neuromuscular junctions, resulting in paralysis.

Bowman's capsule (BOW-manz KAP-sul): Cup-shaped end of a nephron that encloses a glomerulus.

Brain: Central controlling and coordinating organ of the nervous system.

Breathing (BREETH-ing): Process of inhaling and exhaling air.

Bronchi (BRONG-kie): Largest branch of the bronchial tree between the trachea and bronchioles.

Bronchial tree (BRONG-key-uhl TREE): Entire system of air passageways within the lungs formed by the branching of bronchial tubes.

Bronchioles (BRONG-key-ohls): Smallest of the air passageways within the lungs.

Bronchitis (bron-KIE-tis): Inflammation of the mucous membrane of the bronchial tubes.

Bulimia (boo-LEE-me-ah): Eating disorder characterized by eating binges followed by self-induced vomiting or laxative abuse.

C

Calcitonin (kal-si-TOE-nin): Hormone secreted by the thyroid gland that decreases calcium levels in the blood.

Calyces (KAY-li-seez): Cup-shaped extensions of the renal pelvis that enclose the tips of the renal pyramids and collect urine.

Capillary (CAP-i-lair-ee): Minute blood vessel that connects arterioles with venules.

Carcinoma (car-si-NO-ma): Cancerous tumor of the skin, mucous membrane, or similar tissue of the body.

Cardiac cycle (CAR-dee-ack): Series of events that occur in the heart during one complete heartbeat.

Carpal tunnel syndrome (CAR-pal TUN-nel SIN-drome): Disorder caused by the compression at the wrist of the median nerve supplying the hand, causing numbness and tingling.

Cataract (KAT-ah-rakt): Condition in which the lens of the eye turns cloudy, causing partial or total blindness.

Cauda equina (KAW-da ee-KWHY-nah): Spinal nerves that hang below the end of the spinal cord.

Cecum (SEE-kum): Blind pouch at the beginning of the large intestine.

Cell-mediated immunity (CELL MEE-dee-a-ted i-MYOO-ni-tee): Immune response led by T cells that does not involve the production of antibodies.

Central nervous system: Part of the nervous system consisting of the brain and spinal cord.

Cerebral cortex (se-REE-bral KOR-tex): Outermost layer of the cerebrum made entirely of gray matter.

Cerebrum (se-REE-brum): Largest part of the brain, involved with conscious perception, voluntary actions, memory, thought, and personality.

Cholesterol (ko-LESS-ter-ol): Fatlike substance produced by the liver that is an essential part of cell membranes and body chemicals; when present in excess in the body, cholesterol can accumulate on the inside walls of arteries and block blood flow.

Ceruminous glands (suh-ROO-mi-nus GLANDZ): Exocrine glands in the skin of the auditory canal of the ear that secrete earwax or cerumen.

Chemoreceptors (kee-moe-re-SEP-terz): Receptors sensitive to various chemicals substances.

Choroid (KOR-oid): Middle, pigmented layer of the eye.

Chyle (KILE): Thick, whitish liquid consisting of lymph and tiny fat globules absorbed from the small intestine during digestion.

Chyme (KIME): Soupylike mixture of partially digested food and stomach secretions.

Ciliary body (SIL-ee-air-ee BAH-dee): Circular muscle that surrounds the edge of the lens of the eye and changes the shape of the lens.

Cirrhosis (si-ROW-sis): Chronic disease of the liver in which normal liver cells are damaged and then replaced by scar tissue.

Cochlea (KOK-lee-ah): Spiral-shaped cavity in the inner ear that contains the receptors for hearing in the organ of Corti.

Colon (KOH-lun): Largest region of the large intestine, divided into four sections: ascending, transverse, descending, and sigmoid (the term "colon" is sometimes used to describe the entire large intestine).

Colostomy (kuh-LAS-tuh-mee): Surgical procedure where a portion of the large intestine is brought through the abdominal wall and attached to a bag to collect feces.

Cones: Photoreceptors in the retina of the eye that detect colors.

Conjunctiva (kon-junk-TIE-vah): Mucous membrane lining the eyelids and covering the front surface of the eyeball.

Conjunctivitis (kon-junk-ti-VIE-tis): Inflammation of the conjunctiva of the eye.

Cornea (KOR-nee-ah): Transparent front portion of the sclera of the eye.

Corpus callosum (KOR-pus ka-LOW-sum): Large band of neurons connecting the two cerebral hemispheres.

Cortisol (KOR-ti-sol): Hormone secreted by the adrenal cortex that promotes the body's efficient use of nutrients during stressful situations.

Cramp: Prolonged muscle spasm.

Creatinine (kree-AT-i-neen): Waste product in urine produced by the break-down of creatine.

Crohn's disease (CRONES di-ZEEZ): Disorder that causes inflammation and ulceration of all the layers of the intestinal wall, particularly in the small intestine.

Cushing's syndrome (KU-shingz SIN-drome): Disorder caused by an over-production of steroids (mostly cortisol) by the adrenal cortex, resulting in obesity and muscular weakness.

Cystic fibrosis (SIS-tik fie-BRO-sis): Genetic disease in which, among other things, the mucous membranes of the respiratory tract produce a thick, sticky mucus that clogs airways.

Cystitis (sis-TIE-tis): Inflammation of the urinary bladder caused by a bacterial infection.

D

Defecation (def-e-KAY-shun): Elimination of feces from the large intestine through the anus.

Dendrites (DEN-drites): Branchlike extensions of neurons that carry impulses toward the cell body.

Dentin (DEN-tin): Bonelike material underneath the enamel of teeth, forming the main part.

Dermal papillae (DER-mal pah-PILL-ee): Fingerlike projections extending upward from the dermis containing blood capillaries, which provide nutrients for the lower layer of the epidermis; also form the characteristic ridges on the skin surface of the hands (fingerprints) and feet.

Dermatitis (der-ma-TIE-tis): Any inflammation of the skin.

Dermis (DER-miss): Thick, inner layer of the skin.

Diabetes mellitus (die-ah-BEE-teez MUL-le-tus): Disorder in which the body's cells cannot absorb glucose, either because the pancreas does not produce enough insulin or the cells do not respond to the effects of insulin that is produced.

Diaphragm (DIE-ah-fram): Membrane of muscle separating the chest cavity from the abdominal cavity.

Diastole (die-ASS-te-lee): Period of relaxation and expansion of the heart when its chambers fill with blood.

Diencephalon (die-en-SEF-ah-lon): Rear part of the forebrain that connects the midbrain to the cerebrum and that contains the thalamus and hypothalamus.

Diffusion (dif-FEW-shun): Movement of molecules from an area of greater concentration to an area of lesser concentration.

Diverticulosis (di-ver-ti-cue-LOW-sis): Condition in which the inner lining of the large intestine bulges out through its muscular wall; if the bulges become infected, the condition is called diverticulitis.

Duodenum (doo-o-DEE-num or doo-AH-de-num): First section of the small intestine.

Dura mater (DUR-ah MAY-tur): Outermost and toughest of the three meninges covering the brain and spinal cord.

E

Eardrum (EER-drum): Thin membrane at the end of the outer ear that vibrates when sound waves strike it.

Eccrine sweat glands (ECK-rin): Body's most numerous sweat glands, which produce watery sweat to maintain normal body temperature.

Edema (i-DEE-mah): Condition in which excessive fluid collects in bodily tissue and causes swelling.

Emphysema (em-feh-ZEE-mah): Respiratory disease marked by breathlessness that is brought on by the enlargement of the alveoli in the lungs.

Emulsify (e-MULL-si-fie): To break down large fat globules into smaller droplets that stay suspended in water.

Enamel (e-NAM-el): Whitish, hard, glossy outer layer of teeth.

Endocardium (en-doe-CAR-dee-um): Thin membrane lining the interior of the heart.

Enzymes (EN-zimes): Proteins that speed up the rate of chemical reactions.

Epicardium (ep-i-CAR-dee-um): Lubricating outer layer of the heart wall and part of the pericardium.

Epidermis (ep-i-DER-miss): Thin, outer layer of the skin.

Epiglottis (ep-i-GLAH-tis): Flaplike piece of tissue at the top of the larynx that covers its opening when swallowing is occurring.

Epilepsy (EP-eh-lep-see): Disorder of the nervous system marked by seizures that often involve convulsions or the loss of consciousness.

Epinephrine (ep-i-NEFF-rin): Also called adrenaline, a hormone secreted by the adrenal medulla that stimulates the body to react to stressful situations.

Epithelial tissue (ep-i-THEE-lee-al): Tissue that covers the internal and external surfaces of the body and also forms glandular organs.

Erythrocyte (e-RITH-re-site): Red blood cell.

Esophagus (i-SOF-ah-gus): Muscular tube connecting the pharynx and stomach.

Estrogens (ES-tro-jenz): Female steroid hormones secreted by the ovaries that bring about the secondary sex characteristics and regulate the female reproductive cycle.

Eustachian tube (yoo-STAY-she-an TOOB): Slender air passage between the middle ear cavity and the pharynx, which equalizes air pressure on the two sides of the eardrum.

Exhalation (ex-ha-LAY-shun): Also known as expiration, the movement of air out of the lungs.

External auditory canal (ex-TER-nal AW-di-tor-ee ka-NAL): Also called the ear canal, the tunnel in the ear between the pinna and eardrum.

F

Farsightedness: Known formally as hyperopia, the condition of the eye where incoming rays of light reach the retina before they converge to form a focused image.

Fascicle (FA-si-kul): Bundle of myofibrils wrapped together by connective tissue.

Feces (FEE-seez): Solid body wastes formed in the large intestine.

Fever: Abnormally high body temperature brought about as a response to infection or severe physical injury.

Filtration (fill-TRAY-shun): Movement of water and dissolved materials through a membrane from an area of higher pressure to an area of lower pressure.

Flatus (FLAY-tus): Gas generated by bacteria in the large intestine.

Follicle-stimulating hormone (FAH-lik-uhl STIM-yoo-lay-ting HOR-mone): Gonadotropic hormone produced by the anterior pituitary gland that stimulates the development of follicles in the ovaries of females and sperm in the testes of males.

G

Gallstones (GAUL-stones): Solid crystal deposits that form in the gall bladder.

Ganglion (GANG-glee-on): Any collection of nerve cell bodies forming a nerve center in the peripheral nervous system.

Gastric juice (GAS-trick JOOSE): Secretion of the gastric glands of the stomach, containing hydrochloric acid, pepsin, and mucus.

Gigantism (jie-GAN-tizm): Disorder in children in which the anterior pituitary overproduces growth hormone, resulting in abnormal enlargement of the extremities (nose, jaw, fingers, and toes) and the long bones, causing unusual height.

Gland: Any organ that secretes or excretes substances for further use in the body or for elimination.

Glaucoma (glaw-KOE-mah): Eye disorder caused by a buildup of aqueous humor that results in high pressure in the eyeball, often damaging the optic nerve and eventually leading to blindness.

Glomerulonephritis (glah-mer-u-lo-ne-FRY-tis): Inflammation of the glomeruli in the renal corpuscles of the kidneys.

Glomerulus (glow-MER-yoo-lus): Network of capillaries enclosed by a Bowman's capsule.

Glottis (GLAH-tis): Opening of the larynx between the vocal cords.

Glucagon (GLUE-ka-gon): Hormone secreted by the islets of Langerhans that raises the level of sugar in the blood.

Gonad (GO-nad): Sex organ in which reproductive cells develop.

Gonadotropic hormones (gon-ah-do-TROP-ik): Hormones secreted by the anterior pituitary that affect or stimulate the growth or activity of the gonads.

Graves' disease: Disorder in which an antibody binds to specific cells in the thyroid gland, forcing them to secrete excess thyroid hormone.

Gray matter: Grayish nerve tissue of the central nervous system containing neuron cell bodies, neuroglia cells, and unmyelinated axons.

Gustation (gus-TAY-shun): The sense of taste.

Gustatory cells (GUS-ta-tor-ee CELLS): Chemoreceptors located within taste buds.

Gyri (JYE-rye): Outward folds on the surface of the cerebral cortex.

H

Hemoglobin (HEE-muh-glow-bin): Iron-containing protein pigment in red blood cells that can combine with oxygen and carbon dioxide.

Hemophilia (hee-muh-FILL-ee-ah): Inherited blood disease in which the blood lacks one or more of the clotting factors, making it difficult to stop bleeding.

Henle's loop (HEN-leez LOOP): Looped portion of a renal tubule.

Hepatic portal circulation (heh-PAT-ick POR-tal): System of blood vessels that transports blood from the digestive organs and the spleen through the liver before returning it to the heart.

Hepatitis (hep-a-TIE-tis): Inflammation of the liver that is caused mainly by a virus.

Hilus (HIGH-lus): Indentation or depression on the surface of an organ such as a kidney.

Hippocampus (hip-ah-CAM-pes): Structure in the limbic system necessary for the formation of long-term memory.

Histamine (HISS-ta-mean): Chemical compound released by injured cells that causes local blood vessels to enlarge.

HIV: Human immunodeficiency virus, which infects helper T cells and weakens immune responses, leading to the severe AIDS disorder.

Homeostasis (hoe-me-o-STAY-sis): Ability of the body or a cell to maintain the internal balance of its functions, such as steady temperature, regardless of outside conditions.

Huntington's disease: Inherited, progressive disease causing uncontrollable physical movements and mental deterioration.

Hypertension (hi-per-TEN-shun): High blood pressure.

Hyperthyroidism (hi-per-THIGH-roy-dizm): Disorder in which an overactive thyroid produces too much thyroxine.

Hypothalamus (hi-po-THAL-ah-mus): Region of the brain containing many control centers for body functions and emotions; also regulates the pituitary gland's secretions.

Hypothyroidism (hi-po-THIGH-roy-dizm): Disorder in which an underactive thyroid produces too little thyroxine.

I

Ileocecal valve (ill-ee-oh-SEE-kal VALV): Sphincter or ring of muscular that controls the flow of chyme from the ileum to the large intestine.

Ileum (ILL-ee-um): Final section of the small intestine.

Immunity (i-MYOO-ni-tee): Body's ability to defend itself against pathogens or other foreign material.

Inflammation (in-flah-MAY-shun): Response to injury or infection of body tissues, marked by redness, heat, swelling, and pain.

Inhalation (in-ha-LAY-shun): Also known as inspiration, the movement of air into the lungs.

Insulin (IN-suh-lin): Hormone secreted by the islets of Langerhans that regulates the amount of sugar in the blood.

Integument (in-TEG-ye-ment): In animals and plants, any natural outer covering, such as skin, shell, membrane, or husk.

Interferon (in-ter-FIR-on): Protein compound released by cells infected with a virus to prevent that virus from reproducing in nearby normal cells.

Interstitial fluid (in-ter-STI-shul): Fluid found in the spaces between cells.

Iris (EYE-ris): Pigmented (colored) part of the eye between the cornea and lens made of two sets of smooth muscle fibers.

Islets of Langerhans (EYE-lets of LAHNG-er-hanz): Endocrine cells of the pancreas that secrete insulin and glucagon.

J

Jejunum (je-JOO-num): Middle section of the small intestine.

K

Keratin (KER-ah-tin): Tough, fibrous, water-resistant protein that forms the outer layers of hair, calluses, and nails and coats the surface of the skin.

Kidney stones: Large accumulations of calcium salt crystals from urine that may form in the kidneys.

L

Lacrimal gland (LAK-ri-muhl GLAND): Gland located at the upper, outer corner of each eyeball that secretes tears.

Lacteals (LAK-tee-als): Specialized lymph capillaries in the villi of the small intestine.

Lactic acid (LAK-tik ASS-id): Chemical waste product created when muscle fibers break down glucose without the proper amount of oxygen.

Lactose intolerance (LAK-tose in-TOL-er-ance): Inability of the body to digest significant amounts of lactose, the predominant sugar in milk.

Larynx (LAR-ingks): Organ between the pharynx and trachea that contains the vocal cords.

Lens: Clear, oval, flexible structure behind the pupil in the eye that changes shape for the focusing of light rays.

Leukemia (loo-KEE-mee-ah): Type of cancer that affects the blood-forming tissues and organs, causing them to flood the bloodstream and lymphatic system with immature and abnormal white blood cells.

Leukocyte (LUKE-oh-site): White blood cell.

Limbic system (LIM-bik SIS-tem): Group of structures in the cerebrum and diencephalon that are involved with emotional states and memory.

Lipase (LIE-pace): Digestive enzyme that converts lipids (fats) into fatty acids.

Lower esophageal sphincter (LOW-er i-sof-ah-GEE-al SFINGK-ter): Strong ring of muscle at the base of the esophagus that contracts to prevent stomach contents from moving back into the esophagus.

Lungs: Paired breathing organs.

Lunula (LOO-noo-la): White, crescent-shaped area of the nail bed near the nail root.

Luteinizing hormone (loo-tee-in-EYE-zing): Gonadotropic hormone secreted by the anterior pituitary that stimulates, in women, ovulation and the release of estrogens and progesterone by the ovaries and, in men, the secretion of testosterone by the testes.

Lymph (LIMF): Slightly yellowish but clear fluid found within lymph vessels.

Lymphadenitis (lim-fad-e-NIE-tis): Inflammation of lymph nodes.

Lymphangitis (lim-fan-JIE-tis): Inflammation of lymphatic vessels.

Lymph node: Small mass of lymphatic tissue located along the pathway of a lymph vessel that filters out harmful microorganisms.

Lymphocyte (LIM-foe-site): Type of white blood cell produced in lymph nodes, bone marrow, and the spleen that defends the body against infection by producing antibodies.

Lymphoma (lim-FOE-mah): General term applied to cancers of the lymphatic system, which include Hodgkin's lymphoma and non-Hodgkin's lymphomas.

M

Macrophage (MACK-row-fage): Large white blood cell that engulfs and destroys bacteria, viruses, and other foreign substances in the lymph.

Malignant melanoma (ma-LIG-nant mel-ah-NO-ma): Cancer of melanocytes; the most serious type of skin cancer.

Mechanoreceptors (mek-ah-no-re-SEP-terz): Receptors sensitive to mechanical or physical pressures such as sound and touch.

Medulla oblongata (mi-DUL-ah ob-long-GAH-tah): Part of the brain located at the top end of the spinal cord that controls breathing and other involuntary functions.

Megakaryocyte (meg-ah-CARE-ee-oh-site): Large cell in the red bone marrow that breaks up into small fragments that become platelets.

Melanocyte (MEL-ah-no-site): Cell found in the lower epidermis that produces the protein pigment melanin.

Melatonin (mel-a-TOE-nin): Hormone secreted by the pineal gland that helps set the body's twenty-four-hour clock and plays a role in the timing of puberty and sexual development.

Meniere's disease (men-ee-AIRZ): Ear disorder characterized by recurring dizziness, hearing loss, and a buzzing or ringing sound in the ears.

Meninges (meh-NIN-jeez): Membranes that cover the brain and spinal cord.

Metabolism (muh-TAB-uh-lizm): Sum of all the physiological processes by which an organism maintains life.

Micturition (mik-tu-RISH-un): Urination, or the elimination or voiding of urine from the urinary bladder.

Midbrain: Part of the brain between the hypothalamus and the pons that regulates visual, auditory, and rightening reflexes.

Migraine (MY-grain): A particularly intense form of headache.

Multiple sclerosis (skle-ROW-sis): Disorder in which immune cells attack and destroy the insulation covering nerve fibers in the central nervous system, causing muscular weakness and loss of coordination.

Muscle tone: Sustained partial contraction of certain muscle fibers in all muscles.

Muscular dystrophy (MUS-kyu-lar DIS-tro-fee): One of several inherited muscular diseases in which a person's muscles gradually and irreversibly deteriorate, causing weakness and eventually complete disability.

Myasthenia gravis (my-ass-THEH-nee-ah GRA-vis): Autoimmune disease in which antibodies attack acetylcholine, blocking the transmission of nerve impulses to muscle fibers.

Myelin (MY-ah-lin): Soft, white, fatty material that forms a sheath around the axons of most neurons.

Myocardium (my-oh-CAR-dee-um): Cardiac muscle layer of the heart wall.

Myofibrils (my-o-FIE-brilz): cylindrical structures lying within skeletal muscle fibers that are composed of repeating structural units called sarcomeres.

Myofilament (my-o-FILL-ah-ment): Protein filament composing the myofibrils; can be either thick (composed of myosin) or thin (composed of actin).

N

Nasal cavity (NAY-zul KAV-i-tee): Air cavity in the skull through which air passes from the nostrils to the upper part of the pharynx.

Nasal conchae (NAY-zul KAHN-kee): Flat, spongy plates that project toward the nasal septum from the sides of the nasal cavity.

Nasal septum (NAY-zul SEP-tum): Vertical plate made of bone and cartilage that divides the nasal cavity.

Natural killer cell: Also known as an NK cell, a type of lymphocyte that patrols the body and destroys foreign or abnormal cells.

Nearsightedness: Known formally as myopia, the condition of the eye where incoming rays of light are bent too much and converge to form a focused image in front of the retina.

Negative feedback: Control system in which a stimulus initiates a response that reduces the stimulus, thereby stopping the response.

Nephrons (NEFF-ronz): Urine-forming structures in the kidneys.

Nerve: Bundle of axons in the peripheral nervous system.

Neuroglia (new-ROGUE-lee-ah): Also known as glial cells, these cells support and protect neurons in the central nervous system.

Neuromuscular junction (nu-row-MUSS-ku-lar JUNK-shun): Region where a motor neuron comes into close contact with a muscle fiber.

Neuron (NUR-on): Nerve cell.

Neurotransmitter (nur-oh-TRANS-mi-ter): Chemical released by the axon of a neuron that travels across a synapse and binds to receptors on the dendrites of other neurons or body cells.

Node of Ranvier (NODE OF rahn-VEEAY): Small area between Schwann cells on an axon that is unmyelinated or uncovered.

Norepinephrine (nor-ep-i-NEFF-rin): Also called noradrenaline, a hormone secreted by the adrenal medulla that raises blood pressure during stressful situations.

Nose: Part of the human face that contains the nostrils and organs of smell and forms the beginning of the respiratory tract.

Nostril (NOS-tril): Either of the two external openings of the nose.

O

Olfaction (ol-FAK-shun): The sense of smell.

Olfactory epithelium (ol-FAK-ter-ee ep-e-THEE-lee-um): Section of mucous membrane in the roof of the nasal cavity that contains odor-sensitive olfactory nerve cells.

Oligodendrocyte (o-li-go-DEN-dro-site): Cell that produces the myelin sheath around the axons of neurons in the central nervous system.

Organ (OR-gan): Any part of the body formed of two or more tissues that performs a specialized function.

Organ of Corti (OR-gan of KOR-tee): Structure in the cochlea of the inner ear that contains the receptors for hearing.

Osmosis (oz-MOE-sis): Diffusion of water through a semipermeable membrane.

Ossicles (OS-si-kuls): Three bones of the middle ear: hammer, anvil, and stirrup.

Otitis media (oh-TIE-tis ME-dee-ah): Infection of the middle ear.

Ovaries (O-var-eez): Female gonads in which ova (eggs) are produced and that secrete estrogens and progesterone.

Oxytocin (ahk-si-TOE-sin): Hormone produced by the hypothalamus and stored in the posterior pituitary that stimulates contraction of the uterus during childbirth and secretion of milk during nursing.

P

Palate (PAL-uht): Roof of the mouth, divided into hard and soft portions, that separates the mouth from the nasal cavities.

Papillae (pah-PILL-ee): Small projections on the upper surface of the tongue that contain taste buds.

Paranasal sinuses (pair-a-NAY-sal SIGH-nus-ez): Air-filled chambers in the bones of the skull that open into the nasal cavity.

Parasympathetic nervous system (pair-ah-sim-puh-THET-ik NERV-us SIS-tem): Division of the autonomic nervous system that controls involuntary activities that keep the body running smoothly under normal, everyday conditions.

Parathyroid glands (pair-ah-THIGH-roid): Four small glands located on the posterior surface of the thyroid gland that regulate calcium levels in the blood.

Parkinson's disease: Progressive disease in which cells in one of the movement-control centers of the brain begin to die, resulting in a loss of control over speech and head and body movements.

Pericardium (pair-i-CAR-dee-um): Tough, fibrous, two-layered membrane sac that surrounds, protects, and anchors the heart.

Peripheral nervous system (peh-RIFF-uh-ruhl NERV-us SIS-tem): Part of the nervous system consisting of the cranial and spinal nerves.

Peristalsis (per-i-STALL-sis): Series of wavelike muscular contractions that move material in one direction through a hollow organ.

Peyer's patches (PIE-erz): Masses of lymphatic tissue located in the villi of the small intestine.

Phagocyte (FAG-oh-site): Type of white blood cell capable of engulfing and digesting particles or cells harmful to the body.

Phagocytosis (fag-oh-sigh-TOE-sis): Process by which a phagocyte engulfs and destroys particles or cells harmful to the body.

Pharynx (FAR-inks): Short, muscular tube extending from the mouth and nasal cavities to the trachea and esophagus.

Photoreceptors (fo-to-re-SEP-terz): Receptors sensitive to light.

Pinna (PIN-nah): Commonly referred to as the ear, the outer, flaplike portion of the ear.

Pia mater (PIE-ah MAY-tur): Delicate innermost layer of the three meninges covering the brain and spinal cord.

Pineal gland (PIN-ee-al): Gland located deep in the rear portion of the brain that helps establish the body's day-night cycle.

Pituitary gland (pi-TOO-i-tair-ee): Gland located below the hypothalamus that controls and coordinates the secretions of other endocrine glands.

Plaque (PLACK): Sticky, whitish film on teeth formed by a protein in saliva and sugary substances in the mouth.

Plasma (PLAZ-muh): Fluid portion of blood.

Platelets (PLATE-lets): Irregular cell fragments in blood that are involved in the process of blood clotting.

Pleura (PLOOR-ah): Membrane sac covering and protecting each lung.

Pneumonia (noo-MOE-nya): Disease of the lungs marked by inflammation and caused by bacteria or viruses.

Poliomyelitis (po-lee-o-my-eh-LIE-tis; often referred to simply as polio): Contagious viral disease that can cause damage to the central nervous system, resulting in paralysis and loss of muscle tissue.

Pons: Part of the brain connecting the medulla oblongata with the midbrain.

Prime mover: Muscle whose contractions are chiefly responsible for producing a particular movement.

Progesterone (pro-JESS-te-rone): Female steroid hormone secreted by the ovaries that makes the uterus more ready to receive a fertilized ovum or egg.

Prolactin (pro-LAK-tin): Gonadotropic hormone secreted by the anterior pituitary that stimulates the mammary glands to produce milk.

Psoriasis (so-RYE-ah-sis): Chronic skin disease characterized by reddened lesions covered with dry, silvery scales.

Pulmonary circulation (PULL-mo-nair-ee): System of blood vessels that transports blood between the heart and lungs.

Pulmonary surfactant (PULL-mo-nair-ee sir-FAK-tent): Oily substance secreted by the alveoli to prevent their walls from sticking together.

Pupil (PYOO-pil): Opening in the center of the iris though which light passes.

Purkinje fibers (purr-KIN-gee): Specialized cardiac muscle fibers that conduct nerve impulses through the heart.

Pyelonephritis (pie-e-low-ne-FRY-tis): Inflammation of the kidneys caused by a bacterial infection.

Pyloric sphincter (pie-LOR-ick SFINGK-ter): Strong ring of muscle at the junction of the stomach and the small intestine that regulates the flow of material between them.

R

Receptors (re-SEP-terz): Specialized peripheral nerve endings or nerve cells that respond to a particular stimulus such as light, sound, heat, touch, or pressure.

Red blood cells: Most numerous blood cells in the blood, they carry oxygen bonded to the hemoglobin within them.

Reflex (REE-flex): Involuntary and rapid response to a stimulus.

Renal corpuscle (REE-nul KOR-pus-el): Part of a nephron that consists of a glomerulus enclosed by a Bowman's capsule.

Renal cortex (REE-nul KOR-tex): Outermost layer of the kidney.

Renal filtrate (REE-nul FILL-trait): Fluid formed in a Bowman's capsule from blood plasma by the process of filtration in the renal corpuscle.

Renal medulla (REE-nul muh-DUH-luh): Middle layer of a kidney.

Renal pelvis (REE-nul PELL-vis): A cavity at the innermost area of a kidney that connects to the ureter.

Renal pyramids (REE-nul PEER-ah-mids): Triangular or pie-shaped segments of the renal medulla in which urine production occurs.

Renal tubule (REE-nal TOO-byool): Twisting, narrow tube leading from the Bowman's capsule in a nephron.

Renin (REE-nin): Enzyme secreted by the cells of renal tubules that helps to raise blood pressure.

Respiration (res-pe-RAY-shun): Exchange of gases (oxygen and carbon dioxide) between living cells and the environment.

Retina (RET-i-nah): Innermost layer of the eyeball that contains the photoreceptors—the rods and cones.

Rigor mortis (RIG-er MOR-tis): Rigid state of the body after death due to irreversible muscle contractions.

Rods: Photoreceptors in the retina of the eye that detect the presence of light.

Rugae (ROO-jee): Folds of the inner mucous membrane of organs, such as the stomach, that allow those organs to expand.

S

Saccule (SAC-yool): Membranous sac in the vestibule of the inner ear that contains receptors for the sense of balance.

Sarcomere (SAR-koh-meer): Unit of contraction in a skeletal muscle fiber containing a precise arrangement of thick and thin myofilaments.

Schwann cell (SHWAHN SELL): Cell that forms the myelin sheath around axons of neurons in the peripheral nervous system.

Sclera (SKLER-ah): Outermost layer of the eyeball, made of connective tissue.

Sebaceous gland (suh-BAY-shus): Exocrine gland in the dermis that produces sebum.

Seborrheic dermatitis (seh-beh-REE-ik der-ma-TIE-tis): Commonly called seborrhea, a disease of the skin characterized by scaly lesions that usually appear on the scalp, hairline, and face.

Sebum (SEE-bum): Mixture of oily substances and fragmented cells secreted by sebaceous glands.

Semicircular canals (sem-eye-SIR-cue-lar ka-NALZ): Three oval canals in the inner ear that help to maintain balance.

Semilunar valves (sem-eye-LU-nar): Valves located between the ventricles and the major arteries into which they pump blood.

Serous fluid (SIR-us): Clear, watery, lubricating fluid produced by serous membranes, which line body cavities and cover internal organs.

Sickle cell anemia (SICK-el cell ah-NEE-me-yah): Inherited blood disorder in which red blood cells are sickle-shaped instead of round because of defective hemoglobin molecules.

Sinoatrial (SA) node (sigh-no-A-tree-al): Node of specialized tissue lying in the upper area of the right atrium that fires an electrical impulse across the atria, causing them to contract.

Sinusoids (SIGH-nuh-soids): Larger than normal capillaries whose walls are also more permeable, allowing proteins and blood cells to enter or leave easily.

Somatic nervous system (so-MAT-ik NERV-us SIS-tem): Part of the peripheral nervous system that controls the voluntary movements of the skeletal muscles.

Spasm: Sudden, involuntary muscle contraction.

Sphygmomanometer (sfig-moe-ma-NOM-i-tur): Instrument used to measure blood pressure.

Spinal cord: Long cord of nerve tissue running through the spine or backbone that transmits impulses to and from the brain and controls some reflex actions.

Spleen: Lymphoid organ located in the upper left part of the abdomen that stores blood, destroys old red blood cells, and filters pathogens from the blood.

Squamous cell carcinoma (SKWA-mus CELL car-si-NO-ma): Skin cancer affecting the cells of the second deepest layer of the epidermis.

Squamous cells (SKWA-mus): Cells that are flat and scalelike.

Strain: Slight tear in a muscle; also called a pulled muscle.

Subcutaneous (sub-kew-TAY-nee-us): Tissues between the dermis and the muscles.

Sulci (SUL-sye): Shallow grooves on the surface of the cerebral cortex.

Sympathetic nervous system (sim-puh-THET-ik NERV-us SIS-tem): Division of the autonomic nervous system that controls involuntary activities that help the body respond to stressful situations.

Synapse (SIN-aps): Small space or gap where a nerve impulse passes between the axon of one neuron and a dendrite of the next neuron.

Synergist (SIN-er-jist): Muscle that cooperates with another to produce a particular movement.

Systemic circulation (sis-TEM-ick): System of blood vessels that transports blood between the heart and all parts of the body other than the lungs.

Systemic lupus erythematosus (sis-TEM-ick LOU-pus er-i-the-mah-TOE-sis): Also called lupus or SLE, a disorder in which antibodies attack the body's own tissues as if they were foreign.

Systole (SIS-te-lee): Rhythmic contraction of the heart.

T

T cell: Also known as T lymphocyte, a type of lymphocyte that matures in the thymus and that attacks any foreign substance in the body.

Taste buds: Structures on the papillae of the tongue that contain chemoreceptors that respond to chemicals dissolved in saliva.

Tendon (TEN-den): Tough, white, cordlike tissue that attaches muscle to bone.

Testes (TESS-teez): Male gonads that produce sperm cells and secrete testosterone.

Testosterone (tess-TAHS-ter-ohn): Hormone secreted by the testes that spurs the growth of the male reproductive organs and secondary sex characteristics.

Tetanus (TET-n-es): Bacterial disease in which a bacterial toxin causes the repetitive stimulation of muscle fibers, resulting in convulsive muscle spasms and rigidity.

Thalamus (THAL-ah-mus): Part of the brain behind the hypothalamus that acts as the brain's main relay station, sending information to the cerebral cortex and other parts of the brain.

Thoracic duct (tho-RAS-ik): Main lymph vessel in the body, which transports lymph from the lower half and upper left part of the body.

Thrombocyte (THROM-bow-site): Platelet.

Thymosin (thigh-MOE-sin): Hormone secreted by the thymus that changes a certain group of lymphocytes into germ-fighting T cells.

Thymus (THIGH-mus): Glandular organ consisting of lymphoid tissue located behind the top of the breastbone that produces specialized lymphocytes; reaches maximum development in early childhood and is almost absent in adults.

Thyroid gland (THIGH-roid): Gland wrapped around the front and sides of the trachea at the base of the throat just below the larynx that affects growth and metabolism.

Thyroxine (thigh-ROK-seen): Hormone secreted by the thyroid gland that regulates the rate of metabolism and, in children, affects growth.

Tonsillitis (tahn-si-LIE-tis): Infection and swelling of the tonsils.

Tonsils (TAHN-sills): Three pairs of small, oval masses of lymphatic tissue located on either side of the inner wall of the throat, near the rear openings of the nasal cavity, and near the base of the tongue.

Trachea (TRAY-key-ah): Also known as the windpipe, the respiratory tube extending from the larynx to the bronchi.

Trypsin (TRIP-sin): Digestive enzyme that converts proteins into amino acids; inactive form is trypsinogen.

Tuberculosis (too-burr-cue-LOW-sis): Infectious, inflammatory disease of the lungs caused by a bacteria that leads to tissue damage.

U

Ulcer (digestive) (UL-sir): Any sore that develops in the lining of the lower esophagus, stomach, or duodenum.

Ulcerative colitis (UL-sir-a-tiv ko-LIE-tis): Disorder that causes inflammation and ulceration of the inner lining of the large intestine and rectum.

Urea (yoo-REE-ah): Main nitrogen-containing waste excreted in the urine, produced when the liver combines ammonia and carbon dioxide.

Ureter (you-REE-ter): Muscular tube that carries urine from the renal pelvis in a kidney to the urinary bladder.

Urethra (yoo-REE-thrah): Thin-walled tube that carries urine from the urinary bladder to the outside of the body.

Urethritis (yer-i-THRY-tis): Inflammation of the urethra caused by a bacterial infection.

Uric acid (YUR-ik AS-id): Waste product in urine formed by the breakdown of nucleic acids.

Urinary bladder (YER-i-nair-ee BLA-der) Hollow, collapsible, muscular sac that stores urine temporarily.

Urinary incontinence (YER-i-nair-ee in-KON-ti-nence): Involuntary and unintentional passage or urine.

Urine (YUR-in): Fluid formed by the kidneys from blood plasma.

Utricle (YOO-tri-kuhl): Membranous sac in the vestibule of the inner ear that contains receptors for the sense of balance.

Uvula (U-vue-lah): Fleshy projection hanging from the soft palate that raises to close off the nasal passages during swallowing.

V

Vaccine (vack-SEEN): Substance made of weakened or killed bacteria or viruses injected (or taken orally) into the body to stimulate the production of antibodies specific to that particular infectious disease.

Vein (VAIN): Vessel that carries blood to the heart.

Vena cava (VEE-na KAY-va): Either of two large veins that return blood to the right atrium of the heart.

Ventricles (VEN-tri-kuls): Lower chambers of the heart that contract to pump blood into the arteries.

Venule (VEN-yool): Small vein.

Vestibule (VES-ti-byool): Bony chamber of the inner ear that contains the utricle and the saccule.

Vestigial organ (ves-TIJ-ee-al OR-gan): Organ that is reduced in size and function when compared with that of its evolutionary ancestors.

Villi (VILL-eye): Tiny, fingerlike projections on the inner lining of the small intestine that increase the rate of nutrient absorption by greatly increasing the intestine's surface area.

Vitiligo (vit-i-LIE-go): Skin disorder in which the loss of melanocytes results in patches of smooth, milky white skin.

Vitreous humor (VIT-ree-us HYOO-mer): Transparent, gellike substance that fills the cavity of the eye behind the lens.

W

Warts: Small growths caused by a viral infection of the skin or mucous membrane.

White blood cells: Cells in blood that defend the body against viruses, bacteria, and other invading microorganisms.

White matter: Whitish nerve tissue of the central nervous system containing bundles of myelinated axons.

BODY BY DESIGN

From the Digestive System to the Skeleton

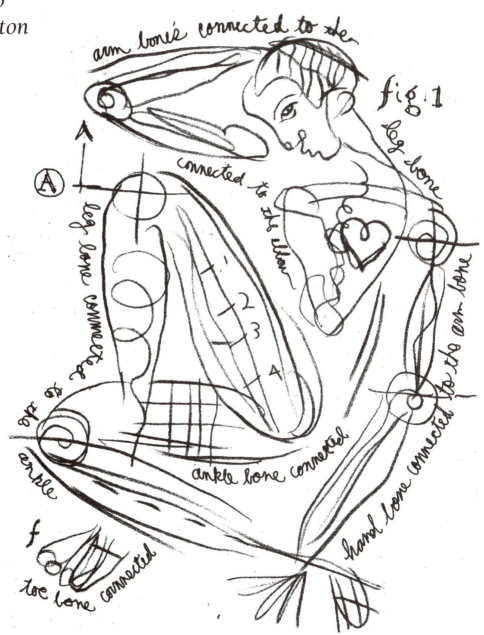

arm bone's connected to the...

fig. 1

leg bone

connected to the elbow

A

leg bone connected to the...

2
3
4

leg bone

hand bone connected to the arm bone

ankle bone connected

ankle

f

toe bone connected

7

The Nervous System

The nervous system is the master controller of the body. Each thought, each emotion, each action—all result from the activity of this system. Through its many parts, the nervous system monitors conditions both within and outside the body. It then processes that information and decides how the body should respond, if at all. Finally, if a response is needed, the system sends out electrical signals that spur the body into immediate action. Although one of the smallest of the body's systems in terms of weight, the nervous system is the most complex and versatile.

DESIGN: PARTS OF THE NERVOUS SYSTEM

The nervous system is a collection of cells, tissues, and organs. It can be split into two separate divisions: the central nervous system and the peripheral nervous system.

The central nervous system (CNS) acts as the command center of the body. It interprets incoming sensory information, then sends out instructions on how the body should react. The CNS consists of two major parts: the brain and the spinal cord.

The peripheral nervous system (PNS) is the part of the nervous system outside of the CNS. It consists mainly of nerves that extend from the brain and spinal cord to areas in the rest of the body. Cranial nerves carry impulses to and from the brain while spinal nerves carry impulses to and from the spinal cord. The PNS can be divided into two systems: the somatic nervous system and the autonomic nervous system. The somatic nervous system controls the voluntary movements of the skeletal muscles. The autonomic nervous system control activities in the body that are involuntary or automatic. These include the actions of the heart, glands, and digestive organs and associated parts.

The autonomic nervous system can be divided further into two subdivisions: the parasympathetic and sympathetic nervous systems. These two subdivisions work against each other. The parasympathetic nervous system regulates involuntary activities that keep the body running smoothly under normal, everyday conditions. The sympathetic nervous system controls involuntary activities that help the body respond to stressful situations.

WORDS TO KNOW

Arachnoid (ah-RAK-noid): Weblike middle layer of the three meninges covering the brain and spinal cord.

Autonomic nervous system (aw-toh-NOM-ik NERV-us SIS-tem): Part of the peripheral nervous system that controls involuntary actions, such as the heartbeat, gland secretions, and digestion.

Axon (AK-son): Taillike projection extending out a neuron that carries impulses away from the cell body.

Basal ganglia (BAY-zul GANG-lee-ah): Paired masses of gray matter within the white matter of the cerebrum that help coordinate subconscious skeletal muscular movement.

Brain: Central controlling and coordinating organ of the nervous system.

Cauda equina (KAW-da ee-KWHY-nah): Spinal nerves that hang below the end of the spinal cord.

Central nervous system: Part of the nervous system consisting of the brain and spinal cord.

Cerebral cortex (se-REE-bral KOR-tex): Outermost layer of the cerebrum made entirely of gray matter.

Cerebrum (se-REE-brum): Largest part of the brain, involved with conscious perception, voluntary actions, memory, thought, and personality.

Corpus callosum (KOR-pus ka-LOW-sum): Large band of neurons connecting the two cerebral hemispheres.

Dendrites (DEN-drites): Branchlike extensions of neurons that carry impulses toward the cell body.

Diencephalon (die-en-SEF-ah-lon): Rear part of the forebrain that connects the midbrain to the cerebrum and that contains the thalamus and hypothalamus.

Dura mater (DUR-ah MAY-tur): Outermost and toughest of the three meninges covering the brain and spinal cord.

Ganglion (GANG-glee-on): Any collection of nerve cell bodies forming a nerve center in the peripheral nervous system.

Gray matter: Grayish nerve tissue of the central nervous system containing neuron cell bodies, neuroglia, and unmyelinated axons.

Gyri (JYE-rye): Outward folds on the surface of the cerebral cortex.

Hippocampus (hip-ah-CAM-pes): Structure in the limbic system necessary for the formation of long-term memory.

Hypothalamus (hi-po-THAL-ah-mus): Region of the brain containing many control centers for body functions and emotions; also regulates the pituitary gland's secretions.

Limbic system (LIM-bik SIS-tem): Group of structures in the cerebrum and diencephalon that are involved with emotional states and memory.

Medulla oblongata (mi-DUL-ah ob-long-GAH-tah): Part of the brain located at the top end of the spinal cord that controls breathing and other involuntary functions.

Meninges (meh-NIN-jeez): Membranes that cover the brain and spinal cord.

Neurons

The cells making up the brain, spinal cord, and nerves are called neurons. They are special cells capable of receiving a stimulus (nerve or electrical impulse), transmitting that stimulus throughout their length, and then delivering that stimulus to other cells next to them. The human body contains about 200 billion neurons. Almost half of them are located in the brain.

Midbrain: Part of the brain between the hypothalamus and the pons that regulates visual, auditory, and rightening reflexes.

Myelin (MY-ah-lin): Soft, white, fatty material that forms a sheath around the axons of most neurons.

Nerve: Bundle of axons in the peripheral nervous system.

Neuroglia (new-ROGUE-lee-ah): Also known as glial cells, cells that support and protect neurons in the central nervous system.

Neuron (NUR-on): Nerve cell.

Neurotransmitter (nur-oh-TRANS-mi-ter): Chemical released by the axon of a neuron that travels across a synapse and binds to receptors on the dendrites of other neurons or body cells.

Node of Ranvier (NODE OF rahn-VEEAY): Small area between Schwann cells on an axon that is unmyelinated or uncovered.

Oligodendrocyte (o-li-go-DEN-dro-site): Cell that produces the myelin sheath around the axons of neurons in the central nervous system.

Parasympathetic nervous system (pair-ah-sim-puh-THET-ik NERV-us SIS-tem): Division of the autonomic nervous system that controls involuntary activities that keep the body running smoothly under normal, everyday conditions.

Peripheral nervous system (peh-RIFF-uh-ruhl NERV-us SIS-tem): Part of the nervous system consisting of the cranial and spinal nerves.

Pia mater (PIE-ah MAY-tur): Delicate innermost layer of the three meninges covering the brain and spinal cord.

Pons: Part of the brain connecting the medulla oblongata with the midbrain.

Reflex (REE-flex): Involuntary and rapid response to a stimulus.

Schwann cell (SHWAHN SELL): Cell that forms the myelin sheath around axons of neurons in the peripheral nervous system.

Somatic nervous system (so-MAT-ik NERV-us SIS-tem): Part of the peripheral nervous system that controls the voluntary movements of the skeletal muscles.

Spinal cord: Long cord of nerve tissue running through the spine or backbone that transmits impulses to and from the brain and controls some reflex actions.

Sulci (SUL-sye): Shallow grooves on the surface of the cerebral cortex.

Sympathetic nervous system (sim-puh-THET-ik NERV-us SIS-tem): Division of the autonomic nervous system that controls involuntary activities that help the body respond to stressful situations.

Synapse (SIN-aps): Small space or gap where a nerve impulse passes between the axon of one neuron and a dendrite of the next neuron.

Thalamus (THAL-ah-mus): Part of the brain behind the hypothalamus that acts as the brain's main relay station, sending information to the cerebral cortex and other parts of the brain.

White matter: Whitish nerve tissue of the central nervous system containing bundles of myelinated axons.

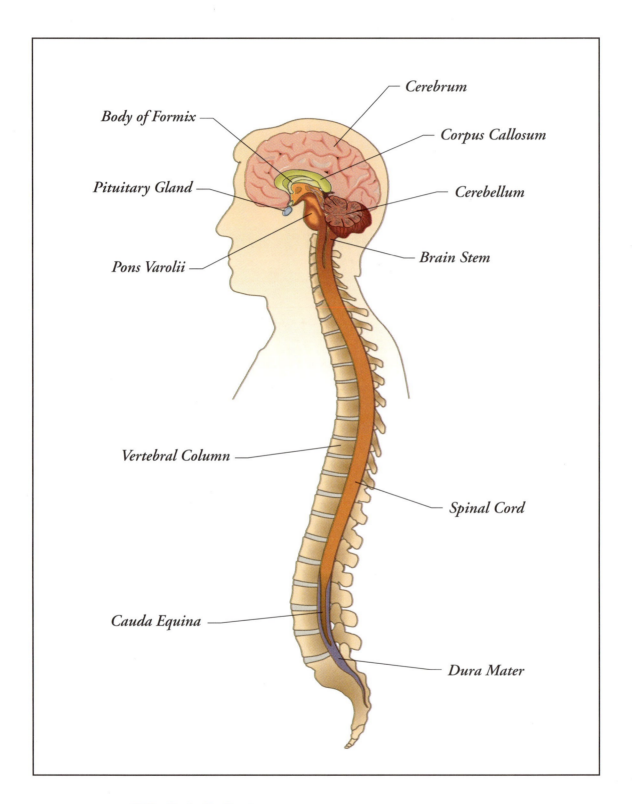

Cerebrum

Body of Formix

Corpus Callosum

Pituitary Gland

Cerebellum

Pons Varolii

Brain Stem

Vertebral Column

Spinal Cord

Cauda Equina

Dura Mater

A neuron consists of three main parts: the cell body, dendrites, and an axon (dendrites and axons are both referred to as nerve fibers). The cell body has most of the same structures found in typical body cells, such as a nucleus (the part of the cell that controls its activities). It is ball shaped, about 0.001 inch (0.002 centimeter) in diameter.

Dendrite comes from the Greek word *dendron,* meaning "tree." Dendrites are hairlike threads branching off of the cell body like branches of a tree. Extensions of the cell body, they contain the same cytoplasm or cellular fluid found in the cell body. Dendrites are the points through which signals from adjacent neurons enter a particular neuron (the signal is then transmitted to the cell body). Since each neuron contains many dendrites, a neuron can receive signals from many other surrounding neurons.

An axon is a taillike projection extending out of one end of the cell body. It ends in a cluster of branches called terminal branches or axon terminals. Axons have the opposite function of dendrites: they carry nerve impulses away from the cell body. Axons vary in length and diameter. Some (such as those in the central nervous system) are very short, no longer than 0.01 inch (0.02 centimeter). Others (such as those in the peripheral nervous system) can be 3 feet (1 meter) long.

Most long axons are surrounded by a white, fatty material called myelin. The tubelike covering formed is known as a myelin sheath. It serves the same kind of function as the wrapping on a telephone line or an electrical cable. It protects the axon and prevents electrical impulses traveling through it from becoming lost.

Special cells form the myelin sheath by wrapping themselves around the axons of neurons. In the CNS, the cells forming the myelin sheath are called oligodendrocytes. In the PNS, special cells known as Schwann cells form the myelin sheath. The gap or indentation on an axon where one Schwann cell ends and another begins is known as a node of Ranvier. The nodes are unmyelinated (lack a myelin sheath), and the nerve or electrical impulse jumps from node to node as it passes along an axon (in unmyelinated axons, the impulse travels continuously along the axon).

Scientists believe Schwann cells produce a chemical that helps regenerate or restore damaged neurons in the peripheral nervous system. For example, if surgeons are able to reattach a person's severed hand, that person may regain some sensation and movement in that hand as neurons grow and make connections. Conversely, oligodendrocytes lack this ability. This is why

OPPOSITE: The brain and the spinal cord are the two major parts of the central nervous system, or CNS. The CNS acts as the command center of the body. (Illustration by Kopp Illustration, Inc.)

LEEMAN AND SUBSTANCE P

Susan E. Leeman. (Reproduced by permission of Dr. Susan Leeman.)

American neuroendocrinologist Susan E. Leeman (1930–) is known for her work with substance P, a peptide that helps govern the functioning of the nervous and lymphatic systems. (A peptide is a compound containing two or more amino acids, the building blocks of proteins.) While doing research on protein-hormones, Leeman found a peptide that could stimulate the secretion of saliva. The chemical turned out to be substance P, which had been discovered in the 1930s but had never been isolated (separated from other substances for individual study).

Leeman and her colleagues, working at Brandeis University in Massachusetts, isolated and characterized the peptide. A nerve transmitter that has many functions in the body, substance P is distributed throughout both the central and peripheral nervous systems. Substance P is important in the interaction between the nervous system and the lymphatic system (which governs body immunity) and seems to play a role in inflammation in the body.

an injury to the brain or spinal cord often results in some permanent loss of function.

TYPES OF NEURONS. Neurons in the body may be divided into three groups: sensory neurons, motor neurons, and interneurons. As their name implies, sensory neurons carry impulses or sensations from receptors to the brain or spinal cord (central nervous system). Receptors, which are located in the skin, skeletal muscles, joints, and internal organs, detect changes both inside and outside the body. Motor neurons work in the opposite direction. They carry impulses from the brain or spinal cord to muscles and glands, causing muscles to contract and glands to secrete. Both sensory and motor neurons make up the peripheral nervous system. Interneurons work entirely within the central nervous system. They conduct impulses from sensory to motor neurons.

Each neuron carries impulses in only one direction. This prevents impulses from traveling both ways in a neuron and canceling each other when they meet.

OPPOSITE: Typical neuron features. A neuron consists of three main parts: the cell body, dendrites, and an axon. (Illustration by Hans & Cassady.)

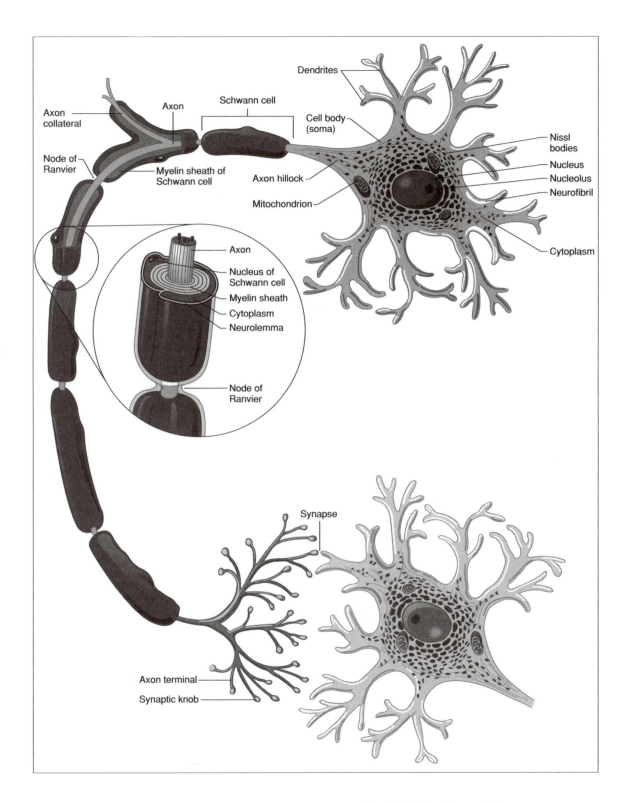

Axon
collateral

Axon

Schwann cell

Dendrites

Cell body
(soma)

Nissl
bodies

Nucleus

Nucleolus

Neurofibril

Node of
Ranvier

Myelin sheath of
Schwann cell

Axon hillock

Mitochondrion

Cytoplasm

Axon

Nucleus of
Schwann cell

Myelin sheath

Cytoplasm

Neurolemma

Node of
Ranvier

Synapse

Axon terminal

Synaptic knob

SUPPORTING CELLS. Neuroglia, or glial cells, are cells that surround neurons in the central nervous system. They do not conduct impulses, but help to support and protect neurons, combining with them to form what is known as nerve tissue. They also supply neurons with nutrients and remove their wastes. Neuroglia are abundant, accounting for some ten times the number of neurons. An example of neuroglia in the CNS are oligodendrocytes.

In the PNS, neurons are supported by Schwann cells and satellite cells (which form around the cell body to protect and cushion it).

Nerves

A nerve is a bundle of axons in the PNS. Each axon or nerve fiber is wrapped in delicate connective tissue. Groups of axons are then bound in coarser connective tissue to form bundles. Finally, many bundles are bound together (along with blood vessels to nourish the axons and Schwann cells) by even tougher connective tissue to form a nerve.

Nerves are categorized like neurons according to the direction in which they conduct impulses. Sensory nerves, made of the axons of sensory neurons, carry impulses to the brain and spinal cord. Motor nerves, made of the axons of motor neurons, carry impulses to the muscles and glands. Mixed nerves contain axons of both sensory and motor neurons. The most abundant nerves, mixed nerves can conduct impulses both to and from the central nervous system.

The brain

The human brain is a soft, shiny, grayish white, mushroom-shaped structure encased within the skull. At birth, a typical human brain weighs between 12 and 14 ounces (350 and 400 grams). By the time an average person reaches adulthood, the brain weighs about 3 pounds (1.36 kilograms). Because of greater average body size, the brains of male are generally about 10 percent larger than those of females. Although brain size varies considerably among humans, there is no correlation or link between brain size and intelligence.

The human brain is composed of up to one trillion nerve cells. One hundred billion of these are neurons, and the remainder are the supporting neuroglia. The brain consists of gray and white matter. Gray matter is nerve tissue in the CNS composed of neuron cell bodies, neuroglia, and unmyelinated axons; white matter is nerve tissue in the CNS composed chiefly of bundles of myelinated axons.

The brain is protected by the skull and by three membranes called the meninges. The outermost membrane is known as the dura mater, the middle as the arachnoid, and the innermost as the pia mater. Also protecting the brain is cerebrospinal fluid, a liquid that circulates between the arachnoid

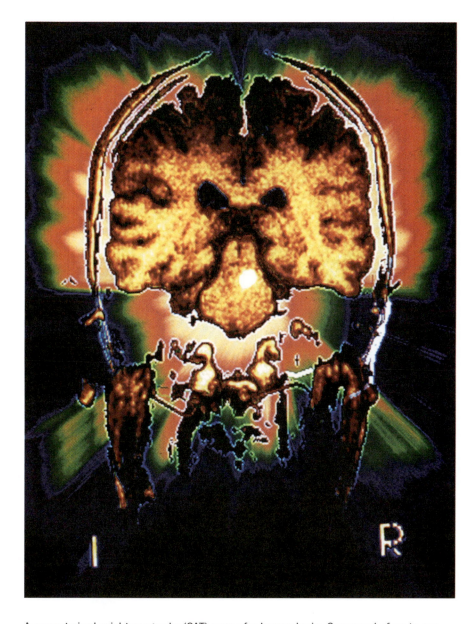

A computerized axial tomography (CAT) scan of a human brain. Composed of up to one trillion nerve cells, the average human brain weighs about 3 pounds. (Photograph by Keith. Reproduced by permission of Custom Medical Stock Photo.)

and pia mater. Many arteries and veins on the surface of the brain penetrate inward. Glucose, oxygen, and certain ions pass easily from the blood into the brain; other substances, such as antibiotics, do not. Scientists believe capillary walls create a blood-brain barrier that protects the brain from a number of biochemicals circulating in the blood.

The parts of the brain can be divided in terms of structure and function. The four principal sections of the human brain are the brain stem, the diencephalon, the cerebrum, and the cerebellum.

THE BRAIN STEM. The brain stem is the stalk of the brain and is a continuation of the spinal cord. It consists of the medulla oblongata, pons, and midbrain. The medulla oblongata is actually a portion of the spinal cord that extends into the brain. All messages that are transmitted between the brain and spinal cord pass through the medulla. Nerves on the right side of the medulla cross to the left side of the brain, and those on the left cross to the right. The result of this arrangement is that each side of the brain controls the opposite side of the body.

Three vital centers in the medulla control heartbeat, rate of breathing, and diameter of the blood vessels. Centers that help coordinate swallowing, vomiting, hiccuping, coughing, sneezing, and other basic functions of life are also located in the medulla. A region within the medulla helps to maintain the conscious state. The pons (from the Latin word meaning "bridge") conducts messages between the spinal cord and the rest of the brain, and between the different parts of the brain. The midbrain conveys impulses from the hypothalamus to the pons and spinal cord. It also contains visual and audio reflex centers involving the movement of the eyeballs and head.

Twelve pair of cranial nerves originate in the underside of the brain, mostly from the brain stem. They leave the skull through openings and extend as peripheral nerves to their destinations. Cranial nerves bring information to the brain from regions in the face, head, and neck. For example, the olfactory nerve transmits messages about smell from the nose and the optic nerve transmits visual information from the eyes. The only exception is the vagus nerve (vagus comes from the Latin word meaning "wandering"). It is the lone cranial nerve that serves other areas of the body. The vagus nerve branches extensively to the larynx, heart, lungs, stomach, and intestines. Among other functions, it helps promote digestive activity and regulate heart activity.

THE DIECEPHALON. The diencephalon lies above the brain stem, and includes the thalamus and hypothalamus. The thalamus is an important relay station for sensory information coming to the cerebral cortex from other parts of the brain. The thalamus also interprets sensations of pain, pressure, temperature, and touch, and is concerned with some of our emotions and memory. It receives information from the outside environment in the form of sound, smell, and taste.

OPPOSITE: The brain conditions that result in coma. Coma is caused by interference with the cerebral cortex or the structures that make up the reticular activating system (such as the thalamus). (Illustration by Hans & Cassady.)

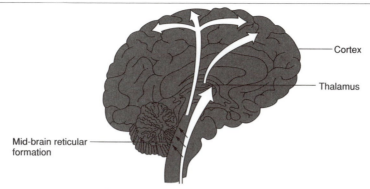

A side-view of the brain, showing movement of the reticular activating substance (RAS) essential to consciousness

Cortex

Thalamus

Mid-brain reticular formation

Diffuse and bilateral damage to the cerebral cortex (relative preservation of brain-stem reflexes)

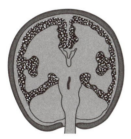

Possible causes
- Damage due to lack of oxygen or restricted blood flow, perhaps resulting form cardiac arrest, an anaesthetic accident, or shock
- Damage incurred from metabolic processes associated with kidney or liver failure, or with hypoglycemia
- Trauma damage
- Damage due to a bout with meningitis, encephalomyelitis, or a severe systemic infection

---

Mass lesions in this region resulting in compression of the brain-stem and damage to the reticular activating substance (RAS)

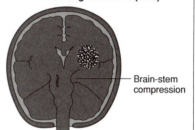

Brain-stem compression

Structural lesions within this region also resulting in compression of the brain-stem and damage to the reticular activating substance (RAS)

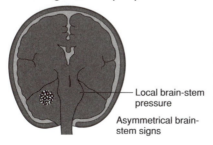

Local brain-stem pressure

Asymmetrical brain-stem signs

Possible causes • Cerebellar tumors, abscesses, or hemorrhages

---

Lesions within the brain-stem directly suppressing the reticular activating substance (RAS)

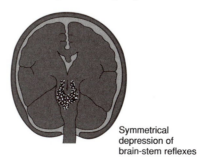

Symmetrical depression of brain-stem reflexes

Possible causes • Drug overdosage

The hypothalamus performs numerous important functions. These include the control of the autonomic nervous system. The hypothalamus controls normal body temperature and helps regulate the endocrine system, which produces hormones or chemical messengers that regulate body functions (for a further discussion of these actions, see chapter 3). It informs the body when it is hungry, full, or thirsty. It helps regulate sleep and wakefulness and is involved in the emotions of anger and aggression.

THE CEREBRUM. The cerebrum makes up about 80 percent of the brain's weight. It lies above the diencephalon. The cerebrum's outer layer, the cerebral cortex, is made entirely of gray matter (white matter makes up the inner portion of the cerebrum). The tissue of the cerebral cortex is about 0.08 to 0.16 inch (2 to 4 millimeters) thick. The cerebral cortex is folded extensively. The folds are called convolutions or gyri, and the shallow grooves between the folds are sulci. Deeper grooves, which are less numerous, are called fissures. The folds greatly increase the surface area of the cerebral cortex—it would have a surface area of about 5 square feet (1.5 square meters) if spread out—and thus the total number of nerve cell bodies it contains.

AVERAGE BRAIN WEIGHTS OF DIFFERENT SPECIES

Sperm whale: 17 pounds (7.8 kilograms)

Elephant: 13.2 pounds (6 kilograms)

Bottle-nosed dolphin: 3.3 pounds (1.5 kilograms)

Human (adult): 3 pounds (1.36 kilograms)

Camel: 1.5 pounds (0.76 kilogram)

Hippopotamus: 1.3 pounds (0.58 kilogram)

Polar bear: 1.1 pounds (0.5 kilogram)

Chimpanzee: 14.7 ounces (420 grams)

Lion: 8.4 ounces (240 grams)

Dog: 2.5 ounces (72 grams)

Cat: 1.1 ounces (30 grams)

Rabbit: 0.4 ounce (11.5 grams)

Squirrel: 0.26 ounce (7.6 grams)

Hamster: 0.05 ounce (1.4 grams)

Bull frog: 0.008 ounce (0.24 gram)

Located deep within the white matter of the cerebrum just above the diencephalon are two paired masses of gray matter known as basal ganglia. They are important in coordinating subconscious skeletal muscular movement, such as swinging of the arms while walking.

A deep fissure separates the cerebrum into a left and right hemisphere or half. The corpus callosum, a bundle of more than 200 million neurons, connects the two cerebral hemispheres and carries vast amounts of information between them—an estimated 4 billion nerve impulses per second. By studying patients whose corpus callosum had been destroyed, scientists have learned that differences exist between the left and right hemispheres. The left side of the brain functions mainly in speech, logic, writing, and arithmetic. The right side of the brain, on the other hand, is more concerned with imagination, art, symbols, and spatial relations.

Scientists have further divided each cerebral hemisphere into lobes named after the overlying bones of the skull: frontal (forehead area), temporal (on the sides above the ears), parietal (top part of the head), and occipital (back of the head) lobes.

The cerebral cortex is the portion of the brain that provides the most important distinctions between humans and other animals. It is responsible for the vast majority of functions that define what is meant by "being human." It enables humans not only to receive and interpret all kinds of sensory information, such as color, odor, taste, and sound, but also to remember, analyze, interpret, make decisions, and perform a host of other "higher" brain functions.

By studying animals and humans who have suffered damage to the cerebral cortex, scientists have found that the various lobes house areas with specific functions. The frontal lobes contain motor areas that generate impulses for voluntary movements. An area usually located in the left frontal lobe is called Broca's area. It coordinates the movements of the mouth involved in speaking. The parietal lobes contain general sensory areas that receive impulses from receptors in the skin. The temporal lobes contain auditory areas (receive impulses from the ears for hearing) and olfactory areas (receive impulses from receptors in the nose for smell). The occipital lobes contain visual areas that receive impulses from the retinas of the eyes. Different areas in the occipital lobes are concerned with judging distance and other spatial relationships.

Association areas, those not involved with a particular movement or sensation, are located in all the lobes. These areas are concerned with emotions and intellectual processes. In association areas, innumerable impulses are processed that result in memory, emotions, judgment, personality, and intelligence: what truly makes each person an individual.

WHY EINSTEIN WAS A GENIUS

German-born American theoretical physicist Albert Einstein (1879–1955), who formulated the theory of relativity (an approach for studying the nature of the universe), is considered by many to have been one of the greatest physicists of all time.

When Einstein died in 1955, the physician who performed the autopsy removed his brain from his body in order to perform scientific studies on it. For years, however, the brain was kept in a jar (for a while, the jar was even placed in a cardboard box behind a beer cooler). Although the physician took measurements of Einstein's brain and cut it into 240 pieces of varying size, he published none of his findings.

In 1996, the physician allowed Canadian researchers to study the remains of Einstein's brain. What the researchers found might explain the reason Einstein was a genius. They discovered that a region in Einstein's brain was 15 percent larger than the same area in people with average intelligence. That region controls mathematical thought, spatial relationships, and other mental processes. Known as the inferior parietal lobe, it is located about the level of the ear, starting in the front of the brain and extending two-thirds of the way back.

The researchers believe the enlarged region created a space for more neurons to make connections between each other and to work together more easily.

THE CEREBELLUM. The cerebellum is located below the cerebrum and behind the brain stem, and is shaped like a butterfly. The "wings" are the cerebellar hemispheres, and each consists of lobes that have distinct grooves or fissures. The cerebellum controls the actions of the muscular system needed for movement, balance, and posture. All motor activity in the body depends on the cerebellum.

THE LIMBIC SYSTEM. The limbic system is a horseshoe-shaped area of the brain located along the border between the cerebrum and diencephalon. Key structures of the limbic system include the almond-shaped amygdala and the sea horse-shaped hippocampus. The limbic system is concerned with emotional states (such as rage, fear, and sexual arousal) and memory. The hippocampus, in particular, plays a vital role in learning and long-term memory.

The spinal cord

The spinal cord, a glistening white rope, is a continuation of the brain stem. It transmits impulses to and from the brain and controls some reflex actions. On average, the spinal cord measures about 18 inches (45 centimeters) in length and about 0.5 inch (14 centimeters) in width. It weighs about 1.25 ounces (35 grams).

The vertebral column or backbone encloses the spinal cord. This long channel, made of individual bones called vertebrae, protects the spinal cord from mechanical injury. Like the brain, the spinal cord is also cushioned and protected by meninges. Arteries run along the surface of the spinal cord, supplying it with a nourishing blood supply.

The spinal cord is composed of roughly 13.5 million neurons. It appears white because its thick outer layer is made of white matter. This layer contains many myelinated axons that form bundles—called tracts—that carry either sensory information or motor commands. Tracts that carry sensory information toward the brain are called ascending tracts. Those that carry motor commands from the brain into the spinal cord are called descending tracts.

Within the spinal cord is an H- or butterfly-shaped gray area composed of gray matter. Cell bodies of neurons and supporting neuroglia make up this gray matter. Many of these cell bodies are those of motor neurons. Their axons pass out of the spinal cord to control skeletal muscles or to regulate the actions of smooth muscles, cardiac muscles, and glands.

Extending out from the spinal cord between the vertebrae are thirty-one pair of spinal nerves. All these nerves are mixed nerves, containing thousands of axons of both sensory and motor neurons. Inside the vertebral column, however, each nerve is split into two branches that connect with the spinal cord. The branch that attaches on the rear (posterior) portion of the spinal cord is called the dorsal root. It contains the axons of sensory neurons. On

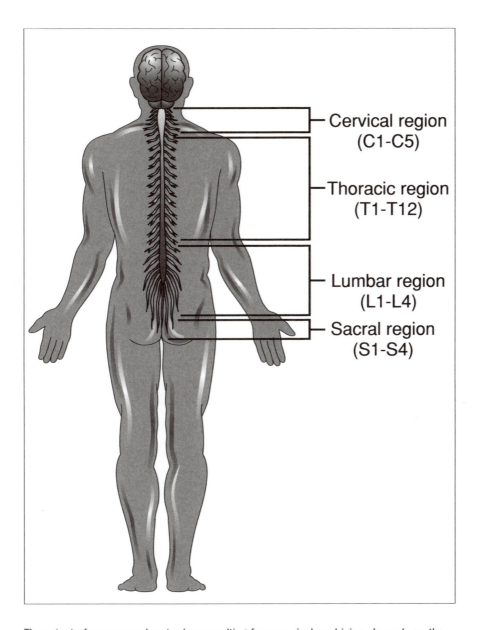

Cervical region
(C1-C5)

Thoracic region
(T1-T12)

Lumbar region
(L1-L4)

Sacral region
(S1-S4)

The extent of sensory and motor loss resulting from a spinal cord injury depends on the level of the injury. This is because nerves at different levels control sensation and movement in different parts of the body. (Illustration by Electronic Illustrators Group.)

each dorsal root is an enlarged area called the dorsal root ganglion (a ganglion is any collection of neuron cell bodies in the PNS). This ganglion contains the cell bodies of the sensory neurons. The branch that attaches on the front (anterior) portion of the spinal cord is called the ventral root. It contains the axons of motor neurons.

The thirty-one pairs of spinal nerves exit the vertebral column to serve the areas of the body close by. The first or top eight pairs (located in the neck area) bring impulses to and from the head, neck, shoulders, arms, and diaphragm. The next twelve pairs (located in the chest area) bring impulses to and from the trunk of the body, including internal organs such as the heart and lungs. The remaining eleven pairs bring impulses to and from the lower part of the body—the hips, pelvic cavity, and legs. Damage to a spinal nerve or either of its roots will result in the loss of sensation and in paralysis of the area of the body being served by that nerve.

The spinal cord does not extend all the way down the vertebral column. In order to reach their proper openings to exit the column, the last eleven pair of spinal nerves hang below the end of the spinal cord like long hairs. Because of their appearance, they are collectively called the cauda equina (in Latin, *cauda equina* means "horse's tail").

WORKINGS: HOW THE NERVOUS SYSTEM FUNCTIONS

Reading a book, walking through a field, playing a musical instrument, digesting a holiday meal, remembering a lost relative—the nervous system regulates all of the body's activities, from the simplest to the most complex. In order to perceive and to respond to the world around us and the changes within us, the body's tissues, organs, and organ systems must function. In order for those body parts to function, they must be stimulated and regulated by nerve impulses.

Neurons have the ability to respond to a stimulus and convert it into a nerve impulse. They also have the ability to transmit that impulse to other neurons or the cells of muscles or glands.

Transmission of nerve impulses

In neurons, information travels in the form of nerve impulses that are conducted along axons. In myelinated axons, a nerve impulse can travel up to about 325 feet (100 meters) per second. In unmyelinated axons, the impulse travels much slower, about 1.5 feet (0.5 meter) per second.

Impulses do not travel in and between neurons like electric currents through telephone wires. For nerve impulses to be transmitted throughout the body, electrochemical reactions must occur in neurons. As stated earlier, dendrites are the points through which signals or impulses from adjacent neurons enter a particular neuron. If a dendrite of a neuron is stimulated, electrical and chemical changes take place throughout the cell.

Every neuron communicates with other neurons or with other types of cells. Neurons that transmit impulses to other neurons do not actually touch one another. The small space or gap where the impulse passes between the axon of one neuron and a dendrite of the next neuron is known as the synapse. A synapse measures about 0.000001 inch (0.0000025 centimeter).

When a neuron is inactive or resting, the tissue fluid that surrounds it contains more positive ions than are inside the neuron (an ion is an atom or group of atoms that has an electrical charge, either positive or negative). The major positive ions outside the cell are sodium; the major positive ions inside the cell are potassium. Because there are more positive ions outside the neuron, its internal surface is slightly negative. As long as the outside remains positive and the inside negative, the neuron remains at rest.

When a dendrite of a neuron is stimulated, tiny "gates" in the membrane of the dendrite and cell body begin to open and close. According to the laws of diffusion, molecules always move from an area where they exist in greater numbers to an area where they exist in lesser numbers. So, when these gates are open, sodium ions flow into the cell body. This temporary movement of ions changes the electrical charges on the membrane of the cell—positive on the inside, negative on the outside. This results in an electrical charge or nerve impulse on the surface of the cell. The impulse rapidly passes from the dendrite, down the length of the cell body, and along the length of the axon. An all-or-nothing response, the nerve impulse never goes partway along a neuron, but along its entire length.

As soon as the gates on the membrane of the neuron open, they close and the body restores the correct balance of sodium and potassium ions

WAVES IN THE BRAIN

The electrical charges (nerves impulses) created by the billions of neurons in the brain combine to generate an electrical field. That field can be measured by a machine called an electroencephalograph. The machine records the electrical activity as horizontal zigzag patterns on a screen or a page. Those patterns are known as brain waves.

As different regions of the brain are stimulated or are quieted down, the brain wave patterns change. There are four major types of brain waves. Alpha waves occur in normal, healthy adults who are awake but relaxed. The waves produce regular, fast patterns, about 8 to 13 cycles per second. Beta waves result when a person is concentrating or thinking about something. They produce patterns that are small and very fast, about 13 to 30 cycles per second. Theta waves are found in the brains of children and in adults who are under emotional stress. In adults, theta waves may also indicate a brain disorder. The patterns of theta waves are large and slow, about 4 to 8 cycles per second. The largest and slowest-moving waves are delta waves. These regular-patterned waves appear in the brains of infants and in the brains of sleeping adults. They are also found in the brains of individuals who have suffered brain damage.

By comparing the brain waves of a person to those found in normal, healthy individuals, physicians can determine if the brain of that person has been injured or infected by a disease.

inside and outside the neuron. Only after the balance has been restored and the neuron is at rest can another impulse be conducted along the neuron.

NEUROTRANSMITTERS. When the impulse or electrical current has reached the terminal branches or end of the axon, it stimulates the branches to release chemicals known as neurotransmitters. As their name suggests, neurotransmitters are the mechanisms by which a nerve impulse travels from one neuron to another or to body cells.

Once released from an axon, a neurotransmitter drifts across the synapse to a second neuron. When it has reached that cell, it attaches itself to specialized parts, called receptors, in the dendrites of the second neuron. This act of attaching creates the stimulus for dendrites in the second neuron. Those

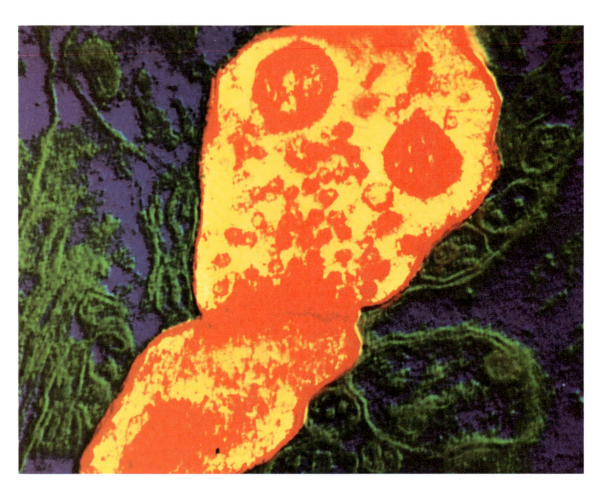

False color typography of a synapse between two neurons in a human cerebral cortex. (Reproduced by permission of CNRI/SPL/Photo Researchers, Inc.)

dendrites then respond to this stimulus just as the first neuron responded to its stimulus, and the nerve impulse continues.

Scientists have identified a number of neurotransmitters, including dopamine, serotonin, and acetylcholine. Each neurotransmitter occurs in certain types of neurons and has specific functions. It can either start an action or stop it, such as causing a muscle to contract or a gland to stop secreting. For example, acetylcholine is the neurotransmitter released at the terminal branches of motor neurons that come in close contact with muscle fibers (in this case, the synapse is called the neuromuscular junction). When acetylcholine attaches to receptors on the membrane of the muscle fiber, it triggers an electrical charge that quickly travels from one end of the muscle fiber to the other, causing it to contract.

The transmission of a nerve impulse—first along a neuron, then to another neuron—is an electrochemical event. The impulse traveling along a neuron is electrical, but the transfer of that impulse (the stimulation of the next neuron by neurotransmitters) is chemical. The actions involved in the creation and transfer of a nerve impulse ensure that it can travel in one direction only in a neuron—from dendrite through axon.

Even though nerve impulses travel in one direction only, a neuron can have as many as 100,000 synapses connecting it to other neurons. Thus, a neuron can receive and transmit many impulses over a variety of pathways, connecting with many different neurons at the same time. The path an impulse takes, from a particular neuron to another one, determines the meaning of that impulse and the action it evokes.

EVEN THOUGH NERVE IMPULSES TRAVEL IN ONE DIRECTION ONLY, A NEURON CAN HAVE AS MANY AS 100,000 SYNAPSES CONNECTING IT TO OTHER NEURONS.

Reflexes

It is not always necessary for a nerve impulse traveling along sensory nerves to reach the brain before a response causes the body to react in some way. When a stimulus causes a response that is involuntary, rapid, and predictable, that response is known as a reflex. Reflexes are classified according to the systems of the PNS: autonomic reflexes and somatic reflexes. Autonomic reflexes control the activity of the smooth muscles, heart, and glands. They also regulate complex body functions such as digestion, blood pressure, sweating, and swallowing. Somatic reflexes control skeletal muscles. In general, reflexes control much of what the body must do every day.

The pathway a nerve impulse travels when a reflex is initiated is called the reflex arc. A typical reflex action begins when a sensory receptor (in the skin, sense organ, or other internal organ) is activated by some kind of stimulus. The receptor generates an impulse in a sensory neuron and the impulse then travels along other sensory neurons to the spinal cord. In the gray matter of the spinal cord, the impulse passes from a sensory neuron through an interneuron into a motor neuron. The motor neuron then transmits the impulse through other motor neurons to a muscle or gland, where some type of response occurs.

For example, if a person touches a hot stove, that person immediately pulls his or her hand away. Heat and pain receptors in the skin were stimulated to send impulses to the spinal cord, where they were transferred to motor neurons that eventually connected to muscles in the hand, which were stimulated to contract and pull the hand away. Although it may seem that the pain caused by the hot stove led to the quick withdrawal of the hand, the movement actually occurred milliseconds before the brain became aware of the pain and initiated some response. This is an example of a somatic reflex.

Reflexes such as this one are important in safeguarding the body against potentially harmful changes outside or inside the body. Reflexes are also a good tool in evaluating the condition of the nervous system. If a reflex is exaggerated or even absent, a nervous system disorder may be present. That is why doctors often perform the knee-jerk reflex test during a routine physical examination: a sharp rap on the tendon below the knee should cause the quadriceps muscle on the front part of the thigh to contract, forcing the lower leg to kick outward.

Autonomic nervous system

Much of what occurs in the body every day occurs without an individual being consciously aware. The heart beats, the lungs expand, blood vessels contract and dilate (widen), and the stomach and intestines break down food and move it through the system. These actions and all others that take place without willful control are regulated by the autonomic nervous system (ANS), a part of the peripheral nervous system.

All body systems contribute to homeostasis or the ability of the body to maintain the internal balance of its functions. The minute-to-minute stability of the body, however, is largely dependent on the workings of the ANS.

The ANS is broken down into two subdivisions. The part that keeps body systems running smoothly on a daily basis is called the parasympathetic nervous system. The part that comes into play when emergencies or stressful situations arise is called the sympathetic nervous system. Both subdivisions service the same body organs and use motor nerves to do so (some glands and skin structures receive only sympathetic motor nerves).

The parasympathetic nervous system is in control when the body is at rest. The neurons for this system originate in the brain stem and in the lower region of the spinal cord. The impulses conducted through this system target body organs in an effort to conserve body energy and promote normal digestion and elimination. In the digestive tract, secretions and peristalsis (series of wavelike muscular contractions that move material in one direction through a hollow organ) increase. Heart rate, the force of heart contractions, and blood pressure all decrease. The pupils of the eyes constrict to limit the amount of light entering the body. Kidneys increase their production of urine. Nutrient levels in the blood increase, and cells throughout the body add the extra nutrients to their energy reserves.

The sympathetic nervous system has the opposite effect on the body. It comes into play when an individual is faced with a "fight-or-flight" situation. The neurons for this system originate from the middle of the spinal cord. Their impulses seek to stimulate the body into using its energy. The activity of the digestive and urinary organs decreases. The liver releases glucose (sugar) into the blood for use by the cells as energy. Heart rate and contraction, blood pressure, and blood flow to skeletal muscles all increase. The eyes dilate to let more light in. In short, the sympathetic nervous system prepares the body to respond to some threat, whether that response is to run, to see better, or to think more clearly.

Rita Levi-Montalcini. (Reproduced by permission of AP/Wide World Photos.)

LEVI-MONTALCINI'S NERVE GROWTH FACTOR

Italian-born American neurobiologist Rita Levi-Montalcini (1909–) is recognized for her groundbreaking research on nerve cell growth.

She discovered a protein in the human nervous system that she named the nerve growth factor (NGF). For her work, which has proven useful in the study of several disorders (including Alzheimer's disease), Levi-Montalcini received the 1986 Nobel Prize for physiology or medicine (she shared the award with biochemist Stanley Cohen).

After graduating from medical school in Italy in 1936, Levi-Montalcini began to research the nervous system. She conducted experiments on chicken embryos (organisms in their earliest stages of development) in order to study how neurons are differentiated, or how they are formed and assigned a particular function in the developing body. Levi-Montalcini believed that a specific nutrient was essential for neuron growth. In the 1950s, she finally isolated or obtained a sample of the substance that caused neurons to grow and labeled it NGF.

The work that Levi-Montalcini began in the late 1930s has been carried on by researchers who realize the important role that NGF can possibly play in treating degenerative diseases (those in which organs or tissue deteriorate and stop functioning).

The parasympathetic and sympathetic nervous systems rarely work independently of each other. Instead, they often work together, especially in affecting vital organs. Their opposing effects help to maintain the dynamic balance of the internal body.

AILMENTS: WHAT CAN GO WRONG WITH THE NERVOUS SYSTEM?

Because of its role as the master controller of the body, when the nervous system becomes disabled, so does the rest of the body. Injuries to the brain and spinal cord can easily occur in contact sports (such as football, hockey, and boxing) and as a result of falls or collisions in other activities (such as bicycling, horseback riding, skiing, and soccer). They may range from mild concussions where the brain is jarred against the skull, resulting in the temporary slight loss of higher mental functions, to severe spinal injuries where the spinal cord is pinch or severed, resulting in permanent paralysis or even death.

The nervous system can be also adversely affected by diseases or disorders. Some may be genetic (hereditary), others caused by an illness or disease. The following are just a few of the many diseases and disorders that can affect this system or its parts.

Alzheimer's disease

Alzheimer's disease (AD) is a progressive (tending to grow worse) neurological disorder that results in dementia—impaired memory, thinking, and

NERVOUS SYSTEM DISORDERS

Alzheimer's disease (ALTS-hi-merz): Disease of the nervous system marked by a deterioration of memory, thinking, and reasoning.

Amyotrophic lateral sclerosis (a-me-o-TROW-fik LA-ter-al skle-ROW-sis): Also known as Lou Gehrig's disease, a disease that breaks down motor neurons, resulting in the loss of the ability to move any of the muscles in the body.

Carpal tunnel syndrome (CAR-pal TUN-nel SIN-drome): Disorder caused by the compression at the wrist of the median nerve supplying the hand, causing numbness and tingling.

Epilepsy (EP-eh-lep-see): Disorder of the nervous system marked by seizures that often involve convulsions or the loss of consciousness.

Huntington's disease: Inherited, progressive disease causing uncontrollable physical movements and mental deterioration.

Migraine (MY-grain): A particularly intense form of headache.

Parkinson's disease: Progressive disease in which cells in one of the movement-control centers of the brain begin to die, resulting in a loss of control over speech and head and body movements.

Poliomyelitis (po-lee-o-my-eh-LIE-tis): Contagious viral disease that can cause damage to the central nervous system, resulting in paralysis and loss of muscle tissue.

reasoning. AD usually occurs in old age. It affects approximately 4 million people in the United States and is the fourth leading cause of death among adults (after heart disease, cancer, and stroke). Scientists believe that 5 to 10 percent of people over the age of sixty-five suffer from some form of the disease. AD affects men and women almost equally.

The primary symptoms of AD are the gradual loss of memory, lessened ability to perform routine tasks, disorientation, difficulty in learning, loss of language skills, impairment of judgment and planning, and mood or behavioral changes. Depression, paranoia, and delusions may also arise. The disease begins slowly and gradually. Most people die within eight years after being diagnosed with AD. Some die within a year, while others may live as long as twenty years.

Scientists do not know the exact cause or causes of AD. Research has shown that in people with AD, the centers of the brain concerned with learning, reasoning, and memory become clogged with abnormal tissue. What triggers this twisted mass of tissue to form is, again, unknown.

There is currently no cure for AD. Treatments, however, are available to alleviate or lessen some of the symptoms. Two drugs that have been approved by the U.S. Food and Drug Administration both increase the levels of the neurotransmitter acetylcholine in the brain. This helps increase the communication ability of the remaining neurons, thereby modestly increasing a person's ability to perform normal daily activities. Research into this disabling disease continues.

Amyotrophic lateral sclerosis

Amyotrophic lateral sclerosis (ALS) is a disease that breaks down tissues in the nervous system, affecting the nerves that control body movement. ALS is also known as motor neuron disease and Lou Gehrig's disease, after the American baseball player (1903–1941) whose career it ended.

The disease affects approximately 30,000 people in the United States. It usually begins between the ages of forty and seventy, although it can begin at a younger age. Men are slightly more likely to develop ALS than women. Eighty percent of those people affected with the disease die within five years. However, noted English theoretical physicist Stephen Hawking (1942–) has lived with ALS for over thirty years.

Technically, ALS causes the destruction of motor neurons that control voluntary muscle movement. For yet unknown reasons, the motor neurons in the spinal cord and brain die. As they die, the muscles they normally control cannot be moved as effectively and begin to waste away. The ability to move virtually any of the muscles in the body is soon lost. ALS principally affects the muscles controlled by conscious thought, such as those in the arms, legs, and trunk.

Weakness in the arms and legs, usually more pronounced on one side than the other, is the earliest symptom of ALS. Later symptoms include the loss of the ability to walk, to use the arms and hands, to speak clearly or at all, to swallow, and to hold the head up. Lung infection, brought on by poor swallowing and the weakness of respiratory muscles, is often the cause of death.

There is currently no cure for ALS, and no treatment that can significantly alter its course.

Carpal tunnel syndrome

Carpal tunnel syndrome is a condition in which the squeezing or compression of the median nerve that passes through the wrist results in numb-

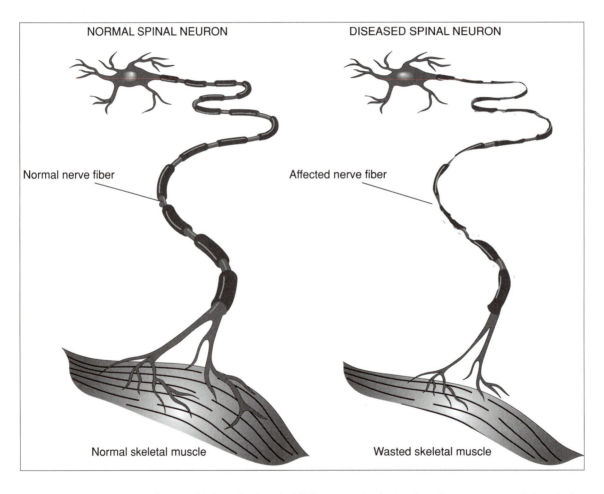

Amyotrophic lateral sclerosis (ALS) causes the destruction of motor neurons that control voluntary muscle movement. The motor neurons in the spinal cord and brain die and the muscles they normally control cannot be moved as effectively and begin to waste away. (Illustration by Electronic Illustrators Group.)

ness, tingling, weakness, or pain in one or both hands. The hands may become so weakened that opening jars or grasping objects becomes difficult and painful. Women between the ages of thirty and sixty have the highest rates of carpal tunnel syndrome.

The carpal tunnel is a space formed by the carpal (wrist) bones and the carpal ligament (a connective tissue that attaches bone to bone). Through this space pass the median nerve and tendons of the fingers and thumb (the median nerve runs from the neck through the middle of the arm to the fingers). When the tendons within the carpal tunnel become inflamed, they swell and press on the median nerve.

Most often, performing a job that requires repeated bending or twisting of the wrists increases the likelihood of developing the disorder. Continuous flexing of the wrist, as when typing on a keyboard or playing a piano, can cause compression of the median nerve. A number of other conditions can also cause swelling of the carpal tunnel and pressure on the median nerve. Such conditions include pregnancy, arthritis, hypothyroidism (reduced function of the thyroid gland), diabetes, menopause (the point in a woman's life when menstruation ceases and childbearing is no longer possible), and pituitary gland abnormalities.

Carpal tunnel syndrome is treated initially by applying a brace or splint, to prevent the wrist from bending and to relieve pressure on the median nerve. If a person's job is causing the disorder, performing other work may be necessary. Treatment of a related medical condition may relieve the symptoms of carpal tunnel syndrome. Severe cases may require surgery to decrease compression of the median nerve.

Epilepsy

Epilepsy comes from the Greek word for seizure. A seizure is a sudden disruption in the brain's normal electrical activity accompanied by a state of altered consciousness. Epilepsy is a condition characterized by recurrent seizures during which a person may lose consciousness and experience convulsions, or violent repetitive muscle contractions. Scientists believe epilepsy

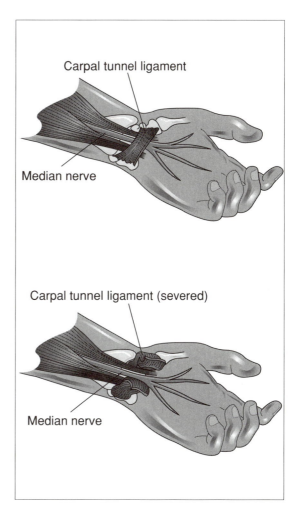

The most severe cases of carpel tunnel syndrome may require surgery to decrease pressure on the median nerve. (Illustration by Electronic Illustrators Group.)

Body By Design   **199**

affects 1 to 2 percent of the population of the United States. One in every two cases develops before the age of twenty-five.

The repeated symptoms associated with epilepsy are the result of unusually large electrical charges from neurons in a particular area of the brain. However, the reason this occurs in 50 to 70 percent of all cases of epilepsy is unknown. Epilepsy is sometimes the result of trauma at the time of birth, such as insufficient oxygen to the brain or head injury. Other causes of the disorder may be head injury resulting from a car accident, alcoholism, inflammation of the meninges, infectious diseases such as measles or mumps, or lead or mercury poisoning.

The best known examples of epilepsy are grand mal and petit mal. The term *mal* comes from the French word meaning "illness," while *grand* and *petit* refer respectively to "large" and "small" episodes of the illness.

THE BEST KNOWN EXAMPLES OF EPILEPSY ARE GRAND MAL AND PETIT MAL.

In the case of grand mal, an epileptic (person suffering from epilepsy) is likely to have some indication (such as a distinctive smell, taste, or other unusual sensation) that a seizure is imminent. This feeling is called an aura. Very soon after feeling the aura, the person will lapse into unconsciousness and experience generalized muscle contractions that may distort the body. The thrashing movements of the limbs that follow are caused by opposing sets of muscles alternately contracting. The person may also lose control of the bladder and or bowels. When the seizures stop, usually after three to five minutes, the person may remain unconscious for up to half an hour. Upon awakening, the person may not remember having had a seizure and may be confused for a time.

In contrast to the grand mal seizure, the petit mal may seem insignificant. The person interrupts whatever he or she is doing and for up to about 20 seconds may show subtle outward signs, such as blinking of the eyes, staring into space, or pausing in conversation. After the seizure has ended, the person resumes his or her previous activity, usually totally unaware that an interruption has taken place. Petit mal seizures generally begin at the age of four and stop by the time a child has become an adolescent. Untreated, petit mal seizures can recur as many as 100 times a day and may progress to grand mal seizures.

Epilepsy is a recurrent, lifelong condition that must be managed on a long-term basis. A number of drugs are available to help eliminate seizures or make the symptoms less frequent and less severe. About 85 percent of all seizure disorders can be partially or completely controlled if an epileptic person takes anti-seizure medications according to directions, gets enough sleep, and eats balanced meals.

Huntington's disease

Huntington's disease (HD) is an inherited, progressive (tending to grow worse) disease that causes uncontrollable physical movements and mental deterioration. It is occasionally referred to as Woody Guthrie's disease, after the American folk singer (1912–1967) who died from it. Approximately 30,000 people in the United States are affected by HD.

Benjamin Carson. (Photograph by Richard T. Nowitz. Reproduced by permission of Photo Researchers, Inc.)

BENJAMIN CARSON: CELEBRATED NEUROSURGEON

American pediatric neurosurgeon Benjamin Carson (1951–) has undertaken many high-risk operations on children involving complex and delicate neurosurgical procedures. In 1987 he gained international acclaim for leading a team of seventy medical personnel that separated a pair of Siamese twins (children who are born physically connected) who were joined at the backs of their heads.

One of Carson's most difficult operations took place in 1985 when he operated on a four-year-old boy with a malignant tumor of the brain stem (a malignant tumor is one that spreads and causes physical harm). Other physicians had stated that the cancer could not be removed with surgery, but Carson disagreed and went ahead with the operation. The boy eventually made a complete recovery.

Another notable operation involved a four-year-old girl who suffered from multiple seizures—up to 120 a day. Her right side was paralyzed, and she had a rare brain disease that, if unchecked, would have left her with serious neurological damage. Carson removed the diseased left hemisphere of her brain during a ten-hour operation. Six months later she had regained nearly complete use of her right arm and leg and was free of seizures. The right side of her brain had taken over functions of the left.

Carson's most famous medical operation occurred in 1987, when he led a team of doctors, nurses, and technicians to separate a pair of German Siamese twins who shared a blood vessel in the back of their heads. Carson devised a plan to separate the twins by completely shutting down their blood flow, severing their common blood vessel, and then restoring their individual vessel systems. While the entire procedure lasted twenty-two hours, Carson and another surgeon had only one hour to conduct the actual surgery and restoration. The operation went smoothly until Carson noticed the vessels that carried blood from the brain of each child were more tangled than had been expected. Twenty minutes after stopping the twins' circulation, Carson made the final cut. He then had forty minutes to reconstruct the severed blood vessels and close. Just a few minutes before the hour limit, the twins were separated and the operating tables were wheeled apart.

The symptoms of HD usually appear in people between the ages of thirty and fifty. They fall into three categories: motor or movement symptoms, personality and behavioral changes, and mental decline. Early motor symptoms include restlessness, twitching, and a desire to move about. As the disease progresses, a person may experience involuntary jerking or twisting, difficulty in speaking and swallowing, impaired balance, depression, anxiety, the inability to plan and carry out routine tasks, slowed thought, and impaired or inappropriate judgment.

In 1993, scientists discovered the exact gene that causes HD. The gene makes a protein. When the gene is defective, the protein it creates interacts with other proteins in brain cells where it occurs, and this interaction ultimately leads to cell death. A parent, either the mother or father, who has the defective gene has a 50 percent chance of passing it on to his or her children. Male and females are affected equally.

There is no cure for HD and no treatment that can slow its rate of progression. Drugs and physical therapy can help reduce the effects of involuntary muscular movements and mental deterioration. Death usually occurs fifteen to twenty years after a person has been diagnosed with the disease.

Migraine

Migraine is a particularly intense form of headache lasting several hours or more. The term does not apply to a single medical condition, but is applied to a variety of symptoms that are often numerous and changeable. Migraine sufferers find that their headaches are provoked by a particular stimulus, such as stress, loud noises, missed meals, or eating particular foods.

Migraines affect as many as 24 million people in the United States. Approximately 18 percent of women and 6 percent of men experience at least one migraine attack per year. Migraines often begin in adolescence, but are rare after the age of sixty.

MIGRAINES AFFECT AS MANY AS 24 MILLION PEOPLE IN THE UNITED STATES.

A migraine condition can generally be divided into four distinct phases. The first phase is known as the prodrome. Symptoms develop slowly over a twenty-four-hour period; they include feelings of heightened or dulled perception, irritability or withdrawal, and cravings for certain foods.

The second phase, known as the aura, is marked by visual disturbances. These are described as flashing lights, shimmering zigzag lines, spotty vision, and other disturbances in one or both eyes. Other symptoms such as tingling or numbness in the hands may occur as well. All these symptoms can be acutely distressing to the patient. This phase usually precedes the actual headache by one hour or less.

Phase three consists of the headache itself, usually described as a severe throbbing or pulsating pain on one or both sides of the head. It may be accompanied by nausea and vomiting. Light, noise, and movement may worsen the condition. This phase may last from four to seventy-two hours.

During the final phase, called the postdrome, the person often feels drained and washed-out. This feeling generally subsides within twenty-four hours.

Migraine appears to involve changes in the patterns of blood circulation and of nerve transmissions in the brain. Scientists currently believe that migraines develop in three phases. The first step takes place in the midbrain. For reasons not fully understood, cells that are otherwise functioning normally in this region begin sending abnormal electrical signals to other brain centers, including the visual cortex. The second step occurs when blood vessels in the brain dilate (expand), increasing blood flow. The third step occurs when nerve cells that control the sensation of pain in the head and face become activated. The pain of migraine is thought to result from this combination of increased pain sensitivity, tissue and blood vessel swelling, and inflammation.

Several drugs may be used to reduce the pain and severity of a migraine attack. Research has shown that a combination of acetaminophen (Tylenol), aspirin, and caffeine can effectively relieve symptoms for many migraine sufferers. Research has also shown a connection between migraine and low levels of serotonin, a neurotransmitter found in the brain. Drugs that chemically resemble serotonin have proven effective in treating migraine.

Parkinson's disease

Parkinson's disease (PD) is a progressive (tending to grow worse) disease in which cells in one of the movement-control centers of the brain begin to die. Nerves and muscles become weak, and the control over speech and head and body movements is lost. Individuals suffering from PD move around very slowly and their hands may tremble. Approximately 500,000 people in the United States, both men and women, are affected by PD.

Scientists have not yet been able to determine exactly what causes the brain cells to die. Certain chemical toxins in illegal drugs have been found to bring on symptoms of PD, but these toxins cannot be linked to the numerous cases of PD that arise each year. A deficiency of the neurotransmitter dopamine has been suggested as a possible cause for PD. In this case, scientists believe that when too little dopamine is produced in the body, neurons are not sufficiently stimulated, which can lead to symptoms characteristic of PD.

Symptoms of PD include tremors (usually beginning in the hands), slow movements, muscle rigidity or stiffness, balance problems, decreased eye-blinking, depression, speech changes, sleep problems, constipation, and irritability.

There is currently no cure for or a way to prevent PD. Most drugs prescribed treat the symptoms of the disease only. Regular, moderate exercise has been shown to improve certain motor functions in people afflicted with PD. Over time, the symptoms of PD worsen and become less responsive to drug treatments.

Poliomyelitis

Poliomyelitis (often referred to simply as polio) is a serious infectious disease that attacks muscle-controlling nerves and can eventually cause paralysis. Poliomyelitis is caused by one of three related viruses, and it primarily affects children. However, adults can also be infected. There is no drug that can cure polio once a person has been infected.

THERE IS NO DRUG THAT CAN CURE POLIO ONCE A PERSON HAS BEEN INFECTED.

Poliomyelitis is infectious, meaning it is spread primarily through contact with the saliva or feces of someone who already has the disease. The virus enters the body through the mouth and multiplies rapidly in the intestines. Eventually it enters the bloodstream, then gains access to the central nervous system where it travels along nerve pathways.

Symptoms usually begin to show one to three weeks after the virus is contracted. In some cases, the attack may be so mild that it goes unnoticed. The body quickly develops immunity and the virus is eliminated. A more severe attack gives rise to symptoms that resemble those of influenza (fever, sore throat, vomiting, diarrhea, stiff neck and back, and muscle pain). About two-thirds of people infected in such a way recover without suffering any paralysis.

A serious attack occurs if the virus reaches the central nervous system and invades motor nerves. Inflammation and the destruction of those nerves can result. Without stimulation from those nerves, muscle tissue then weakens and paralysis develops. Usually the paralysis is only temporary, and about 50 percent of people infected recover without permanent disability. However, if any of the cells attacked by the virus are destroyed, they cannot be replaced and muscle function is permanently impaired. About 25 percent of people who recover after being seriously infected have severe permanent disability. If the nerve cells of the brain stem are attacked, the muscles controlling swallowing, heartbeat, and breathing are paralyzed. The result is death.

In the 1950s, two types of vaccines were developed to provide the body immunity to the poliomyelitis virus. The first contains components or parts of the virus while the second contains live but weakened virus. Both vaccines prompt the body's lymphatic system to produce antibodies that will attack any future invading forms of the disease. Poliomyelitis is now a rare disease in the United States.

TAKING CARE: KEEPING THE NERVOUS SYSTEM HEALTHY

The growth of the brain stops once an individual reaches young adulthood. As aging takes place, neurons become damaged and die. Since they cannot reproduce themselves, their number in the brain continually decreases. However, the number lost under normal conditions is only a small percentage of the total.

THE GROWTH OF THE BRAIN STOPS ONCE AN INDIVIDUAL REACHES YOUNG ADULTHOOD.

As in all body systems, though, aging brings about structural changes in the brain and nervous system. With the loss of neurons, brain size and weight decrease. Blood flow to the brain also decreases. Again, these changes are normal and usually are not the cause of mental disabilities in elderly people.

However, certain activities in life can accelerate the aging process of the brain, leading to mental impairment. Boxers and alcoholics are prime candidates to suffer from slurred speech, tremors, and dementia (impaired memory, thinking, and reasoning) long before others. Certain drugs, high blood pressure, arteriosclerosis (diseased condition in which the walls of arteries become thickened and hard, interfering with the circulation of blood), poor nutrition, depression, and stress can also lead to premature loss of mental abilities.

Learning can continue throughout life as neural pathways are always available and ready to be developed. Like the muscles of the body, the mind can remain strong if used regularly. The following activities, if maintained on a life-long basis, can help keep the nervous system operating at peak efficiency: eating a proper diet low in fat and high in fiber, maintaining a healthy weight, consuming proper amounts of good-quality drinking water, getting adequate rest, engaging in regular exercise, not smoking or taking illegal drugs, drinking only moderate amounts of alcohol (if at all), and reducing stress levels.

FOR MORE INFORMATION

Books

Barmeier, Jim. *The Brain.* San Diego, CA: Lucent Books, 1996.

Edelson, Edward. *The Nervous System.* New York: Chelsea House, 1991.

Greenfield, Susan A. *The Human Mind Explained.* New York: Henry Holt, 1996.

Parker, Steve. *The Brain and Nervous System.* Austin, TX: Raintree/Steck-Vaughn, 1997.

Simon, Seymour. *The Brain: Our Nervous System.* New York: Morrow, 1997.

Silverstein, Alvin, Virginia Silverstein, and Robert Silverstein. *The Nervous System.* New York: Twenty-First Century Books, 1994.

Turkington, Carol. *The Brain Encyclopedia.* New York: Facts on File, 1996.

Wade, Nicholas, ed. *The Science Times Book of the Brain.* New York: Lyons Press, 1998.

WWW Sites

American Academy of Neurology
http://www.aan.com/
Homepage of the American Academy of Neurology, which includes information about neurology and the academy.

A Brief Tour of the Brain
http://suhep.phy.syr.edu/courses/modules/MM /Biology/biology.html
Site provides information about the brain, beginning with a brief history of the study of the brain, then describing the brain's large-scale features, building blocks, and organization.

Cyber Anatomy: Nervous System
http://tqd.advanced.org/11965/html /cyber-anatomy_nervous.html
Site provides detailed information on the nervous system that is divided into two levels: the first geared for students in grades 6-9, the other for students in grades 10-12.

Mind Over Matter: The Brain's Response to Drugs
http://www.nida.nih.gov/MOM/TG/momtg-index.html
From the National Institute on Drug Abuse, a site that explains the effects of legal and illegal drugs, such as nicotine and marijuana, on the brain. Also includes a section on brain anatomy.

Nervous System
http://www.fm.cnyric.org/Wellwood/humansystems/Nervous%20System /nervsyst.html
Site provides links to other sites that provide information such as a description of the nervous system and facts on the brain.

Neuroscience for Kids
http://faculty.washington.edu/chudler/neurok.html
Highly recommended site provides an extensive amount of information on the nervous system and the brain. Includes experiments and activities, a list of on-line and off-line books and articles, current events and new discoveries in brain research, and links to other sites.

8

The Reproductive System

The reproductive system makes life possible. An individual does not need the system to survive, but the human race does. Without the reproductive system, babies would not be born to grow into adults to give birth to more babies. The human cycle would end. All living things on the planet reproduce more of their own kind, and they do so in one of two ways. Some organisms reproduce by splitting in half or by growing buds that eventually turn into copies of the original organism. This method, in which a single organism reproduces itself, is called asexual reproduction. The reproductive method whereby a male and female of a particular species interact and exchange genetic material to create offspring is called sexual reproduction. Humans reproduce by this latter method.

DESIGN: PARTS OF THE REPRODUCTIVE SYSTEM

The male and female reproductive systems form the halves that come together to create new human life. Each system is composed of primary and accessory reproductive organs. In both, the primary sex organs are called gonads. These gonads produce reproductive or sex cells called gametes; they also secrete sex hormones. Despite their joint purpose to produce offspring, the two systems are quite different in structure and function.

The male reproductive system

The primary organs in the male reproductive system are the testes. Their main function is to produce male gametes or sperm, which fertilize ova or female eggs (they also produce the male hormone testosterone). The reproductive ducts—epididymis, ductus deferens, ejaculatory duct, and urethra—carry sperm from the testes to the exterior of the body. Accessory glands—seminal vesicles, prostate gland, and bulbourethral glands—produce secretions that combine with sperm to create semen. The male genitalia (external sex organs) are the scrotum and penis.

WORDS TO KNOW

Acrosome (AK-ro-sohm): Tip of the head of a sperm cell that contains enzymes to digest the membrane of an ovum.

Adenosine triphosphate (ah-DEN-o-seen try-FOS-fate): High-energy molecule found in every cell in the body.

Amnion (AM-nee-on): Fluid-filled sac that surrounds a developing embryo/fetus.

Areola (ah-REE-oh-lah): Circular, darkened area surrounding the nipple of each breast.

Alveolar glands (al-VEE-o-lar GLANDZ): Glands within the lobes of mammary glands that produce milk.

Bulbourethral glands (bull-bo-yoo-REE-thruhl GLANDZ): Glands located underneath on either side of the prostate gland in males that secrete fluid that becomes part of semen.

Cervix (SIR-viks): Lower necklike portion of the uterus leading into the vagina.

Chromosomes (kro-meh—somes): Threadlike structures found in the nucleus of cells that carry the genetic material or genes that determine heredity.

Circumcision (sirnkum-SIZH-un): Surgical removal of the prepuce or foreskin of the penis.

Clitoris (KLI-to-ris): Small protruding mass of erectile tissue at the top of the labia minora.

Corpus luteum (KOR-pus LOU-tee-um): Yellowish remains of a burst ovarian follicle that secretes progesterone.

Ductus deferens (DUK-tus DEF-e-renz): Passageway that carries sperm from the epididymis to the ejaculatory duct.

Ejaculation (ee-jack-you-LAY-shun): Sudden ejection of semen from the penis.

Ejaculatory duct (ee-JACK-yoo-la-tor-ee DUKT): Duct formed by the union of the ductus deferens and the duct of the seminal vesicle.

Endometrium (en-doe-MEE-tree-um): Inner layer of the uterus that provides nourishment for a developing embryo and fetus and that sloughs off during the regular menstrual cycle.

Epididymis (ep-i-DID-i-mis): Portion of the male reproductive duct system in which sperm mature or fully develop.

Estrogens (ES-tro-jenz): Female steroid hormones secreted by the ovaries that bring about the secondary sex characteristics and regulate the female reproductive cycle.

Fallopian tube (fah-LOH-pee-an TOOB): Tube connecting an ovary to the uterus and through which an ovum is transported.

Fimbriae (FIM-bree-ee): Fingerlike projections at the end of a fallopian tube that partially surround an ovary.

Flagellum (flah-JELL-um): Long, whiplike tail that helps provide locomotion in certain cells, such as sperm cells.

Follicle-stimulating hormone (FAH-lik-uhl STIM-yoo-lay-ting HOR-mone): Gonadotropic hormone produced by the anterior pituitary gland that stimulates the development of follicles in the ovaries of females and sperm in the testes of males.

Gamete (GAM-eat): Female or male reproductive or sex cell (egg or sperm).

Genitalia (jen-i-TAY-lee-ah): External organs of the reproductive system.

Gonad (GO-nad): Sex organ in which reproductive cells develop.

Greater vestibular glands (GRAY-ter ves-TI-byoo-lar GLANDZ): Pair of mucus-secreting glands that lubricate the lower portion of the vagina.

Hymen (HI-men): Thin membrane partially covering the external opening of the vagina.

Hysterectomy (his-teh-REK-teh-mee): Surgical removal of the uterus.

Labia majora (LAY-bee-ah ma-JOR-ah): Outer skin folds of the vagina.

Labia minora (LAY-bee-ah my-NOR-ah): Inner skin folds of the vagina.

Lactiferous ducts (lak-TIF-er-us): Ducts that carry milk from the alveolar glands to the surface of the nipple of a breast.

Luteinizing hormone (loo-tee-in-EYE-zing): Gonadotropic hormone secreted by the anterior pituitary that stimulates, in women, ovulation and the release of estrogens and progesterone by the ovaries and, in men, the secretion of testosterone by the testes.

Mammary glands (MAM-uh-ree GLANDZ): Milk-producing glands in female breasts.

Menarche (meh-NAR-key): Beginning of menstruation or the first menstrual period.

Menopause (MEN-ah-paws): Period in a woman's life when menstrual activity ceases.

Menstruation (men-stroo-A-shun): Also known as menses, periodic (monthly) discharge of blood, secretions, tissue, and mucus from the female uterus in the absence of pregnancy.

Mons pubis (MONZ PYU-bes): Fatty, rounded area at the top of the vulva.

Myometrium (my-oh-MEE-tree-um): Outer layer of the uterus composed of interwoven smooth muscle cells.

Oocyte (OH-oh-site): Immature or developing egg cell.

Ova (O-va): Female gametes or eggs (singular: ovum).

Ovarian follicles (o-VAR-ee-an FOL-i-kulz): Structures within an ovary consisting of a developing egg surrounded by follicle cells.

Ovaries (O-var-eez): Female gonads in which ova (eggs) are produced and that secrete estrogens and progesterone.

Ovulation (ov-yoo-LAY-shun): Release of a mature ovum from an ovary.

Oxytocin (ahk-si-TOE-sin): Hormone produced by the hypothalamus and stored in the posterior pituitary that stimulates contraction of the uterus during childbirth and secretion of milk during nursing.

Penis (PEE-nis): Male organ of reproduction and urination.

Placenta (plah-SEN-tah): Temporary organ that provides nutrients and oxygen to a developing fetus, carries away wastes, and produces hormones such as estrogens and progesterone.

Prepuce (PREE-pyus): Also called foreskin, the fold of skin over the glans or tip of the penis.

Progesterone (pro-JESS-te-rone): Female steroid hormone secreted by the ovaries that makes the uterus more ready to receive a fertilized ovum or egg.

Prolactin (pro-LAK-tin): Gonadotropic hormone secreted by the anterior pituitary that stimulates the mammary glands to produce milk.

Prostate gland (PRAHS-tate GLAND): Muscular gland in males that surrounds the first inch of the urethra and secretes a fluid that becomes part of semen.

Scrotum (SKROW-tum): External sac enclosing the testes.

Semen (SEE-men): Thick, whitish, somewhat sticky fluid composed of sperm and glandular secretions that is propelled out of a male's reproductive tract during ejaculation.

Seminal vesicles (SEM-i-nuhl VESS-i-kulls): Glands in males located at the base of the bladder that secrete fluid that becomes part of semen.

Seminiferous tubules (sem-i-NIFF-er-us TOO-by-oolz): Tightly coiled tubes within the testes that produce sperm.

Sperm: Mature male sex or reproductive cell.

Testes (TESS-teez): Male gonads that produce sperm cells and secrete testosterone.

Testosterone (tess-TAHS-ter-ohn): Hormone secreted by the testes that spurs the growth of the male reproductive organs and secondary sex characteristics.

Umbilical cord (um-BILL-i-kull KORD): Structure that connects the embryo/fetus to the placenta.

Uterus (YOU-ter-us): Also known as the womb, the hollow organ in females that receives, retains, and nourishes a fertilized ovum or egg.

Vagina (vuh-JIGH-nah): Muscular tube in women that extends from the cervix of the uterus to the vaginal opening.

Vulva (VUL-vah): Female external genital organs.

Zygote (ZIE-goat): Fertilized ovum.

THE TESTES. The testes are two small, egg-shaped structures suspended in the scrotum, a loose sac of skin that hangs outside the pelvic cavity between the upper thighs. In a male fetus, the testes develop near the kidneys, then descend into the scrotum just before birth.

Each testis measures about 1.5 inches (3.8 centimeters) long and 1 inch (2.5 centimeters) wide. Internally, a testis is subdivided into many lobes. Each lobe contains one to four tightly coiled tubes, called seminiferous tubules, in which sperm is produced. Each tubule averages about 31.5 inches (80 centimeters) in length. The combined length of all the seminiferous tubules in a testis equals about 0.5 mile (0.8 kilometer).

Mature sperm cells are the smallest cells in the body. Each tadpolelike sperm cell consists of three regions: the head, middle piece, and flagellum. The helmetlike head contains the male genetic material essential for reproduction. On the tip of the head is the acrosome, which contains enzymes to break down the membrane of an ovum so fertilization can occur. The middle piece contains a supply of adenosine triphosphate (ATP), a high-energy molecule found in every cell in the body. The sperm cell uses the ATP to power its flagellum, the long whiplike tail, to move the cell along.

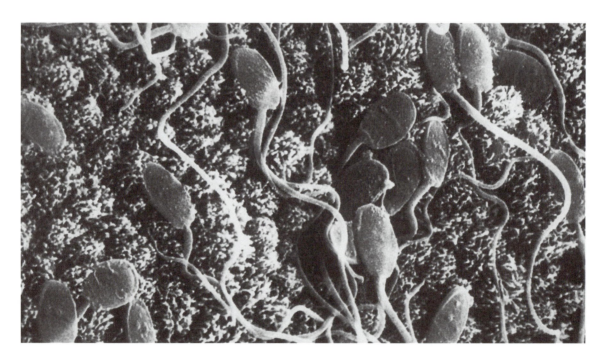

Human sperm cells. Each tadpolelike sperm cell consists of three regions: the head, middle piece, and flagellum. (Photograph by Fawcett/Philips. Reproduced by permission of Photo Researchers, Inc.)

Sperm from the seminiferous tubules are carried along by fluids through a network of tubes before entering the epididymis, the first of the male reproductive ducts.

THE EPIDIDYMIS. The epididymis is a tube about 20 feet (6 meters) in length. Tightly coiled on the posterior or back side of each testis, each epididymis takes up very little room. As sperm cells move through this tube, they absorb nutrients and become mature or fully developed, a process that takes about two weeks. The walls of the epididymis are made of smooth muscle cells, which helps propel sperms cells into the ductus deferens.

THE DUCTUS DEFERENS. The ductus deferens, also called the vas deferens, extends from each epididymis upward over the top of the bladder, then down its back side. The paired ducts measure between 16 and 18 inches (40 and 45 centimeters) in length. Their smooth muscular walls move the sperm along through peristaltic contractions, or a series of wavelike muscular contractions that move material in one direction through a hollow organ.

THE EJACULATORY DUCT. The ejaculatory duct is a short passageway that is formed by the union of a ductus deferens and the duct of a seminal vesicle. Each ejaculatory duct measures just under 1 inch (2.5 centimeters) in length. Both ejaculatory ducts empty sperm (from the ductus deferens) and fluid (from the seminal vesicle) into the single urethra.

THE URETHRA. The urethra extends from the base of the urinary bladder to the tip of the penis, a distance of 6 to 8 inches (15 to 20 centimeters). In males, the urethra serves both the reproductive and urinary systems. It transports sperm (with its fluid) and urine to the body exterior, but never both at the same time. When sperm enters the urethra from the ejaculatory ducts, a sphincter or ring of muscle at the junction of the bladder and urethra closes, keeping urine in the bladder (and also preventing sperm from entering the bladder).

ACCESSORY GLANDS AND SEMEN. The three accessory glands produce secretions that combine with sperm to create a whitish, somewhat sticky mixture called semen. Those secretions (the fluid part of semen) are known collectively as seminal fluid. Ejaculation is the sudden ejection of semen from the penis. A typical ejaculation releases between 0.07 and 0.17 ounce (2 and 5 milliliters) of semen. Although as many as 400 to 600 million sperm are contained in a typical ejaculation, they make up only about 1 percent of the volume of the semen because of their extremely small size.

The seminal vesicles are the first accessory glands to add secretions to sperm. Located at the base of the bladder, their ducts join with the paired ductus deferens to form the ejaculatory ducts. Their thick, yellowish secretion, which makes up about 60 percent of the seminal fluid, contains high amounts of fructose (sugar), vitamin C, and other substances. The secretion helps nourish and activate the sperm as its passes through the reproductive tract.

Male Reproductive System

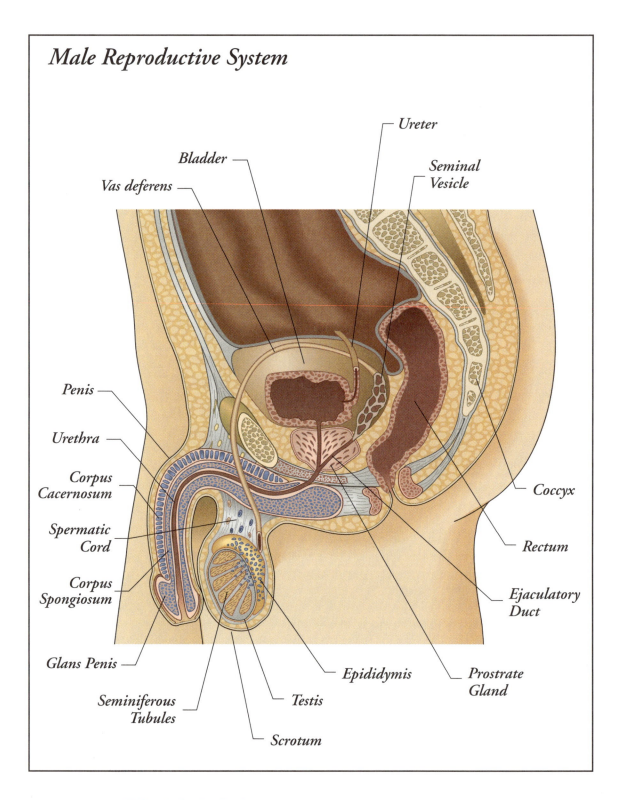

Ureter

Bladder

Seminal
Vesicle

Vas deferens

Penis

Urethra

Corpus
Cacernosum

Coccyx

Spermatic
Cord

Rectum

Corpus
Spongiosum

Ejaculatory
Duct

Glans Penis

Epididymis

Prostrate
Gland

Seminiferous
Tubules

Testis

Scrotum

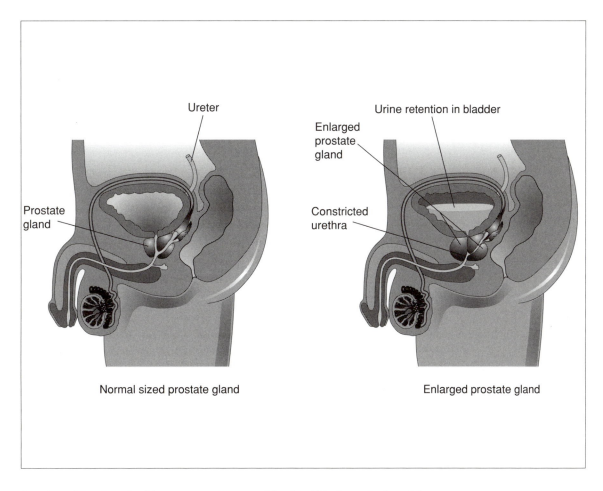

Ureter

Prostate gland

Normal sized prostate gland

Urine retention in bladder

Enlarged prostate gland

Constricted urethra

Enlarged prostate gland

An enlarged prostate gland is a non-cancerous condition in which the narrowing of the urethra makes the elimination of urine more difficult. (Illustration by Electronic Illustrators Group.)

The prostate gland is a single, rounded gland that has a diameter of about 1.6 inches (4 centimeters). It surrounds the urethra as the urethra leaves the bladder. It produces an acidic, milky secretion that enters the urethra through several small ducts. This secretion makes up about 30 percent of the seminal fluid.

The bulbourethral glands are the last glands to add secretions to the seminal fluid. The tiny, pea-shaped glands are located underneath on either side of the prostate gland. Their secretion—a thick, clear mucus—enters the urethra when a man becomes sexually aroused before the secretions of the other

OPPOSITE: The male reproductive system. (Illustration by Kopp Illustration Inc.)

accessory glands. The secretion coats the lining of the urethra and cleanses it of any traces of acidic urine that might be present. It also serves as a lubricant during sexual intercourse.

The secretion of all three accessory glands are slightly alkaline or basic (solutions containing a high number of hydrogen ions are acidic, those with a low number are alkaline or basic). This is important because the bacteria present in the female vagina create an acidic environment there. The alkaline seminal fluid neutralizes the acid in the vagina, allowing sperm in the semen to exist and move in the vagina so fertilization may take place.

MALE GENITALIA. The scrotum and penis are the male genitalia that hang outside the body. As stated earlier, the scrotum is a loose sac of skin that hangs outside the pelvic cavity between the upper thighs. It is divided into two compartments, each holding a testis. The scrotum holds the testes away from the body since normal body temperature is too warm for sperm to be produced. The temperature inside the scrotum is a few degrees cooler than inside the rest of the body. If the external temperature becomes very cold, muscles in the scrotum pull the testes closer to the body, maintaining the proper temperature for sperm production.

The penis is a tubular organ that surrounds the latter part of the urethra. It serves two purposes: to conduct urine outside the body and to deliver semen into the female reproductive tract. The two main parts of the penis are the glans (enlarged tip) and shaft (body). A fold of skin called the prepuce or foreskin covers the glans. It is common practice in certain cultures and religions to remove the foreskin surgically soon after birth, a procedure called a circumcision. The shaft contains three masses or columns of erectile tissue. Normally, this spongy tissue is not filled with much blood. During sexual arousal, however, blood flow to the tissue increases. The penis, engorged with blood, becomes longer, wider, and rigid. This event, called an erection, allows the penis to enter the female vagina and deliver semen to the female's reproductive tract.

The female reproductive system

The reproductive system in females is more complex than that in males. The system produces female gametes, called ova or eggs, and provides a protective space for an ovum to be fertilized and to develop until birth. The primary organs in this system are the ovaries. The accessory organs include the fallopian tubes, the uterus, the vagina, the genitalia, and the mammary glands.

THE OVARIES. The ovaries are two almond-shaped structures measuring about 1.5 inches (3.8 centimeters) in length. They are located on each side of the pelvis, one at the end of each fallopian tube. Ligaments attach the

OPPOSITE: The female reproductive system. (Illustration by Kopp Illustration Inc.)

Female Reproductive System

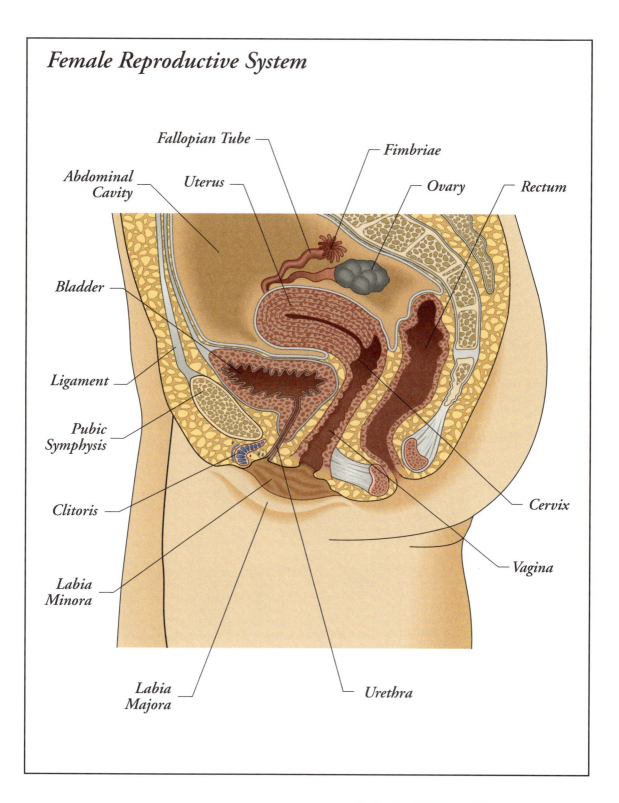

Fallopian Tube

Fimbriae

Abdominal Cavity

Uterus

Ovary

Rectum

Bladder

Ligament

Pubic Symphysis

Clitoris

Cervix

Vagina

Labia Minora

Labia Majora

Urethra

ovaries to the walls of the pelvis and to the uterus (these latter ligaments are called ovarian ligaments).

Within each ovary are many tiny saclike structures called ovarian follicles. An ovary contains several hundred thousand of these follicles, which are present from birth. Each follicle consists of an immature or developing egg called an oocyte surrounded by one or more layers of cells called follicle cells. During a woman's life, however, only about 360 to 480 ovarian follicles will produce mature eggs or ova.

FALLOPIAN TUBES. The fallopian tubes, also called uterine tubes, connect the ovaries to the uterus. Each fallopian tube is about 4 inches (10 centimeters) in length and extremely narrow. The end of the tube that attaches

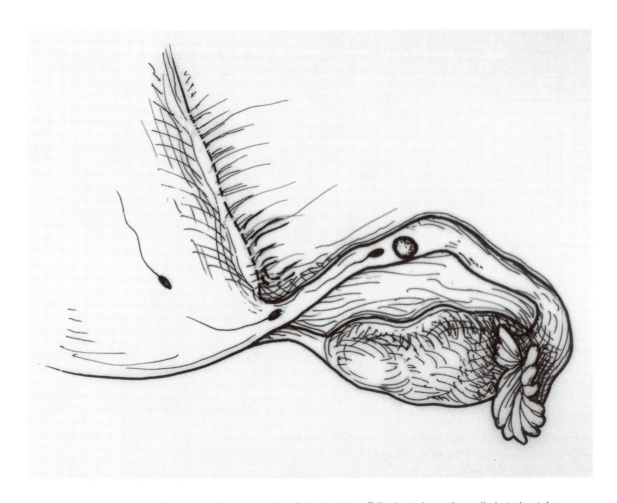

Sperm meets an ovum in a fallopian tube. Fallopian tubes, also called uterine tubes, connect the ovaries to the uterus. (Illustration by June Hill Pedigo. Reproduced by permission of Custom Medical Stock Photo.)

to an ovary has fingerlike projections called fimbriae that partially surround the ovary. The inner surfaces of the tubes are carpeted with cilia, microscopic hairlike structures projecting in from the inner lining.

THE UTERUS. The uterus, or womb, is a hollow, muscular chamber shaped like an upside-down pear. An average uterus measures about 3 inches (7.6 centimeters) in length and 2 inches (5 centimeters) in width. It weighs approximately between 1 and 1.4 ounces (30 and 40 grams). The uterus lies in the pelvis between the urinary bladder and rectum and is anchored in place by various ligaments.

The part of the uterus above where the fallopian tubes attach is called the fundus. The body is the large central portion. The narrow, lower end that projects a short distance and opens into the vagina is called the cervix.

The thick wall of the uterus is composed of two main layers: the myometrium and the endometrium. The myometrium, the outer layer, is made of smooth muscle cells (among the strongest in the body) that are interwoven to allow the uterus to expand to accommodate a growing fetus and to contract to force the fetus out at the end of pregnancy. The endometrium, the inner layer, provides a site for a fertilized egg to attach to receive nourishment during its development. If an egg is not fertilized, the endometrium sloughs off or is shed during the regular menstrual cycle.

THE VAGINA. The vagina is a muscular tube extending from the uterus to the genitalia. It lies parallel to the rectum. The vagina serves as a exit for menstrual fluids, receives the penis during intercourse, and forms the birth canal through which the fetus passes at the end of pregnancy. Normally, it measures about 4 inches (10 centimeters) in length, but to accommodate all of its activities, its length and width vary widely.

The external opening of the vagina (vaginal opening) is usually partially covered by a thin membrane called the hymen. This membrane is usually ruptured or broken during a women's first sexual intercourse, by the use of tampons during the menstrual period, or during a sports activity.

Bacteria normally exist in the vagina, living on nutrients found in the mucus secreted by the cervix. They are quite beneficial. Through their activities, they create an acidic environment in the vagina that inhibits or prevents the growth of pathogens (disease-causing organisms).

FEMALE GENITALIA. In females, the external sex organs are collectively called the vulva. The parts making up the vulva include the mons pubis, labia majora and minora, clitoris, and greater vestibular glands.

The mons pubis is the prominent fatty bulge at the top of the vulva. Beginning at puberty, this area is covered with pubic hair. Running down from the mons pubis are two hair-covered skin folds or flaps called the labia majora. They enclose two delicate, hair-free skin folds called the labia minora.

The area within the labia minora, referred to as the vestibule, contains the openings of the urethra (through which urine passes) and the vagina.

At the top of the labia minora (above the urethral opening) lies the clitoris. A small protruding mass of erectile tissue, it is similar to the male penis. During sexual arousal or excitement, the sensitive clitoris becomes engorged with blood. Located in the floor of the vestibule on either side of the vaginal opening are a pair of glands called the greater vestibular glands. During sexual arousal, these glands secrete a mucus that lubricates the lower portion of the vagina.

MAMMARY GLANDS. Mammary glands are found in the breasts of both women and men. However, they normally function only in women. Mammary glands are modified sweat glands that are actually part of the integumentary system (skin). Although not directly involved in the reproduction process, mammary glands play an important role in providing nourishment for a newborn baby and their activities are controlled by hormones of the reproductive system. For these reasons, they are considered accessory reproductive organs.

> MAMMARY GLANDS ARE FOUND IN THE BREASTS OF BOTH WOMEN AND MEN. HOWEVER, THEY NORMALLY FUNCTION ONLY IN WOMEN.

On the outside of each breast, slightly below center, is a darkened, reddish brown area called the areola. In the center of the areola is a small protruding nipple.

Within each mammary gland are 15 to 25 lobes radiating inward from the nipple. The lobes are separated by connective tissue and fat. Within each lobe are chambers containing alveolar glands, which produce milk after a woman has given birth. Lactiferous ducts carry milk from the alveolar glands to small openings on the surface of each nipple. The milk is a mixture of water, proteins, fats, sugars, salts, and enzymes that have immune properties.

When a baby suckles a mother's nipple, nerve impulses are sent to the mother's hypothalamus. It then signals the posterior portion of the pituitary gland to secrete the hormone oxytocin. The hormone stimulates the contraction of the muscle cells around the lactiferous ducts, causing the ejection of milk through the nipple.

WORKINGS: HOW THE REPRODUCTIVE SYSTEM FUNCTIONS

The main functions of the male reproductive system are to produce sperm and to introduce that sperm into the female reproductive tract. The main functions of the female reproductive system are to produce ova, receive sperm from the male penis, house and provide nutrients to the developing embryo and fetus, give birth, and produce milk to feed offspring.

The activities of both reproductive systems are controlled by hormones (chemicals produced by the body that affect various bodily processes) released from the pituitary gland, which is located at the base of the brain behind the nose, and from the gonads in each system.

Hormones and the male reproductive system: Sperm production

In males, the testes produce male sex hormones called androgens (from the Greek word *andros,* meaning "man"). Testosterone is the most important of these. It spurs the growth of the male reproductive organs and the production of sperm. In addition, testosterone brings about the male secondary sex characteristics: deepening of the voice; appearance of hair under the arms, on the face, and in the genital area; and increased growth of muscles and heavy bones.

Testosterone is produced in the male fetus to stimulate the formation of the male duct system and accessory organs. Its production then declines and does not increase until puberty.

At puberty (usually occurring between the ages of twelve and sixteen in boys), the anterior portion of the pituitary gland releases luteinizing hormone. This hormone activates the cells surrounding the seminiferous tubules in each testis to begin secreting testosterone. The anterior pituitary then releases follicle-stimulating hormone, which stimulates the cells of the seminiferous tubules to begin producing sperm. In the presence of testosterone, the sperm are able to mature.

MILLIONS OF SPERM ARE FORMED EACH DAY IN THE TESTES. ALTHOUGH THIS NUMBER DECREASES AS A MAN AGES, THE PRODUCTION OF SPERM NEVER COMPLETELY STOPS.

This process, begun at puberty, continues throughout a man's life. Millions of sperm are formed each day in the testes. Although this number decreases as a man ages, the production of sperm never completely stops.

Hormones and the female reproductive system: The menstrual cycle

In women, the ovaries secrete two groups of steroid hormones, estrogens and progesterone. Estrogens spur the development of the female secondary sex characteristics: enlargement of the breasts, appearance of hair under the arms and in the genital area, and the accumulation of fat in the hips and thighs. Estrogens also act with progesterone to stimulate the growth of the lining of the uterus, preparing it to receive a fertilized egg.

The ovaries do not begin to function until puberty (usually occurring between the ages of eleven and fourteen in girls). At this time, the anterior pituitary gland secretes follicle-stimulating hormone (FSH). This hormone stimulates a small number of ovarian follicles in an ovary to grow and mature. It also stimulates the follicle cells in those follicles to secrete estrogens.

Together, FSH and estrogens help the oocyte (immature ovum) in each stimulated follicle to mature.

About fourteen days after the anterior pituitary secreted FSH, only one follicle in the ovary has developed to maturity with a mature ovum inside. The anterior pituitary then releases luteinizing hormone (LH), which causes the mature follicle to burst open and release its ovum through the ovary wall. This event is known as ovulation.

The cilia carpeting the inner surfaces of the fallopian tubes wave back and forth, creating a current in the fluid that fills the tubes and spaces around the ovaries. The mature ovum that is released is drawn by these currents into the fallopian tube attached to the ovary. Muscle contractions in the walls of the tube also help propel the ovum along.

Min-Chueh Chang. (Reproduced by permission of AP/Wide World Photos.)

DEVELOPING "THE PILL"

Reproductive biologist Min-Chueh Chang (1908–1991) is best known for developing an oral contraceptive—commonly known as the birth control pill—in collaboration with American endocrinologist Gregory Goodwin Pincus (1903–1967) and American gynecologist and obstetrician John Rock (1890–1984).

In the early 1950s, Chang and Pinkus began to study the female hormone progesterone, believing it could provide them with clues about how to create an oral contraceptive (a substance that prevents conception). Through their research the scientists soon realized that increasing blood levels of progesterone could stop ovulation. They experimented with more than two hundred substances in order to find natural compounds that imitated the combined actions of progesterone and another female hormone, estrogen. At that point, they began a collaboration with John Rock of the Rock Reproduction Clinic in Brookline, Massachusetts. The team developed a pill made of three compounds, including estrogen and progesterone derived from a wild Mexican yam. They began testing their pill on human subjects, using groups of women in Brookline, as well as in Haiti and Puerto Rico.

Their trials were successful in stopping ovulation, but the researchers decided to slightly alter the pill they had developed. They wanted to try to eliminate estrogen from the pill because they considered it to be unnecessary. They thought that progesterone was the key ingredient they needed. Trials of this no-estrogen pill, however, had seriously negative results, including pregnancies and breakthrough bleeding (bleeding between menstrual periods) in the women they tested. The scientists restored estrogen to the pill, creating a form of contraception that was over 99 percent effective and relatively safe. The combined estrogen-progesterone pill was approved by the U.S. Food and Drug Administration in 1960.

While the ovum is in a fallopian tube, the ovarian follicle that burst undergoes another transformation. LH, which triggered ovulation, also causes the ruptured follicle to change into another structure. This small yellow structure is known as the corpus luteum. It begins secreting another hormone, progesterone. The new hormone prevents the other stimulated follicles with their eggs from reachig full maturity. In combination with estrogens, it also causes the endometrium (lining of the uterus) to grow in size and secrete nutrients into the cavity of the uterus (to help nourish a developing embryo, if one is present). As the endometrium grows, so does its supply of blood vessels.

The mature ovum in the fallopian tube can only survive for twelve to twenty-four hours. Fertilization of the ovum by male sperm must occur within the fallopian tube within that time. If fertilization does not occur, the ovum enters the uterus and begins to break down. Blood levels of LH and FSH decrease dramatically. The corpus luteum continues to secrete progesterone for about ten to twelve days after ovulation. It then stops and begins to degenerate or shrivel up.

Without the presence of progesterone, the thickened endometrium begins to detach from the uterus and break apart. After a while, the tissue pieces of the endometrium (along with the blood vessels that nourished it) are discharged from the body in a flow of blood through the vaginal opening. This event is referred to menstruation or menses. The flow of blood, which is commonly called a period, usually lasts four or five days. The average amount of blood lost during a period ranges from 1.7 to 5 ounces (50 to 150 milliliters). Once menstruation ends, the endometrium begins to regenerate.

The beginning of menstruation marks the end of what is known as the menstrual cycle. The cycle begins with the secretion of FSH spurring ovarian follicles to mature. The time period of a menstrual cycle is normally about twenty-eight days (the length can vary from nineteen to thirty-seven days). As menstruation is occurring, new follicles in the other ovary are being stimulated by FSH and a new menstrual cycle is underway.

The first menstruation or menstrual period a girl undergoes at puberty is known as menarche. Menstrual cycles continue one after the other (unless a woman becomes pregnant) from puberty until a woman reaches her forties or fifties. At that time, the number of ovarian follicles in the ovaries has been exhausted and the ovaries no longer respond to FSH. Ovulation and menstruation cease, and blood levels of estrogens and progesterone decline. A decline in estrogen levels leads to a reduction in the size of the uterus and breasts. The walls of the vagina and uterus also become thinner. This change in a woman's reproductive system and organs is known as menopause.

Fertilization

The only time a woman does not experience a menstrual cycle between puberty and menopause is when she is pregnant (certain illnesses, emotional stress, and extensive physical activity can also stop menstrual cycles from occurring). For pregnancy to occur under normal conditions, an ovum must be fertilized by a sperm in a fallopian tube.

When a man ejaculates semen into a woman's vagina, the millions of sperm swim through the watery fluid inside the vagina and uterus. Of the multitude of sperm, only a relative few will reach an ovum in a fallopian tube, if one is present. A vast majority of sperm will be destroyed by white blood cells in the walls of the vagina and uterus. Of those that survive, many may not be able to swim to the top of the uterus. Of those that are able, half then swim into the wrong fallopian tube.

About 100 sperm eventually reach an ovum in a fallopian tube. They then attached themselves to the ovum's outer membrane. Enzymes in the acrosomes of the sperms begin to break down the membrane. Eventually,

---

BIRTH CONTROL METHODS

Birth control or contraception is the deliberate effort to keep a woman from becoming pregnant. Attempts to prevent pregnancy date back to ancient times and cultures. Some form of contraception is currently used by more than half the women in the United States. Although widespread, contraception remains controversial, with some religious and political groups opposed to the distribution of contraceptives.

There are a number of contraceptive devices to prevent pregnancy, some more effective than others. The following are a few common devices:

Birth control pills: The most popular contraceptive in the United States. The pills contain hormones that are released into a woman's system on a regular basis to prevent pregnancy, either by inhibiting ovulation, preventing implantation of a fertilized egg, or by thickening the secretions throughout a woman's reproductive system so that her partner's sperm has less of a chance to meet her egg.

Condom: A sheath used to cover the penis to prevent semen from entering a woman's reproductive tract. Modern condoms are made of latex (rubber). Also used as an effective barrier against sexually transmitted diseases.

Contraceptive sponge: Device used to cover the cervix to prevent the passage of semen into the uterus. Was taken off the market in the United States in the early 1990s because of potential health risks, but has recently begun to be reintroduced.

Diaphragm: Rubber, cap-shaped device that fits over the cervix and prevents the passage of semen into the uterus.

IUD: Intrauterine device, a small plastic device placed inside the uterus of a women by a physician that prevents an embryo from developing in the wall of the uterus.

A permanent form of birth control—sterilization—can be achieved through surgical procedures. Men can undergo an operation called a vasectomy, in which both vas deferens are cut and tied so that sperm cannot be ejaculated. Women can undergo an operation called a tubal ligation, in which the fallopian tubes are either cut or tied so that an egg cannot pass down into the uterus.

Probably the most common contraceptive method in the world is coitus interruptus, in which a man withdraws his penis from a woman's vagina before ejaculating. Unfortunately, this practice has resulted in numerous accidental pregnancies. The rhythm method (in which intercourse is avoided on the days of the month when a woman is most likely to become pregnant) was and remains the only form of birth control approved by the Roman Catholic Church. Abstinence, or the complete avoidance of sexual activity, remains the most effective way to prevent pregnancy.

---

one sperm makes it through to the interior of the ovum. After it does, electrical changes occur in the membrane of the ovum that prevent the other sperm from entering.

The sperm and ovum each carry the genetic material that is necessary to generate and maintain human life. The threadlike structures that carry that genetic material (or genes) are called chromosomes. While all other body cells contain 46 chromosomes (23 pair), a sperm and an ova each contain only 23 single chromosomes. When the genetic material of a sperm combines with that of an ovum, fertilization or conception occurs. The fertilized egg, called a zygote, contains the normal human number of 46 chromosomes.

The zygote then travels down the fallopian tube and enters the uterus. By the time it has reached the uterus, the zygote (now called an embryo) is

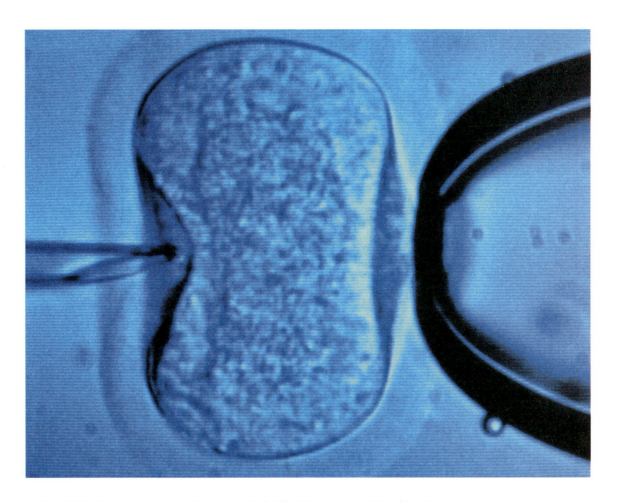

In vitro fertilization, a process by which an egg is fertilized by sperm outside of the body. (Photograph by Hank Morgan. Reproduced by permission of Photo Researchers, Inc.)

a tiny ball of cells that are continually growing and dividing. About a week after fertilization, the embryo becomes embedded in the endometrium. Cells of the embryo then release a hormone that prevents the corpus luteum from degenerating. Estrogens and progesterone continue to be secreted and the endometrium remains intact. Menstruation does not occur and the menstrual cycle is stopped.

Other cells from the embryo combine with tissues from the uterus to form a temporary organ called the placenta. The placenta serves as the site where oxygen and nutrients pass from a woman to the embryo and where

Patrick Steptoe. (Reproduced by permission of Archive Photos, Inc.)

STEPTOE AND THE FIRST TEST TUBE BABY

English gynecologist Patrick Steptoe (1913–1988) is best known for helping develop the technique of in vitro fertilization, a process by which an egg is fertilized by sperm outside of the body. Steptoe and his colleague, English physiologist Robert G. Edwards, received international recognition (both positive and negative) when their work led to the birth of the first so-called test tube baby in 1978.

In 1966, while working on fertility problems (the inability of a woman and man to conceive a child),

Steptoe teamed up with Edwards. Using ovaries that had been removed for medical reasons, Edwards had previously pioneered the fertilization of eggs outside of the body, a procedure called in vitro fertilization. In this operation, a mature egg is removed from the female ovary and is fertilized with sperm in a petri (glass) dish. After a short incubation or development period, the fertilized egg is implanted in the uterus, where it develops as in a typical pregnancy. This procedure gives hope to women who cannot become pregnant because their fallopian tubes are damaged or missing.

For a decade, Steptoe and Edwards pursued their research, but met with little success. In addition, as news of their work began to spread, Steptoe and Edwards faced intense criticism. Scientists and religious leaders raised ethical and moral questions about tampering with the creation of human life. Members of British Parliament demanded an investigation, and the scientists' research funds were cut off. Nevertheless, Steptoe and Edwards continued their work.

Finally, in 1976, Steptoe met Leslie Brown, a thirty-year-old woman who had experienced problems with her fallopian tubes and could not conceive a child. Steptoe removed a mature egg from her ovary, and Edwards fertilized the egg in a petri dish using the sperm of her husband, Gilbert. After two days, Steptoe implanted the fertilized egg in Brown's uterus, where it continued to thrive as a normal pregnancy. On July 25, 1978, Brown gave birth to Joy Louise, a healthy 5.75 pound (2.61 kilogram) baby girl, the first human conceived outside of a woman's body.

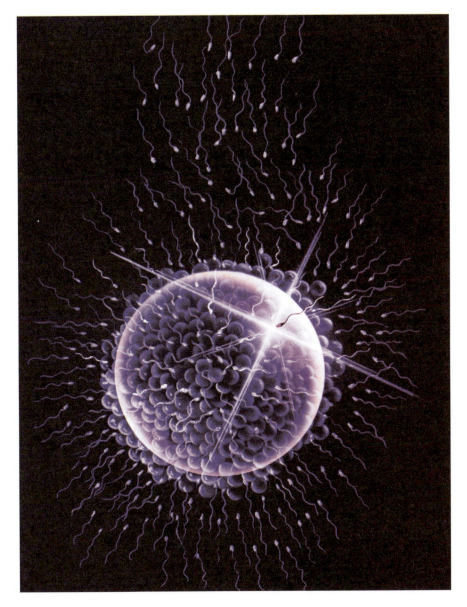

A human ovum at the moment of fertilization. (Illustration by Bryson Biomedical
Illustrations. Reproduced by permission of Custom Medical Stock Photo.)

wastes are taken away from the embryo. The placenta also produces hormones—estrogens, progesterone, and others—that help maintain pregnancy.

A fluid-filled sac, the amnion or amniotic sac, develops around the embryo. In this sac, the embryo will continue to develop, connected to the placenta by a blood vessel-containing tube called the umbilical cord. Nine weeks

after fertilization, the developing embryo is referred to as a fetus. Approximately 270 days after fertilization, the fetus is ready to be born.

AILMENTS: WHAT CAN GO WRONG WITH THE REPRODUCTIVE SYSTEM

Many ailments and disorders can affect the male and female reproductive systems, preventing them from functioning properly. These conditions can range from mild to moderate to severe. Some are life-threatening.

Vaginal yeast infections, caused by a species of yeast found in virtually all normal people, are common infections in women. While not serious, they can be uncomfortable and irritating until treated. Impotence, a condition in which a man is unable to maintain an erection, may be due to some physical or psychological problem. Again, this disorder does not threaten life, but

THE DEVELOPMENT OF A HUMAN FETUS

An embryo is an organism in its earliest stages of development, produced when an ovum is fertilized by a sperm. Shortly after fertilization, the ovum begins to grow and develop. It divides to form two cells, then four, then eight, and so on. The cells then combined to form structures and systems. A developing human individual is considered an embryo from the time of fertilization until the ninth week of pregnancy. At that point, it is considered a fetus.

The following is a list of changes or appearances that mark each month in the development of a fetus:

Month 3: Head is abnormally large in proportion of the body. Facial features are present in crude form. Bone development increases. Brain continues to enlarge. Sex can be readily determined from the genitals. Approximate overall size: 3 inches (7.6 centimeters).

Month 4: Head still quite large, but arms and legs lengthen. Hair appears on head. Face begins to look more human. Eyes, ears, nose, and mouth are well-formed. Body systems continue to develop. Approximate overall size: 5 to 7 inches (13 to 18 centimeters).

Month 5: Body begins to grow more rapidly than head. Body is covered with silklike hair (lanugo). Skin is covered with a grayish-white, cheese-like coating (vernix). Skeletal muscles become active. Approximate overall size: 10 to 12 inches (25 to 30 centimeters).

Month 6: Eyelashes and eyebrows form. Eyelids begin to open. Lanugo has largely disappeared. Skin is wrinkled and red. Approximate overall size: 12 to 14 inches (30 to 35 centimeters).

Month 7: Body and head approach normal proportions. Weight increases substantially. Fat deposits are laid out beneath the skin, which becomes less wrinkled. Fingernails and toenails are present. In males, testes descend into the scrotum. Approximate overall size: 14 to 17 inches (35 to 43 centimeters).

Month 8: More fat is deposited under the skin. Most body systems are fully functional. Approximate overall size: 18 inches (46 centimeters).

Month 9: Skin appears whitish pink. Nails are fully developed. Lungs are more mature. Lanugo is shed. Fetus ready to be born. Approximate overall size: 19 to 21 inches (48 to 53 centimeters).

it is a cause of concern to a man (and to his spouse or partner) as it prevents him from engaging in sexual intercourse.

The organs of the male and female reproductive systems are often sites where tumors or other growths develop. Many of these growths are cancerous. The following are some of the more serious diseases and disorders that can afflict the reproductive systems in males and females.

Breast cancer

Breast cancer develops when cells of the breast become abnormal and grow uncontrollably, forming tumors. The cancer cells can invade and destroy surrounding tissue, then spread throughout the body by way of the blood or lymph vessels. Every woman is at risk for breast cancer. Regardless of family history, a woman's risk for developing this type of cancer increases as she ages. In fact, 80 percent of all breast cancers are found in women over the age of fifty.

A woman's chance for developing breast cancer increases if her mother or sister have had breast cancer, if she has gone through menopause late in life, if she did not breastfeed her children, or if she did not have children or had them late in life. However, more than 70 percent of women who get breast cancer have none of these risk factors.

The following are all indications of possible breast cancer: a lump in the breast, changes in the nipple of the breast, dimpled or reddened skin over the breast, and change in size or shape of the breast.

More than 90 percent of all breast cancers are detected by mammography (a low-dose X ray of the breast). The American Cancer Society recommends that women between the ages of forty and forty-nine have a mammogram done every year or two; women aged fifty or over should have one every year.

Treatment options for breast cancer include surgery, chemotherapy, and radiation. During surgery, surgeons may remove only a portion of a woman's breast, her entire breast and some underarm lymph nodes, or her entire breast along with all of the underarm lymph nodes and chest muscles. The extent of the surgery depends on the type of breast cancer, whether the disease has spread, and the woman's age and health. After the cancer has been removed, the physician may recommend the woman undergo chemotherapy

AVERAGE GESTATION PERIOD OF DIFFERENT ANIMALS

Animal	Period (months)
African elephant	22
Giraffe	15.25
Humpback whale	10 to 12
Bison (buffalo)	9.5
Human	9
Hippopotamus	8
Grizzly bear	7
Baboon	5 to 6
Giant panda	4 to 5
Jaguar	3.5
Dog	2
Cat	2
Squirrel	1.33
Rabbit	1
Hamster	0.5 to 1

(using a combination of drugs to kill any remaining cancer cells and shrink any tumors) or radiation therapy (using X rays or other high-energy rays to kill any remaining cancer cells and shrink any tumors) or a combination of both.

Breast cancer cannot be prevented, but it can be treated successfully if diagnosed from a mammogram at an early stage.

Endometriosis

Endometriosis is a condition in which bits of tissue similar to the endometrium (lining of the uterus) grow in other parts of the body. Like the endometrium, this tissue builds up and sheds in response to monthly hormonal cycles. However, the blood discarded from these tissue implants has no natural outlet. It falls onto surrounding organs, causing swelling and inflammation. Eventually, scar tissue and adhesions develop in these areas.

The exact cause of endometriosis is unknown and there is no way to prevent the disease. It most commonly strikes women who are between the ages of twenty-five and forty. About 7 percent of the women in this age group in the United States are affected by the disorder.

The most common symptoms of endometriosis include menstrual pain beginning a day or two before the true menstrual period starts, abnormal bleeding during menstrual periods, and pain during sexual intercourse.

If endometriosis is discovered, treatment depends on a woman's symptoms, her age, and the extent of the disease. For mild cramping and menstrual pain, over-the-counter pain relievers are taken. Medications similar to hormones may be given to reduce pain and shrink or stop the spread or growth of the condition. The only permanent method to eliminate endometriosis is the surgical removal of the uterus, ovaries, and fallopian tubes. For women with minimal endometriosis, laser surgery to remove the endometrial tissue implants and ovarian cysts may be employed.

Ovarian cancer

Ovarian cancer develops when cells in the ovaries become abnormal and grow uncontrollably, forming tumors. Ninety percent of all ovarian cancers develop in the cells that line the surface of the ovaries. This type of cancer is the fifth most common cancer among women in the United States. However, the death rate due to this cancer is higher than that of any other cancer among women.

REPRODUCTIVE SYSTEM DISORDERS

Chlamydia (kla-MI-dee-ah): Sexually transmitted disease caused by a bacterium.

Endometriosis (en-doe-mee-tree-OH-sis): Condition in which bits of tissue similar to the endometrium grow in other parts of the body.

Gonorrhea (gah-nuh-REE-ah): A highly contagious sexually transmitted disease caused by a bacteria.

Syphilis (SIF-uh-lis): Sexually transmitted disease caused by a coil-shaped bacterium

Uterine fibroids (YOU-ter-in FIE-broydz): Also called myomas, benign (nonthreatening) growths of the muscle in the uterus.

Ovarian cancer can develop at any age, but more than half the cases occur in women who are sixty-five or older. It is difficult to diagnose ovarian cancer early because often there are no warning symptoms. Also, the disease spreads relatively quickly.

The actual cause of ovarian cancer is not known. However, several risk factors are known to increase a woman's chances of developing the disease. These factors include age, race (cancer is highest among white women), a high-fat diet, a family history of ovarian cancer, and having a first period at a young age, or going through menopause at a late age.

OVARIAN CANCER CAN DEVELOP AT ANY AGE, BUT MORE THAN HALF THE CASES OCCUR IN WOMEN WHO ARE SIXTY-FIVE OR OLDER.

In the early stages of ovarian cancer, there may be no noticeable symptoms. Later, a woman may experience pain or swelling in the abdomen, constipation, vomiting, loss of appetite, fatigue, and unexplained weight gain.

If cancer is detected, surgery is the main treatment. The type of surgery depends on the extent of the disease. In most cases, the ovaries, uterus, and fallopian tubes are completely removed. In rare cases, only one ovary may be removed with the uterus and fallopian tubes left intact. After surgery, chemotherapy (using a combination of drugs to kill any remaining cancer cells and shrink any tumors) is usually administered.

More than 50 percent of the women who are diagnosed with ovarian cancer die within five years. If the disease is diagnosed before it has spread beyond an ovary, more than 90 percent of those women will survive five years or more. Since ovarian cancer cannot be prevented, the American Cancer Society recommends that all women over the age of forty undergo annual pelvic examinations to increase the chance of detecting the disease early.

Prostate cancer

Prostate cancer develops when cells in the prostate gland become abnormal and grow uncontrollably, forming tumors. It is the most common cancer among men in the United States, and it is the second leading cause of cancer deaths. Prostate cancer affects African American men twice as often as it does white men. In fact, African Americans have the highest rate of prostate cancer in the world.

Prostate cancer is found mainly in men over the age of fifty-five. As men grow older, the chance of developing the disease increases. Although the cause of this type of cancer is unknown, evidence suggests that age, race, a high-fat diet, and increased blood levels of testosterone may play a part in the development of the disease.

FREQUENTLY, PROSTATE CANCER HAS NO SYMPTOMS.

Frequently, prostate cancer has no symptoms. When the tumor is enlarged or the cancer has spread, the following symptoms may appear: weak or interrupted urine flow, frequent urination (especially at night), difficulty starting urination, inability to urinate, pain or burning sensation when urinating, blood in the urine, persistent pain in the lower back, and painful ejaculation.

If prostate cancer is detected (either through a rectal examination or blood test), surgery to remove the prostate gland completely is the most common treatment. The seminal vesicles are also removed during the procedure. If the prostate cancer is detected at an early stage, radiation therapy (using X rays or other high-energy rays to kill cancer cells and shrink any tumors) may be used instead of surgery. Chemotherapy (using a combination of drugs to kill any remaining cancer cells and shrink any tumors) is sometimes used to treat prostate cancer that has recurred after initial treatments.

Nearly 87 percent of men who are treated for prostate cancer survive. If the disease is detected early, that percentage increases. Prostate cancer cannot be prevented. To increase the chance of detecting the disease early, the American Cancer Society recommends that all men over the age of forty have an annual rectal examination (men over the age of fifty should have a blood test, in addition).

Sexually transmitted diseases

Sexually transmitted diseases (also called STDs or venereal diseases) are infections transmitted through various forms of sexual activity. More than twenty-five STDs exist, caused by many different organisms. About 12 million new STD infections occur in the United States each year. Almost 65 percent of all STD infections affect people under the age of twenty-five.

STDs can cause birth defects, blindness, brain damage, cancer, heart disease, infertility, mental retardation, and death. Symptoms of STDs vary according to the virus or bacteria causing the disease and the body system affected. In general, a woman who has an STD may bleed when she is not menstruating. She may also have an abnormal vaginal discharge. In addition, vaginal burning, itching, and odor are common. A man afflicted with an STD may have a discharge from the tip of his penis. Urinating may also cause a painful or burning sensation. Both women and men may develop skin rashes, sores, bumps, or blisters near the mouth, genitals, or anal area.

SEXUALLLY TRANSMITTED DISEASES CAN CAUSE BIRTH DEFECTS, BLINDNESS, BRAIN DAMAGE, CANCER, HEART DISEASE, INFERTILITY, MENTAL RETARDATION, AND DEATH.

Perhaps the most deadly and frightening STD is AIDS or acquired immune deficiency syndrome. It is caused by the human immunodeficiency virus or HIV. The virus is transmitted between humans in blood, semen, and vaginal secretions. The two main ways to contract the virus are by sharing a needle with a drug user who is HIV-positive (infected with the virus) or by having unprotected sexual relations with a person who is HIV-positive. (For a more detailed discussion of HIV and AIDS, see chapter 5.)

Other common and potentially serious STDs in the United States include chlamydia, genital herpes, genital warts, gonorrhea, and syphilis.

Chlamydia is the most common STD in the United States. It is caused by a microscopic organism that lives as a parasite in human cells. It is transmitted through vaginal intercourse. A common symptom for both men and women is frequent and painful urination. The disease can be successfully treated with antibiotics.

Genital herpes is an incurable infection caused by a virus that is similar to the one responsible for cold sores. The infection is marked by the formation of fluid-filled, painful blisters in the genital area. The virus stays in the body for life. Over 25 million people in the United States are infected with the disease. It can be transmitted by oral and vaginal intercourse. Drugs are available to lessen symptoms and reduce outbreaks of the disease.

Genital warts, also called venereal warts, are caused by a virus that produces growths (warts) on the skin. In women, the growths occur on the genitals and on the walls of the vagina and cervix. In men, they develop in the urethra and on the shaft of the penis. The disease is transmitted by sexual contact. In addition to the visible warts, bleeding, pain, and odor are common symptoms. No treatment for genital warts is completely effective because it is necessary to destroy the skin infected by the virus.

Gonorrhea, commonly referred to as "the clap," is a highly contagious STD caused by a bacteria. It is transmitted through vaginal and anal intercourse. In men, the disease begins as an infection of the urethra. In women, it will most likely infect the cervix. If left untreated, the disease can travel through the reproductive tract (causing sterility) and spread to the bloodstream, infecting the brains, heart valves, and joints. Symptoms of the disease in women include bleeding between menstrual periods, painful urination, abdominal pain, and a cloudy and yellow vaginal discharge. Symptoms in men include painful and frequent urination and a thick, cloudy discharge from the penis. Gonorrhea is usually treated with a variety of antibiotics, but the bacteria that causes it is developing an increased resistance to routine medications.

Syphilis is an infectious disease caused by a coil-shaped bacterium. Spread by vaginal and anal intercourse, syphilis has been a public health problem since the sixteenth century. It currently affects an estimated 50 million people worldwide. The earliest symptom in both women and men is a chancre sore in the mouth or on the genitals. The fluid in the sore is very infectious. Lymph nodes near the chancre swell in most people afflicted with

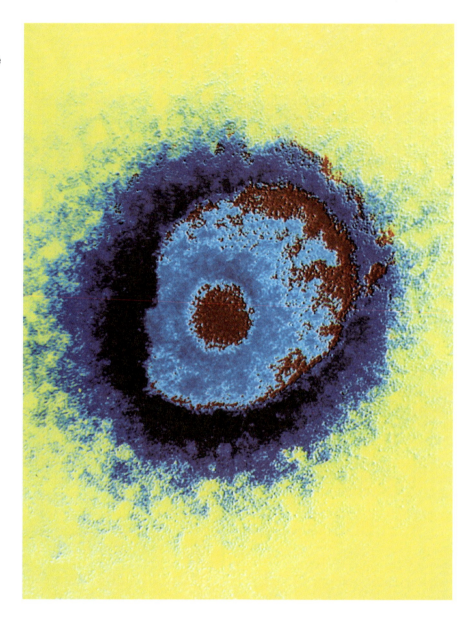

A microscan of the herpes simplex virus. Genital herpes—usually passed from person to person by sexual contact—is caused by Type 2 herpes simplex virus, or HSV2. (Reproduced by permission of Custom Medical Stock.)

the disease. As syphilis progresses, lymph nodes in the armpits, groin, and neck areas may also swell and skin lesions may erupt. If not treated, syphilis may cause damage years later to the heart and blood vessels, lungs, and central nervous system. The disease is usually treated with sufficiently large doses of antibiotics such as penicillin.

Testicular cancer

Testicular cancer develops when cells in the testes become abnormal and grow uncontrollably, forming tumors. Although a rare type of cancer, it often grows very quickly. It is the most common type of cancer to occur in young males under the age of thirty. The cause of testicular cancer is unknown.

This type of cancer usually shows no early symptoms. A mass in the testes usually indicates testicular cancer, but this may not be true in every case. In advanced stages of the cancer, symptoms include lower back pain, difficulty in urinating, a cough, and breathing problems. Sometimes there is pain in the testes.

TESTICULAR CANCER IS THE MOST COMMON TYPE OF CANCER TO OCCUR IN YOUNG MALES UNDER THE AGE OF THIRTY.

If testicular cancer is discovered, surgery to remove the mass is the first line of treatment. If the cancer has spread to other parts of the body, chemotherapy (using a combination of drugs to kill

William Augustus Hinton. (Reproduced by permission of UPI/Bettmann.)

HINTON'S FIGHT AGAINST SYPHILIS

William Augustus Hinton (1883–1859), the first African American professor at Harvard Medical School, earned an international reputation as a medical researcher for his work on the detection and treatment of sexually transmitted diseases. He was integral in developing two common diag-

nostic (identification) procedures for syphilis, the Hinton test and the Davies-Hinton test.

From the time he graduated from Harvard Medical School in 1912 until his retirement, Hinton concentrated his research on the diagnosis and treatment of syphilis. The first diagnostic test for the disease had been developed by German physician August von Wassermann in 1906. However, the test took two days to complete. In 1923, a Russian-American researcher, Reuben Leon Kahn, produced a modified syphilis test that took only a few minutes to complete. However, these blood tests for the disease often resulted in false diagnoses and consequent medical mistreatments.

In 1927, Hinton perfected a syphilis test—subsequently known as the Hinton test—that was simpler, less expensive, and more accurate than the previous procedures. As a result, the Hinton test was adopted as the standard method for diagnosing syphilis. Later, with J. A. V. Davies, Hinton developed an even more accurate diagnostic test, the Davies-Hinton test. In 1936, Hinton wrote *Syphilis and Its Treatment,* in which he outlined correct procedures for using laboratory tests for syphilis. Although the book at first had little support in the medical community, within twenty years it had become widely accepted and acclaimed.

any remaining cancer cells and shrink any tumors) or radiation therapy (using X rays or other high-energy rays to kill any remaining cancer cells and shrink any tumors) or a combination of both may be used following surgery.

The cure rate for testicular cancer that has not spread is 95 percent. Since the cancer cannot be prevented, it is important for men to perform regular examinations of their testes in order to detect any mass at an early stage.

Uterine cancer

Uterine cancer, also called endometrial cancer, develops when cells of the endometrium become abnormal and grow uncontrollably, forming tumors. It is a common type of cancer among women, generally occurring in those women who have gone through menopause and are forty-five years old or older.

The exact cause of uterine cancer is unknown. Medical researchers believe, however, that several factors increase a woman's chance of developing this type of cancer. Among those factors are age, obesity, diabetes, high blood pressure, irregular menstrual periods, family history of uterine cancer, and having a first period at a young age or going through menopause at a late age.

Symptoms of uterine cancer are present at an early stage in the disease. The most common symptom is unusual bleeding or discharge from the vagina. Pain and the presence of a lump or mass in the pelvic region are symptoms that occur late in the disease.

If uterine cancer is discovered, the standard treatments are surgery, radiation therapy, chemotherapy, and hormonal therapy. The type of procedure used depends on the stage of the disease. When the disease is detected early, surgery to remove the uterus is the procedure most often employed. This type of surgery is called a hysterectomy. If the cancer has spread, the ovaries and fallopian tubes are also surgically removed. Radiation therapy (using X rays or other high-energy rays to kill any cancer cells and shrink any tumors) may be used in place of or in addition to surgery. Chemotherapy (using a combination of drugs to kill any cancer cells and shrink any tumors) is usually reserved for women with advanced or recurrent uterine cancer. In hormonal therapy, drugs similar to the hormone progesterone are give to help slow the growth of endometrial cells. Again, this procedure is usually reserved for women with advanced or recurrent uterine cancer.

If uterine cancer is found and treated in its early stages, approximately 96 percent of women so treated survive five years or more. That survival rate falls to 66 percent if the cancer has spread before it is treated. Early detection is extremely important in helping to cure this disease. Controlling obesity, high blood pressure, and diabetes may also help to reduce the risk of developing uterine cancer.

Uterine fibroids

Uterine fibroids, also called myomas, are benign (nonthreatening) growths of the muscle in the uterus. They are not cancerous, nor are they related to cancer. Uterine fibroids are extremely common. They usually develop in women between the ages of thirty and fifty. About 25 percent of the women in this age group have noticeable fibroids.

No one knows exactly what causes fibroids, which grow in three locations: in the uterine cavity, on the wall of the uterus, and on the outside of the uterus. Not all fibroids cause symptoms, but when they do, the symptoms include the following: heavy uterine bleeding, pelvic pressure and pain, and complications during pregnancy.

Even fibroids that do cause symptoms may not require treatment. When the fibroids grow large enough to cause serious problems, surgery may be necessary. The only real cure for fibroids is the surgical removal of the uterus,

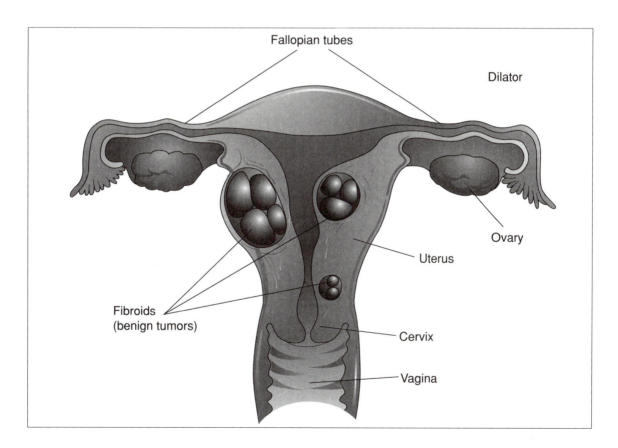

Locations of uterine fibroids. Also called myomas, uterine fibroids are benign growths of the muscle in the uterus. (Illustration by Electronic Illustrators Group.)

a procedure called a hysterectomy. If only the fibroids are removed and the uterus is repaired and left in place, the surgical procedure is called a myomectomy.

Uterine fibroids cannot be prevented. Luckily, many women who have fibroids have either no symptoms or only minor symptoms. Unfortunately, fibroids tend to grow over time, and many women ultimately decide to have some form of treatment.

TAKING CARE: KEEPING THE REPRODUCTIVE SYSTEM HEALTHY

As humans age, the functioning of their reproductive systems decline. Although testosterone and sperm continue to be produced in men, both decrease with advancing age. For women, there is a definite end to the ability to reproduce. With menopause, estrogens levels decrease and ovulation and menstrual cycles cease.

It is important, then, to keep the reproductive system operating at peak efficiency. As in all other body systems, the following play a key part: eating a proper diet low in fat and high in fiber, maintaining a healthy weight, consuming proper amounts of good-quality drinking water, getting adequate rest, engaging in regular exercise, not smoking or taking illegal drugs, drinking only moderate amounts of alcohol (if at all), and reducing stress levels.

Stress taxes all body systems. Any condition that threatens the body's homeostasis or steady state is a form of stress. Conditions that cause stress may be physical, emotional, or environmental. Stress can be particularly taxing on the reproductive system. In women, long-term stress can interrupt or even stop the menstrual cycle. In men, long-term stress can reduce the number of sperm produced or cause impotence. Combining exercise with proper amounts of sleep, relaxation techniques, and positive thinking will help reduce stress and prevent these disorders.

Because the organs of the reproductive system are susceptible to infection, it is especially important to practice good hygiene by keeping the genital area clean. When engaging in sexual relations, it is vital to practice safe sex. This includes choosing a partner carefully and forming a monogamous relationship (having only one sexual partner). If an individual engages in sexual intercourse with numerous partners, that individual should be tested for any sexually transmitted disease. While having sex, a man should wear a latex condom (condoms for females have been developed). Wearing a condom will help prevent the spread of sexually transmitted diseases and prevent unwanted pregnancies. Of course, practicing abstinence (refraining from sexual activity) is the only sure way to prevent sexual diseases and pregnancies.

FOR MORE INFORMATION

Books

Avraham, Regina. *The Reproductive System.* New York: Chelsea House, 1991.

Parker, Steve, and Aziz Khan. *Reproduction.* Brookfield, CT: Copper Beech Books, 1998.

Parker, Steve. *The Reproductive System.* Austin, TX: Raintree/Steck-Vaughn, 1997.

Silverstein, Alvin, Virginia Silverstein, and Robert Silverstein. *The Reproductive System.* New York: Twenty-First Century Books, 1994.

WWW Sites

Cyber Anatomy: Reproductive System
http://tqd.advanced.org/11965/html /cyber-anatomy_reproductive.html
Site provides detailed information on the reproductive system that is divided into two levels: the first geared for students in grades 6–9, the other for students in grades 10–12. In each of those levels, textual information and illustrations are presented separately for the female and male reproductive systems.

Human Reproduction
http://www.epigee.org/guide/reproduction.html
Site gives a clear description of the process of the female reproductive system, ovulation, and contraception. Also provides a short list of recommended books and a few links to other sites.

Reproductive System
http://hyperion.advanced.org/2935/Natures_Best/Nat_Best_Low_Level/Reproductive_page.L.html
Site offers an extensive discussion of the reproductive systems of both males and females with some illustrations (the high band width selection offers more illustrations).

The Reproductive System
http://gened.emc.maricopa.edu/bio/bio181/BIOBK /BioBookReprod.html
Site presents a detailed chapter on the reproductive system—both female and male parts—from the On-Line Biology textbook.

The Reproductive System
http://www.msms.doe.k12.ms.us/biology/anatomy/reproductive /reproductive.html
Site provides links to pages offering text and illustrations that describe the organs and accessory parts of the female and male reproductive systems and how they function.

Sexually Transmitted Diseases
http://www.epigee.org/guide/stds.html
Site provides links to discussions of the most common sexually
transmitted diseases, along with consequences, preventions, tips, and
related links.

9

The Respiratory System

Breathing, controlled by the respiratory system, is a continuous process of which a person is normally unaware. If breathing stops, however, a person becomes acutely aware of the fact. An individual can go days without food and water and hours without sleep, but only five or six minutes without air. Anything beyond that would be fatal. The trillions of cells in the body need a constant and generous amount of oxygen to carry out their vital functions. As they use that oxygen, they give off carbon dioxide as a waste product. It is the role of the respiration system, working in conjunction with the cardiovascular system, to supply the oxygen and dispose of the carbon dioxide.

DESIGN: PARTS OF THE RESPIRATORY SYSTEM

Breathing describes the process of inhaling and exhaling air. The exchange of gases (oxygen and carbon dioxide) between living cells and the environment is a process known as respiration. The respiratory system, which controls breathing and respiration, consists of the respiratory tract and the lungs.

The respiratory tract cleans, warms, and moistens air on its way to the lungs. The tract can be divided into an upper and a lower part. The upper part consists of the nose, nasal cavity, pharynx (throat), larynx, and upper part of the trachea (windpipe). The lower part consists of the lower part of the trachea, bronchi, and lungs (which contain bronchioles and alveoli).

The nose and nasal cavity

The nose is the only external part of the respiratory system. It is made of bone and cartilage (tough connective tissue) and is covered with skin. The two openings to the outside, called nostrils, allow air to enter or leave the body during breathing. The nostrils are lined with coarse hairs that prevent large particles such as dust, insects, and sand from entering.

The nostrils open into a large cavity, the nasal cavity. This cavity is divided into right and left cavities by a thin plate of bone and cartilage called the nasal septum. The hard portion of the palate forms the floor of the entire nasal cavity, separating it from the mouth or oral cavity below. Three flat, spongy folds or plates project toward the nasal septum from the sides of the nasal cavity. These plates, called nasal conchae, help to slow down the passage of air, causing it to swirl in the nasal cavity.

The nasal cavity is lined by mucous membrane containing microscopic hairlike structures called cilia. The cells of the membrane produce mucus, a

WORDS TO KNOW

Alveoli (al-VEE-oh-lie): Air sacs of the lungs.

Breathing (BREETH-ing): Process of inhaling and exhaling air.

Bronchi (BRONG-kie): Largest branch of the bronchial tree between the trachea and bronchioles.

Bronchial tree (BRONG-key-uhl TREE): Entire system of air passageways within the lungs formed by the branching of bronchial tubes.

Bronchioles (BRONG-key-ohls): Smallest of the air passageways within the lungs.

Epiglottis (ep-i-GLAH-tis): Flaplike piece of tissue at the top of the larynx that covers its opening when swallowing is occurring.

Esophagus (i-SOF-ah-gus): Muscular tube connecting the pharynx and stomach.

Exhalation (ex-ha-LAY-shun): Also known as expiration, the movement of air out of the lungs.

Glottis (GLAH-tis): Opening of the larynx between the vocal cords.

Hemoglobin (HEE-muh-glow-bin): Iron-containing protein pigment in red blood cells that can combine with oxygen and carbon dioxide.

Inhalation (in-ha-LAY-shun): Also known as inspiration, the movement of air into the lungs.

Larynx (LAR-ingks): Organ between the pharynx and trachea that contains the vocal cords.

Lungs: Paired breathing organs.

Nasal cavity (NAY-zul KAV-i-tee): Air cavity in the skull through which air passes from the nostrils to the upper part of the pharynx.

Nasal conchae (NAY-zul KAHN-kee): Flat, spongy plates that project toward the nasal septum from the sides of the nasal cavity.

Nasal septum (NAY-zul SEP-tum): Vertical plate made of bone and cartilage that divides the nasal cavity.

Nose: Part of the human face that contains the nostrils and organs of smell and forms the beginning of the respiratory tract.

Nostril (NOS-tril): Either of the two external openings of the nose.

Paranasal sinuses (pair-a-NAY-sal SIGH-nus-ez): Air-filled chambers in the bones of the skull that open into the nasal cavity.

Pharynx (FAR-inks): Short, muscular tube extending from the mouth and nasal cavities to the trachea and esophagus.

Pleura (PLOOR-ah): Membrane sac covering and protecting each lung.

Pulmonary surfactant (PULL-mo-nair-ee sir-FAK-tent): Oily substance secreted by the alveoli to prevent their walls from sticking together.

Respiration (res-pe-RAY-shun): Exchange of gases (oxygen and carbon dioxide) between living cells and the environment.

Trachea (TRAY-key-ah): Also known as the windpipe, the respiratory tube extending from the larynx to the bronchi.

thick, gooey liquid. As the nasal conchae cause air to swirl in the nasal cavity, the mucus moistens the air and traps any bacteria or particles of air pollution. The cilia wave back and forth in rhythmic movement, and pieces of mucus with their trapped particles are swept along to the throat. The mucus is then either spat out or (more often) swallowed. Any bacteria present in the swallowed mucus is destroyed by the hydrochloric acid in the gastric juice of the stomach.

Air is not only moistened in the nasal cavity but warmed, as well. A rich network of thin-walled capillaries permeates the mucus membrane (especially the uppermost concha), and the incoming air is warmed as it passes over the vessels. When air finally reaches the lungs, it is similar to the warm, damp air found in the tropics.

The bones that surround the nasal cavity contain hollow spaces known as paranasal sinuses. The sinuses are also lined with mucous membrane containing cilia. The mucus produced in the sinuses drains into the nasal cavity. The main functions of the sinuses are to lighten the skull and to provide resonance (sound quality) for the voice.

The pharynx

The pharynx or throat is a short, muscular tube extending about 5 inches (12.7 centimeters) from the nasal cavity and mouth to the esophagus and trachea. It serves two separate systems: the digestive system (by allowing the passage of solid food and liquids) and the respiratory system (by allowing the passage of air).

The larynx

The larynx, commonly called the voice box, forms the upper part of the trachea. The larynx is made of nine pieces of cartilage connected by ligaments. The largest of these cartilages is the shield-shaped thyroid cartilage, which may protrude at the front of the neck, forming the so-called Adam's apple. The upper cartilage is the epiglottis, a flaplike piece of tissue. During swallowing, the larynx rises up and the epiglottis folds down to cover the glottis, or the larynx's opening. This prevents food or liquids from passing into the lower respiratory tract.

Mucous membrane lines the larynx. A pair of elastic folds in that lining form the vocal cords. During silent breathing, the vocal cords lie against the walls of the larynx. During speech, the cords are stretched across the opening of the larynx and air that passes through causes them to vibrate, generating sound waves. Various muscles produce tension on the cords, making them tighter (shorter) or looser (longer). The tighter the tension, the higher the pitch of the sound produced. Since men's larynges tend to be larger than women's, their vocal cords tend to be thicker and longer. The male voice thus tends to be lower in pitch.

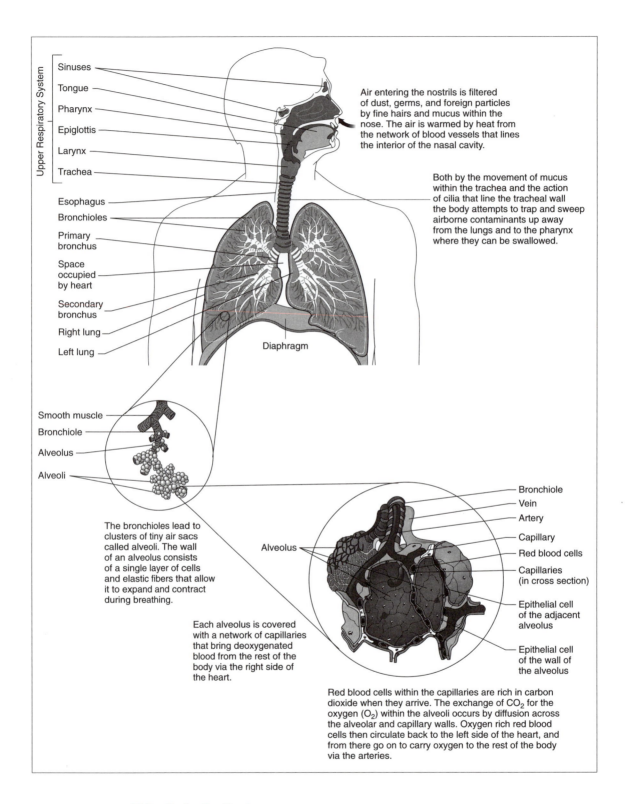

Upper Respiratory System

Sinuses

Tongue

Pharynx

Epiglottis

Larynx

Trachea

Esophagus

Bronchioles

Primary bronchus

Space occupied by heart

Secondary bronchus

Right lung

Left lung

Diaphragm

Air entering the nostrils is filtered of dust, germs, and foreign particles by fine hairs and mucus within the nose. The air is warmed by heat from the network of blood vessels that lines the interior of the nasal cavity.

Both by the movement of mucus within the trachea and the action of cilia that line the tracheal wall the body attempts to trap and sweep airborne contaminants up away from the lungs and to the pharynx where they can be swallowed.

Smooth muscle

Bronchiole

Alveolus

Alveoli

The bronchioles lead to clusters of tiny air sacs called alveoli. The wall of an alveolus consists of a single layer of cells and elastic fibers that allow it to expand and contract during breathing.

Each alveolus is covered with a network of capillaries that bring deoxygenated blood from the rest of the body via the right side of the heart.

Alveolus

Bronchiole

Vein

Artery

Capillary

Red blood cells

Capillaries (in cross section)

Epithelial cell of the adjacent alveolus

Epithelial cell of the wall of the alveolus

Red blood cells within the capillaries are rich in carbon dioxide when they arrive. The exchange of CO_2 for the oxygen (O_2) within the alveoli occurs by diffusion across the alveolar and capillary walls. Oxygen rich red blood cells then circulate back to the left side of the heart, and from there go on to carry oxygen to the rest of the body via the arteries.

The trachea

The trachea is a tough, flexible tube about 1 inch (2.5 centimeters) in diameter and 4.5 inches (11.4 centimeters) in length. Located in front of the esophagus, it is the principal tube that carries air to and from the lungs. The walls of the trachea are supported by 16 to 20 C-shaped cartilage rings. Elastic fibers in the tracheal walls allow the trachea to expand and contract during breathing, while the cartilage rings prevent it from collapsing. Mucous membrane containing cilia lines the trachea. The mucus produced by the membrane traps dust particles and other debris. The cilia move continuously in a direction opposite that of the incoming air, helping propel the mucus away from the lungs to the throat where it can be swallowed or spat out.

The bronchi

The trachea divides behind the sternum (breastbone) to form a right and left branch called primary bronchi (singular: bronchus). Each bronchus passes into a lung—the right bronchus into the right lung and the left bronchus into the left lung. The right bronchus is wider, shorter, and straighter than the left. As a result, accidentally inhaled objects (such as pieces of food) most often enter the right primary bronchus.

By the time incoming air reaches the primary bronchi, it is warm, moistened, and cleansed of most particles or other impurities.

The lungs

The lungs are two broad, cone-shaped organs located on either side of the heart in the thoracic or chest cavity. They extend from the collarbones to the diaphragm, a membrane of muscle separating the thoracic cavity from the abdominal cavity. The base of each lung rests directly on the diaphragm. The rib cage forms a wall around the lungs, protecting them.

At birth, the lungs are pale pink in color. As people age, their lungs grow darker. The inhaling of dirt and other particles increases this aging process, even scarring the delicate tissue of the lungs.

Each lung is divided into lobes separated by deep grooves or fissures. The right lung, which is larger, is divided into three lobes. The left lung is divided into only two lobes. Combined, the two soft and spongy lungs weigh about 2.5 pounds (1.1 kilograms).

A membrane sac, called the pleura, surrounds and protects each lung. One layer of the pleura attaches to the wall of the thoracic cavity; the other layer encloses the lung. A fluid (pleural fluid) between the two membrane

---

OPPOSITE: The human respiratory system. (Illustration by Hans & Cassady.)

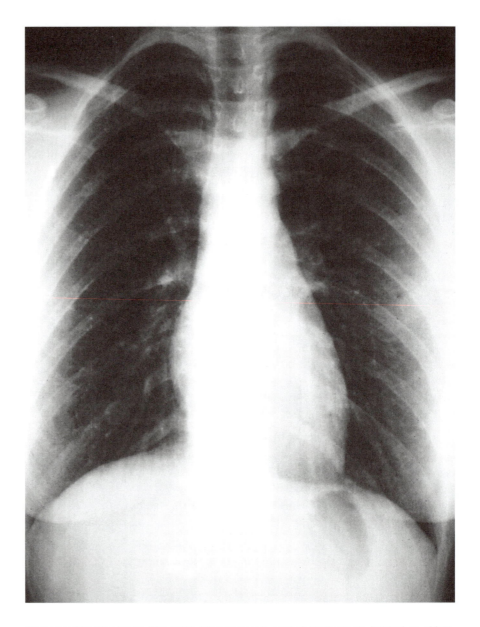

An X ray of healthy lungs. The lungs are two broad, cone-shaped organs located on either side of the heart in the chest cavity. (Photograph by John Smith. Reproduced by permission of Custom Medical Stock Photo.)

layers reduces friction and allows smooth movement of a lung during breathing.

After the bronchi enter the lungs, they subdivide repeatedly into smaller and smaller bronchi or branches. Eventually they form thousands of tiny branches called bronchioles, which have a diameter of about 0.02 inch (0.5 millimeter). This branching network of bronchial tubes within the lungs is called the bronchial tree.

The bronchioles branch to form even smaller passageways that open into clusters of cup-shaped air sacs called alveoli (singular: alveolus). The average person has a total of about 700 million alveoli (which resemble clusters of grapes) in his or her lungs. These provide an enormous surface area-roughly the size of a tennis court—for gas exchange. A network of capillaries surrounds each alveolus. As blood passes through these vessels and air fills the alveoli, the exchange of gases takes place: oxygen passes from the alveoli into the capillaries while carbon dioxide passes from the capillaries into the alveoli.

The membranes of the alveoli are extremely delicate and thin to allow the gases to pass easily through them. The inner lining of those membranes is coated with a thin layer of tissue fluid (a gas must be dissolved in a liquid in order to enter or leave a cell). To prevent the walls of the alveoli from sticking together (like the inside walls of a wet plastic bag), cells in the alveoli also produce an oily secretion, called pulmonary surfactant, that mixes with the tissue fluid (pulmonary refers to anything relating to or affecting the lungs).

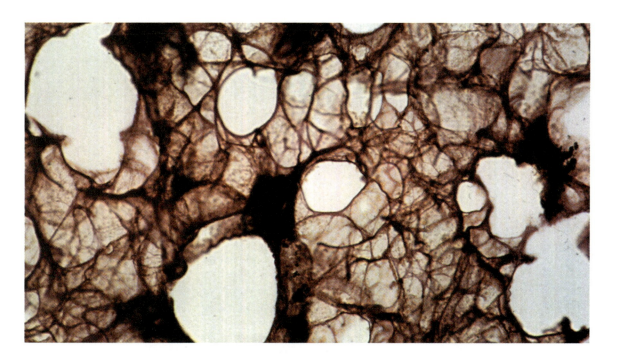

An electron micrograph scan of coal dust (marked by dark patches) in lung tissue infected with black lung disease. A disease found primarily in older coal workers, black lung is characterized by thickening and scarring of lung tissue. (Photograph by Hans-Freider and Astrid Michler. Reproduced by permission of Photo Researchers, Inc.)

WORKINGS: HOW THE RESPIRATORY SYSTEM FUNCTIONS

The main function of the respiratory system is to provide oxygen for the body's cells and remove the carbon dioxide they produce. Oxygen is the most important energy source for the cells. They need it for cellular respiration: the process by which the simple sugar glucose is oxidized (combined with oxygen) to form the energy-rich compound adenosine triphosphate (ATP). Glucose is produced in cells by the breakdown of more complex carbohydrates, including starch, cellulose, and complex sugars such as sucrose (cane or beet sugar) and fructose (fruit sugar). ATP is the compound used by all cells to carry out their ordinary functions: growth, the production of new cell parts and chemicals, and the movement of compounds through cells and the body as a whole.

Breathing

The mechanical process by which the body takes in oxygen and then releases carbon dioxide is called breathing or pulmonary ventilation. Inhalation (or inspiration) occurs when air flows into the lungs. Exhalation (or expiration) occurs when air flows out of the lungs. A single breath, called a respiratory cycle, consists of an inhalation followed by an exhalation. Breathing is brought about by the actions of the nervous system and the respiratory muscles.

The respiratory muscles are the diaphragm and the intercostal muscles. When the diaphragm (the dome-shaped sheet of muscle beneath the lungs that separates the thoracic chest cavity from the abdominal cavity) contracts,

BREATHING IN AND OUT: THE COMPOSITION OF AIR

When Earth was new, its atmosphere was probably composed of hydrogen, methane, and ammonia gases—much like the other planets in our solar system. Over billions of years, the composition of the atmosphere has changed considerably. Scientists theorize that a series of events that began when gases were released by early volcanic activity led to the formation of Earth's current atmosphere.

The air humans breathe in is Earth's atmosphere. The air humans breathe out, however, has a different composition. The following list breaks down the major components of those two types of air and their approximate percentages:

Nitrogen: 78% (inhaled air)/ 78% (exhaled air)

Oxygen: 21% (inhaled air)/ 16% (exhaled air)

Carbon dioxide: 0.04% (inhaled air)/ 4.5% (exhaled air)

Although most of Earth's atmosphere is composed of nitrogen, the human body cannot utilize this gas, so it is simply exhaled. Exhaled air has a decreased amount of oxygen and an increased amount of carbon dioxide. These amounts show how much oxygen is retained within the body for use by the cells and how much carbon dioxide is produced as a by-product of cellular metabolism.

it flattens and moves downward. The intercostal muscles are found between the ribs. When the external intercostal muscles contract, they pull the ribs upward and outward. When the internal intercostal muscles contract, they pull the ribs downward and inward. The actions of all these muscles produce changes in the pressure within the alveoli and the bronchial tree.

All forms of matter—solid, liquid, and gas—exert pressure. In the case of a gas (like air), that pressure is caused by the motion of the gas particles. Gas particles have a tendency to fly away rapidly from each other and fill any container in which they are placed. As they do so, they constantly collide against the walls of that container and each other. The collisions of the gas particles causes gas pressure. In a large container, the gas particles in a certain amount of gas will be far apart and less collisions will occur. As a result, the gas pressure will be low. In a smaller container, the gas particles in that same amount of gas will be closer together and more collisions will occur. This will result in high gas pressure.

Inhalation occurs when motor nerves from the medulla oblongata in the brain carry impulses to the diaphragm and intercostal muscles, stimulating them to contract. When the diaphragm is stimulated to contact, it moves downward. Its dome is flattened and the size of the chest cavity is increased. The external intercostal muscles are also stimulated to contract, and they move the ribs up and outward. This also increases the size of the chest cavity. Since the lungs are attached to the chest (thoracic) walls, as the chest expands, so do the lungs. This action reduces the pressure inside the lungs relative to the pressure of the outside atmospheric air. As a consequence, a partial vacuum is created in the lungs and air rushes in from the outside to fill them. The quantity of fresh air taken in during an inhalation is referred to as tidal air.

The reverse occurs in exhalation. In healthy people, exhalation is mostly a passive process that depends more on the elasticity of the lungs than on muscle contraction. During exhalation, motor nerve stimulation from the brain decreases. The diaphragm relaxes and its dome curves up into the chest cavity, while the external intercostal muscles relax and the ribs move back down and inward. As the chest cavity decreases in size, so do the lungs. The air in the lungs is forced more closely together and its pressure increases. When that pressure rises to a point higher than atmospheric pressure, the air is expelled or forced out of the lungs until the two pressures are equal again.

Under normal circumstances, energy is expended during inhalation, but not during exhalation. However, air can be forcefully expelled, such as during talking, singing, or playing a musical wind instrument. Forced exhalation is an active process that requires muscle contraction. In such a case, the internal intercostal muscles are stimulated to contract, pulling the ribs down and in. This forces more air out of the lungs. The abdominal muscles (rectus abdominis) may also be stimulated to contract, compressing the abdominal organs and pushing the diaphragm upward. This action forces even more air out of the lungs.

A healthy adult at rest breathes in and out—one respiratory cycle—about twelve to sixteen times per minute (children breathe more rapidly, about eighteen to twenty times per minute). Exercise and other factors can change this rate. Total lung capacity is about 12.5 pints (6 liters). Under normal circumstances, an individual inhales and exhales about 1 pint (475 milliliters) of air in each respiratory cycle. Only about three-quarters of this air reaches the alveoli. The rest of the air remains in the respiratory tract. Regardless of the volume of air breathed in and out (called the tidal volume), about 2.5 pints (1200 milliliters) remains in the respiratory passageways and alveoli. This amount of air, called the residual volume, keeps the alveoli inflated and allows gas exchange between the lungs and blood vessels to go on continuously.

Respiration

Once air has filled the lungs, the oxygen in that air must be transported to all the cells in the body. In return, all cells in the body release carbon dioxide that must be transported back to the lungs to be exhaled. The exchanges of gases in the body is known as respiration. External respiration is the exchange of gases through the thin membranes of the alveoli and those of the blood capillaries surrounding them. Internal respiration is the exchange of gases between the blood capillaries and the tissue cells of the body. Within the body, all gases are exchanged through the process of diffusion.

Diffusion is the movement of molecules from an area of greater concentration (existing in greater numbers) to an area of lesser concentration (existing in lesser numbers). Diffusion takes place because molecules have free energy, meaning they are always in motion. This is the case especially with molecules in a gas, which move quicker than those in a solid or liquid. Oxygen and carbon dioxide, the gases that pass between the alveoli and their capillaries and between the blood and the interstitial fluid (fluid surrounding cells of the body), move by diffusion.

EXTERNAL RESPIRATION. After inhalation, the air in the alveoli contains a high concentration of oxygen and a low concentration of carbon dioxide. Conversely, the blood in the pulmonary capillaries surrounding the alveoli

BREATHING UNDERWATER

In 1943, French oceanographer Jacques-Yves Cousteau (1910–1997) and French engineer Emile Gagnan developed the aqualung or scuba gear. This scuba (an acronym for **s**elf-**c**ontained **u**nderwater **b**reathing **a**pparatus) system not only benefitted recreational divers, but scientists as well. It has become an indispensable tool in the study of marine biology.

The aqualung allows a diver to swim freely down to about 180 feet (55 meters). Record-setting dives of over 300 feet (91 meters) have been made with scuba gear. It consists of a canister or canisters of highly compressed air that the diver wears on his or her back. The unit is connected to a demand regulator that automatically supplies air at the same pressure as that of the surrounding water. A mouthpiece attached to the regulator allows the diver to breathe.

(which has come from the body) has a low concentration of oxygen and a high concentration of carbon dioxide. Following the law of diffusion, oxygen molecules in the air in the alveoli flow into the pulmonary capillaries. Carbon dioxide molecules flow in the opposite direction, from the blood in pulmonary capillaries into the air in the alveoli.

After gas exchange occurs in the lungs, the pulmonary capillaries carry the oxygenated (carrying oxygen) blood toward the heart. They merge to form venules, which merge to form larger and larger veins. Finally, the oxygenated blood reaches the left atrium of the heart through the four pulmonary veins. After flowing into the left ventricle, the blood is pumped out to the rest of the body.

Almost all the oxygen that diffuses into the pulmonary capillaries attaches to red blood cells in the blood. The primary element of red blood cells is a protein pigment called hemoglobin. Hemoglobin molecules account for one-third the weight of each red blood cell. At the center of each hemoglobin molecule is a single atom of iron, which gives red blood cells their color. The oxygen molecules bond to the iron atoms to create compounds called oxy-hemoglobins. The main function of red blood cells is to transport this form of oxygen to the cells throughout the body.

INTERNAL RESPIRATION. Internal respiration occurs between the cells in the body and the systemic capillaries (capillaries in the body outside of the lungs). The bond between the oxygen molecules and the iron atoms of hemoglobin is not a very strong or stable one. When red blood cells enter tissues in the body where the concentration of oxygen is low, the bond is readily broken and the oxygen molecules are released.

This occurs when the systemic capillaries pass among the body cells. The blood in the systemic capillaries has a high concentration of oxygen

HOW DO FISH BREATHE?

Fish and most other aquatic animals use gills for respiration. In fish, these external respiratory organs are located in gill chambers at the rear of the mouth. Gills are specialized tissues with many infoldings. Each gill is covered by a thin layer of cells and filled with blood capillaries.

Water taken in through a fish's mouth is forced through openings called gill slits. It then washes over the delicate gills. The exchange of gases—oxygen and carbon dioxide—occurs through diffusion, much like in human lungs. Oxygen that is dissolved in the water diffuses through the thin membranes of the gills and passes into the capillaries. Carbon dioxide, produced as a waste product by the fish's cells, diffuses from the capillaries through the gills into the passing water.

All higher vertebrates or animals that have a backbone or spinal column (including humans) have immature gill slits when they are in an embryo stage or initially developing. However, these gill slits never fully mature and become functional. They disappear as the vertebrate embryo develops.

molecules and a low concentration of carbon dioxide molecules. The body cells and the interstitial fluid surrounding them have just the opposite: a low concentration of oxygen molecules and a high concentration of carbon dioxide molecules (because cells use oxygen to create energy, giving off carbon dioxide as the waste product of human metabolism).

Thus, in internal respiration, oxygen diffuses from the capillaries into the interstitial fluid to be taken up by the cells. At the same time, carbon dioxide diffuses from the interstitial fluid into the capillaries. Red blood cells in the now deoxygenated (carrying very little oxygen) blood then transport the carbon dioxide molecules back to the heart through ever larger veins. Finally, the blood returns to the right atrium of the heart via the venae cavae. After flowing into the right ventricle, the deoxygenated blood is pumped through the pulmonary arteries to the lungs, where the cycle of respiration begins once again.

AILMENTS: WHAT CAN GO WRONG WITH THE RESPIRATORY SYSTEM

Since the respiratory system is open to airborne microorganisms and outside pollution, many ailments or maladies can afflict it. Some respiratory disorders are relatively mild and, unfortunately, very familiar. Excess mucus (runny nose), coughing, sneezing, nasal congestion, headache, sore throat, muscle aches, and tiredness are all symptoms of the common cold. A viral infection of the upper respiratory system, the common cold can be caused by one of over 200 different viruses. An average individual usually suffers from between 50 and 100 colds during his or her life. Almost all colds clear up in less than two weeks without complications.

DO PLANTS BREATHE?

Plants do not "breathe" like animals. All animals have some mechanism for removing oxygen from the air and transmitting it into their bloodstreams, while expelling carbon dioxide from their bloodstreams in the process. Plants exchange oxygen and carbon dioxide with Earth's atmosphere, but in a different process.

Plants create energy for their cells through the process known as photosynthesis. Simply put, a plant absorbs sunlight into chlorophyll (green pigment located in plant cells called chloroplasts) and takes in carbon dioxide from the air through stomata (microscopic openings on the underside of its leaves). It also absorbs water from the soil through its roots. Using the energy from sunlight, the plant combines carbon dioxide and water to create the simple sugar glucose (which is later used to form more complex carbohydrates such as starch and cellulose). Oxygen is a by-product of this process.

In the second phase of photosynthesis, called respiration, the plant combines glucose and oxygen with enzymes to create adenosine triphosphate (ATP), a high-energy molecule used by cells of all organisms to store energy. Since plants use less oxygen during respiration than is created during photosynthesis, they expel that oxygen through their stomata. This action occurs mainly at night when photosynthesis cannot take place.

When a cold lingers beyond that time period, the cause may be an inflammation of the sinuses, a condition called sinusitis. Caused by a bacterial infection, sinusitis is often mistaken for a common cold because the symptoms are somewhat similar. With sinusitis, congestion may be the same or even worse. While drainage from the nose during a common cold is often clear, drainage due to sinusitis is often thick and yellowish-green in color. Sinus pain and pressure is frequent. A sore throat and bad breath, resulting from drainage dripping down the back of the throat, may also occur. Antibiotic medications are often necessary to treat sinusitis.

Allergies, abnormal immune reactions to otherwise harmless substances, are among the most common of medical disorders. Symptoms depend on the specific type of allergic reaction. In the most common type of reaction, symptoms can mimic those of a nasal cavity infection: pressure, pain, a runny nose, congestion, and a scratchy or irritated throat.

The following are some of the more serious—and often fatal—disorders and diseases that can impair the functioning of the respiratory system or its parts.

Asthma

Asthma is a chronic (long-term) inflammatory disease of the airways. Although the cause for the condition is unknown, it is known that allergies can trigger an asthma attack. Continuing inflammation makes the airways hypersensitive to stimuli such as cold air, exercise, dust mites, air pollutants, and even stress and anxiety. All can then give rise to an asthma attack.

Asthma usually begins in childhood or adolescence, but it also may first appear during adult years. An estimated 15 million people in the United States suffer from asthma. More than 5,600 people die of severe asthma attacks each year.

In an asthma attack, the muscle tissue in the walls of the bronchi and bronchioles go into spasm. As a result, the cells lining the airways swell and secrete mucus into the air spaces. Both these actions cause the bronchi and bronchioles to become narrowed. This, in turn, produces a tightness in the chest, wheezing, and breathlessness, sometimes to the point where an individual gasps for air. Asthma attacks come

RESPIRATORY SYSTEM DISORDERS

Asthma (AZ-ma): Respiratory disease often caused by an allergy that is marked by tightness in the chest and difficulty in breathing.

Bronchitis (bron-KIE-tis): Inflammation of the mucous membrane of the bronchial tubes.

Cystic fibrosis (SIS-tik fie-BRO-sis): Genetic disease in which, among other things, the mucous membranes of the respiratory tract produce a thick, sticky mucus that clogs airways.

Emphysema (em-feh-ZEE-mah): Respiratory disease marked by breathlessness that is brought on by the enlargement of the alveoli in the lungs.

Pneumonia (noo-MOE-nya): Disease of the lungs marked by inflammation and caused by bacteria or viruses.

Tuberculosis (too-burr-cue-LOW-sis): Infectious, inflammatory disease of the lungs caused by a bacteria that results in tissue damage.

and go in irregular patterns, and they vary in degree of severity. Some may last only a few minutes; others may go on for much longer.

Treatment for asthma usually includes identifying the specific substance causing the allergic reaction and subsequently avoiding contact with it. Drugs are often given to relax the muscles of the bronchial tubes and allow increased air flow. They may be taken by mouth or inhaled through a nebulizer, a device that delivers a regulated flow of medication into the airways.

Bronchitis

Bronchitis is an inflammation of the mucous membranes of the lower respiratory passages, especially the trachea and bronchi. Bronchitis can either be acute (short-term) or chronic (long-term).

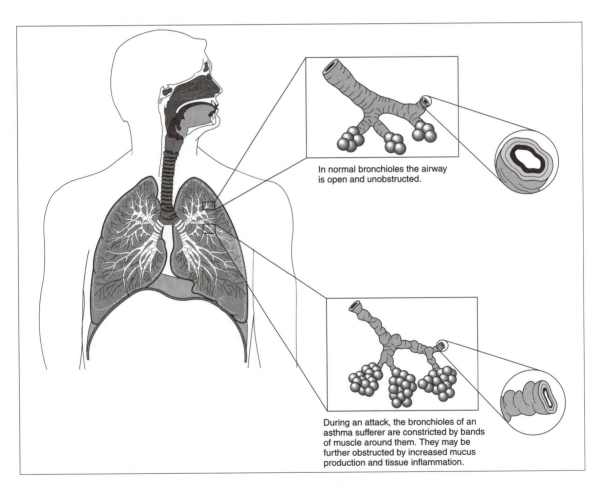

In normal bronchioles the airway is open and unobstructed.

During an attack, the bronchioles of an asthma sufferer are constricted by bands of muscle around them. They may be further obstructed by increased mucus production and tissue inflammation.

A comparison of normal bronchioles and those of an asthma sufferer. (Illustration by Hans & Cassady.)

Acute bronchitis usually follows a viral infection such as a cold or the flu. Anyone can be afflicted with the disorder, but infants, young children, and the elderly are more susceptible because their body immunity (ability to fight disease) is generally weaker. Acute bronchitis usually begins with the symptoms of a cold: runny nose, sneezing, and a dry cough. However, the cough soon becomes deep and painful, and it will bring up greenish-yellow phlegm. High fever and wheezing are also common.

If no additional infection is present, acute bronchitis is treated in the same way as the common cold: drinking plenty of fluids, resting, not smoking, and taking acetaminophen for fever and pain. If an additional infection exists, the infection is treated with an antibiotic. When treated, acute bronchitis usually resolves in one to two weeks without complications.

Chronic bronchitis is a major cause of disability and death in the United States, affecting an estimated 14 million people. The disorder is caused by inhaling respiratory irritants, especially cigarette smoke. The American Lung Association estimates that 80 to 90 percent of all cases are caused by smoking. Other irritants include chemical fumes, air pollution, mold, and dust.

Chronic bronchitis develops slowly over time. When smoke or other irritants are inhaled, the cilia projecting from the mucous membrane lining the respiratory tract become paralyzed or snap off. Airways then become inflamed, narrowed, and clogged with mucus, making breathing difficult. A mild cough, sometimes called smokers' cough, is usually the first symptom. Wheezing and shortness of breath may accompany the cough. As the disease advances, breathing becomes even more difficult and activity decreases.

There is no cure for chronic bronchitis and treatment to help reduce symptoms is complex. As in asthma attacks, drugs may be given to relax the muscles of the bronchial tubes and allow increased air flow. The drugs may be taken by mouth or inhaled through a nebulizer, a device that delivers a regulated flow of medication into the airways. To further reduce the swelling of airway tissue, anti-inflammatory drugs may also be prescribed. As the disease progresses, an individual may be required to breathe supplemental oxygen.

The best way to prevent either type of bronchitis is to stop smoking or not even to begin.

An electron micrograph scan of mucous membranes inflamed by bronchitis. (Reproduced by permission of Custom Medical Stock.)

Cystic fibrosis

Cystic fibrosis is an inherited or genetic disease, meaning it is caused by a defect in a person's genes. It affects the lungs, digestive system, sweat glands, and male fertility (ability to produce offspring or children). The disease affects about 30,000 children and young adults in the United States. Approximately 3,000 babes are born each year with cystic fibrosis.

Cystic fibrosis affects the body's ability to move salt and water in and out of cells. This defect causes the lungs and pancreas to secrete thick mucus, blocking passageways and preventing proper functioning. The disease derives its name from the fibrous scar tissue that develops as a result in the pancreas.

In the lungs, the thickened mucus increases irritation and inflammation of lung tissue. This inflammation swells the passageways, partially closing them down. At the same time, infection from bacteria or viruses becomes more likely since the mucus is a rich source of nutrients. Bronchitis and pneumonia frequently develop in individuals with cystic fibrosis.

The body's response to the infection is to increase mucus production. White blood cells fighting the infection thicken the mucus even further as they break down and release their cell contents. These white blood cells also provoke more inflammation. The process is a downward spiral as a person suffering from the disease experiences ever-increasing shortness of breath and tiredness. Untreated, cystic fibrosis leads to severe lung infection, which is the primary cause of death.

There is no cure for cystic fibrosis. Regular monitoring and early treatment are key to maintaining respiratory health. Good general health, especially good nutrition and exercise, can keep the body's immune response working properly. This, in turn, can help decrease the number of infections started by the bacteria always present in the lungs of infected individuals.

Clearing mucus from the lungs also helps to prevent infection, and devices and techniques have been developed to help in this regard. Several drugs are available to prevent the airways from becoming clogged with mucus. Lung transplants have become increasingly common for people with cystic fibrosis. About 50 percent of adults and 80 percent of children who receive lung transplants live longer than two years.

Emphysema

Emphysema is a respiratory disease marked by breathlessness that is brought on by the enlargement of the alveoli in the lungs. It is the most common cause of death from respiratory disease in the United States. Emphysema occurs mainly among people who are fifty years of age or older. Heavy cigarette smoking is the primary cause of the disease, although a few cases are caused by an inherited defect.

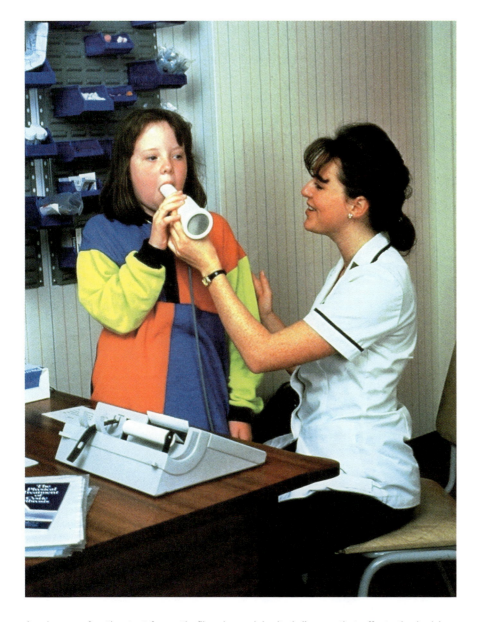

A pulmonary function test for cystic fibrosis, an inherited disease that affects the body's ability to move salt and water in and out of cells. (Reproduced by permission of Custom Medical Stock Photo.)

When a person inhales cigarette smoke, that person's body releases substances that are meant to defend the lungs against the smoke. These substances can also attack the cells of the lungs. Normally, the body prevents such action by releasing other substances. In smokers and those with the inherited defect, no such prevention occurs. Lung tissue is then damaged in such a way that it loses its elasticity. Bronchioles collapse, trapping air in the alveoli. Unable to contract efficiently and move air out, the alveoli overexpand and rupture. The alveoli blend together, forming large air pockets from which air cannot escape. This cuts down the surface area for gas exchange.

As the disease progresses, coughing and shortness of breath occur. Exhaling becomes difficult. Over several years, the extra work of exhaling can cause the chest to enlarge and become barrel-shaped.

Emphysema is a serious and long-term disease that cannot be reversed. The body cannot repair the damage to the lungs. Ultimately, the disease can lead to respiratory failure. If emphysema is detected early, medications may be given to help relax and open air passages, thus reducing some of the symptoms. Mild exercise may be ordered to help strengthen muscles involved in

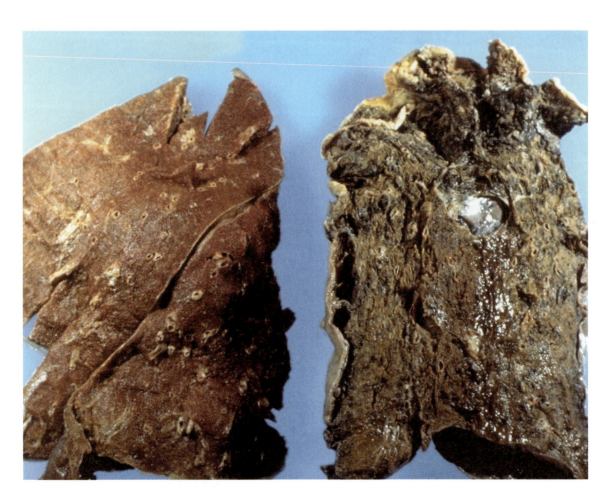

A healthy lung (on the left) and a smoker's lung (on the right). (Photograph by A. Glauberman. Reproduced by permission of Photo Researchers, Inc.)

breathing. An individual suffering from emphysema must stop smoking immediately or no treatments will be effective at all.

the respiratory

Lung cancer

Lung cancer develops when cells of the lung tissues become abnormal and grow uncontrollably, forming tumors. It is the leading cause of death from cancer among both men and women in the United States. Approximately 160,000 people die from the disease each year.

Tobacco smoking is the leading cause of lung cancer. Ninety percent of lung cancers can be prevented by giving up tobacco. Smoking marijuana cigarettes is considered yet another risk factor for lung cancer. These cigarettes have a higher tar content than tobacco cigarettes. In addition, they are inhaled very deeply. As a result, the smoke is held in the lungs for a longer time.

Other causes of lung cancer include exposure to asbestos, toxic chemicals, radioactive minerals, environmental pollution (such as auto exhaust fumes), and a family history of lung cancer.

Lung cancers tend to spread very quickly to other parts of the body. Early symptoms to watch for include a cough that does not go away, chest pain, shortness of breath, persistent hoarseness,

LUNG CANCERS TEND TO SPREAD VERY QUICKLY TO OTHER PARTS OF THE BODY.

swelling of the neck and face, significant weight loss, unexplained fever, bloody or brown-colored spit or phlegm, and recurrent lung infections.

The most common treatment options for lung cancer include surgery, chemotherapy, and radiation. During surgery, surgeons may remove a small part of the lung, one lobe of the lung, or the entire lung. The extent of the surgery depends on how much of the lung is affected. After the cancer has been removed, the physician may recommend chemotherapy (using a combination of drugs to kill any remaining cancer cells and shrink any tumors) or radiation therapy (using X rays or other high-energy rays to kill any remaining cancer cells and shrink any tumors) or a combination of both. Either or both of these methods may be used to shrink the tumor before surgery is attempted.

Almost 50 percent of lung cancer patients survive if the cancer is detected before it has had a chance to spread to other organs and it is treated appropriately. Only 15 percent of lung cancers, however, are found at this early stage. The best way to prevent lung cancer is not to smoke at all or to quit smoking if one has already started. Secondhand smoke from other people's cigarettes should also be avoided.

Pneumonia

Pneumonia is an infection of lung tissues. It can be caused by nearly any organism known to cause human infections. This includes bacteria, viruses,

Body By Design   **257**

fungi, and parasites. Pneumonia is the sixth most common disease leading to death in the United States. It is also the most common fatal infection acquired by people who are already hospitalized.

Pneumonia develops when the several types of immune substances in the respiratory tract are weakened to the point where invading organisms can take over. Once they do so, an infection develops in the normally sterile environment of the lungs. Symptoms include fever, cough, chest pain, shortness of breath, and increased respirations (number of breaths per minute). Many people cough up sputum (commonly known as spit) streaked with pus or blood.

The invading organism causes symptoms by provoking the body to launch an overly strong immune response in the lungs. That response, which should help fight the infection, instead damages lung tissue and makes it more susceptible to infection. Capillaries in the lungs become leaky and the fluid seeps into the alveoli. Mucus production in the lungs is increased. The alveoli further fill with fluid and debris from the large number of white blood cells being produced by the body to fight the infection. The amount of oxygen delivered to the rest of the body is then decreased.

BEFORE THE DISCOVERY OF PENICILLIN ANTIBIOTICS, BACTERIAL PNEUMONIA WAS ALMOST ALWAYS FATAL.

MOVING AIR BY OTHER MEANS

Breathing is not the only process by which humans move air in and out of the lungs. Some processes or actions are reflexes initiated to clear air passages. Others are indications or extensions of emotional states. The following is a list of these common actions and how they are brought about:

Coughing: Reflex that removes irritants from the mucous membrane of the pharynx, larynx, or trachea. A deep inhalation is suddenly followed by an exhalation with the glottis temporarily closed. After pressure has built up, the glottis suddenly opens and an explosive exhalation is directed out of the mouth.

Crying: Action brought on by an emotional state. Inhalation followed by a number of short exhalations while the glottis is open and the vocal cords vibrate.

Hiccuping: Sudden inhalations when the diaphragm abruptly contracts. Sound produced when glottis closes suddenly to stop the inhalation. May be caused by an irritation of the diaphragm or the nerves that serve the diaphragm.

Laughing: Action brought on by an emotional state that produces basically the same air movements as crying.

Sneezing: Reflex that removes irritants from the mucous membrane of the nasal cavity. Action is the same as in coughing, except that oral cavity is closed off by the uvula (fleshy projection hanging from the soft palate) and the explosive exhalation is directed out of the nose.

Yawning: Reflex whose purpose or stimulus is not fully known. Tiredness, boredom, and seeing another person yawn all seem to trigger yawning. Very deep inhalation with jaws wide open brings tidal air to all alveoli.

Before the discovery of penicillin antibiotics, bacterial pneumonia was almost always fatal. Today, antibiotics are very effective against bacterial causes of pneumonia when given early in the course of the disease.

Tuberculosis

Tuberculosis (TB) is a potentially fatal infectious disease caused by a bacterium that can affect almost any part of the body. However, it is mainly an infection of the lungs. Although TB can be treated, cured, or even prevented if persons at risk take certain drugs, scientists have never come close to wiping it out. Popularly known throughout history as consumption, TB currently affects an estimated 8 to 10 million people worldwide each year. Roughly 3 million people die from the disease each year.

TB is usually contracted by inhaling air sneezed or coughed by someone who is suffering from the disease. Once inhaled, the bacterium reaches the alveoli. Actual tissue damage in the lungs is not caused directly by the bacterium, but by the reaction of a person's tissues to its presence. The infection may progress until large areas of the lung have been destroyed.

An infected person may at first feel vaguely ill or develop a cough blamed on smoking or a cold. A small amount of greenish or yellow sputum (spit) may be coughed up upon arising in the morning. In time, more sputum is produced that is streaked with blood. Chest pain, a low-grade fever, night sweats, loss of weight, difficulty breathing, and weakness are symptoms in advanced cases.

Individuals with TB can be treated at home with a combination of prescribed drugs. If the drugs are not effective, surgery to repair the damaged lung or remove part or all of it may be performed. If the disease is diagnosed early and prompt treatment is given, the recovery rate for TB sufferers is very good.

TAKING CARE: KEEPING THE RESPIRATORY SYSTEM HEALTHY

As people age, elastic tissue throughout the body begins to break down. The lungs begin to lose their elasticity, and the ability to ventilate the lungs (breathe in) becomes more difficult. In addition, many of the defenses set up to protect the respiratory system become less efficient, leaving the system open to infections.

These effects of aging can be delayed or even minimized by taking care of not only the respiratory system but the body as a whole. The following all play a vital part in keeping the body healthy and its immune response functioning at peak efficiency: proper nutrition, healthy amounts of good-quality drinking water, adequate rest, regular exercise, and stress reduction.

All forms of air pollution have some harmful effect on humans, especially on the respiratory system and its parts. For example, prolonged exposure to carbon monoxide can cause heart and respiratory disorders. The oxides of both sulfur and nitrogen attack the human respiratory system. At low concentrations, they can leading to an irritated throat and impaired breathing. At higher concentrations, they can lead to emphysema, bronchitis, and lung cancer. Although it is almost impossible to be free from air pollution in modern urban areas, steps can be taken to reduce the amount of pollutants breathed in. Avoiding polluted areas (if possible) and wearing a mask while working in dusty or dirty places are two such steps.

The single most important thing an individual can do to protect and preserve the respiratory system is to not smoke. Tobacco smoking is perhaps the single worst activity an individual can do in regards to health. In addition to nicotine, a powerful drug that affects the heart and blood vessels, tobacco smoke contains carbon monoxide. Carbon monoxide is a well-known toxic gas that reduces the ability of hemoglobin in red blood cells to carry oxygen to all the cells in the body.

THE SINGLE MOST IMPORTANT THING AN INDIVIDUAL CAN DO TO PROTECT AND PRESERVE THE RESPIRATORY SYSTEM IS TO NOT SMOKE.

Tobacco smoke also contains tars and other chemicals that damage the delicate cells in the mucous membrane lining the respiratory tract. Cilia projecting from that membrane are either paralyzed or destroyed by cigarette smoke. Pollutants and other particles, which then cannot be removed, settle in the lungs. The extra mucus produced in response to an irritated respiratory tract provides an ideal breeding ground for harmful bacteria.

Many illnesses or disorders result from smoking tobacco. If smoking is continued over a period of time, those illnesses become progressively worse. Chronic bronchitis, emphysema, and lung cancer are a few of the serious disorders that can result from smoking. All can lead to death.

FORE MORE INFORMATION

Books

Bryan, Jenny. *Breathing: The Respiratory System.* Minneapolis, MN: Dillon Press, 1993.

Parker, Steve. *The Lungs and Respiratory System.* Austin, TX: Raintree/Steck-Vaughn, 1997.

Roca, Nuria Bosch, and Marta Serrano. *The Respiratory System.* New York: Chelsea House, 1995.

Silverstein, Alvin, Virginia Silverstein, and Robert Silverstein. *The Respiratory System.* New York: Twenty-First Century Books, 1994.

Smolley, Laurence A., Debra Fulghum Bruce, and Rob Muzzio. *Breathe Right Now: A Comprehensive Guide to Understanding and Treating the Most Common Breathing Disorders.* New York: Norton, 1998.

WWW Sites

Anatomy of the Respiratory System
> http://www.jeffersonhealth.org/diseases/pulmonary/anatomy.htm
> Site from the Jefferson Health System, a collective of member hospitals and healthcare organizations in the greater Philadelphia region. Includes information on the anatomy of the respiratory system, and includes a discussion of how the various parts work. Also includes links to diseases and disorders of the respiratory system.

Cyber Anatomy: Respiratory System
> http://tqd.advanced.org/11965/html /cyber-anatomy_resboth.html
> Site provides detailed information on the respiratory system that is geared for students in grades 6 through 12.

Human Respiratory System
> http://www.stemnet.nf.ca/~dpower/resp/main.htm
> Site provides links that give information on the exchange of gases in the human body. Also has a link that details the structure of the respiratory system.

Respiratory System
> http://hyperion.advanced.org/2935/Natures_Best /Nat_Best_Low_Level /Respiratory_page.L.html
> Site offers an extensive discussion of the respiratory system, its organs, and various parts. Also includes a discussion of the breathing process (the high band width selection offers more illustrations).

The Respiratory System
> http://gened.emc.maricopa.edu/bio/BIO181/BIOBK/ BioBookRESPSYS.html
> Site presents a detailed chapter on the respiratory system from the On-Line Biology textbook.

Your Gross and Cool Body—Respiratory System
> http://www.yucky.com/body/index.ssf?/systems/respiratory/
> Site presents facts and answers questions about the respiratory system and its various parts.

10

The Skeletal System

The word skeleton comes from the Greek word *skeletos,* meaning "dried up." The parts of the skeletal system—the bones and other structures that make up the joints of the skeleton—are anything but dried up. Strong yet light, the skeletal system is made of living material, with networks of blood vessels running throughout. The system protects body organs, supports the body, and provides attachment points for muscles to enable body movement. All bones act as storage sites for minerals such as calcium and phosphorus, and certain bones also produce blood cells.

DESIGN: PARTS OF THE SKELETAL SYSTEM

Because the bones making up the human skeleton are inside the body, the skeleton is called an endoskeleton (*endo* means "within"). In animals that have an external skeleton, such as the crab, the skeleton is called an exoskeleton (*exo* means "outside"). Exoskeletons restrict the movement of an organism and must be shed periodically in order for that organism to grow. Endoskeletons allow for freer movement and grow along with an organism.

All humans are born with over 300 bones. As an individual ages, certain bones (such as those in the skull and lower spine) fuse or join together, thereby reducing the number. By the time an individual reaches adulthood, the number of bones in the body totals about 206.

Structure of bones

Bone is living tissue that is constantly being renewed throughout life. Three types of bone cells take part in this process: osteoblasts, osteocytes, and osteoclasts (*osteon* is the Greek word meaning "bone").

Osteoblasts are the principal bone-building cells. They produce hard calcium compounds and flexible collagen (a fibrous protein), which combined form the nonliving part of bone called the bone matrix. The matrix makes

WORDS TO KNOW

Appendicular skeleton (ap-en-DIK-yoo-lar SKEL-i-ton): Portion of the skeleton consisting of the pectoral girdle, the pelvic girdle, and the bones of the arms and legs.

Axial skeleton (ACK-see-uhl SKEL-i-ton): Portion of the skeleton consisting of the skull, vertebral column, and rib cage.

Bursa (BURR-sah): Sac filled with synovial fluid that decreases friction between a tendon and a bone.

Diaphysis (die-AFF-i-sis): Shaft of a long bone containing a narrow canal filled with yellow bone marrow.

Epiphysis (e-PIFF-i-sis): End of a long bone.

Fontanels (fon-tah-NELZ): Also known as soft spots, fibrous connective tissue between flat bones in the developing cranium.

Joint: Area where adjacent bones meet or articulate.

Ligament (LIG-a-ment): Fibrous connective tissue that connects bone to bone.

Ossification (ah-si-fi-KAY-shun): Process of bone formation.

Osteoblasts (OS-tee-oh-blasts): Principal bone-building cells.

Osteoclasts (OS-tee-oh-klasts): Large cells that break down bone matrix.

Osteocytes (OS-tee-oh-sites): Mature bone cells.

Periosteum (per-ee-OS-tee-um): Dense fibrous membrane covering the surface of bones except at the joints.

Synovial membrane (sin-OH-vee-uhl MEM-brain): Connective tissue membrane that lines joint cavities and secretes synovial fluid.

Tendon (TEN-den): Tough, white, cordlike tissue that attaches muscle to bone.

bone strong, hard, and slightly elastic. In the process of forming the bone matrix, osteoblasts become trapped in it. Once they are trapped, they develop into osteocytes or mature bone cells. Osteocytes help maintain the hard bone tissue by removing and replacing the calcium compounds in the matrix. In mature adults (whose bones are no longer growing), osteocytes are the most numerous bone cells. Finally, osteoclasts are the bone-destroying cells. They break down bone matrix, releasing calcium and phosphate ions into the blood (this is important when blood calcium levels drop below normal).

About 98 percent of the calcium and 90 percent of the phosphorus in the body are stored in bones and teeth. Although mature bones consist largely of calcium, most bones in the human skeleton begin as cartilage. Cartilage is a type of connective tissue that contains collagen and elastin fibers, which make it tough and elastic. In a developing fetus, cells in the cartilage skeleton begin to break down. They are replaced by osteoblasts, which begin producing bone matrix around the outer portion of the cartilage. For a while, the fetus has cartilage "bones" enclosed by "bony" bones. This bone formation process, known as ossification, continues until almost all the cartilage

OPPOSITE: Some of the major bones in the human body. By the time an individual reaches adulthood, the number of bones in the body totals about 206. (Illustration by Kopp Illustration, Inc.)

Skeletal System

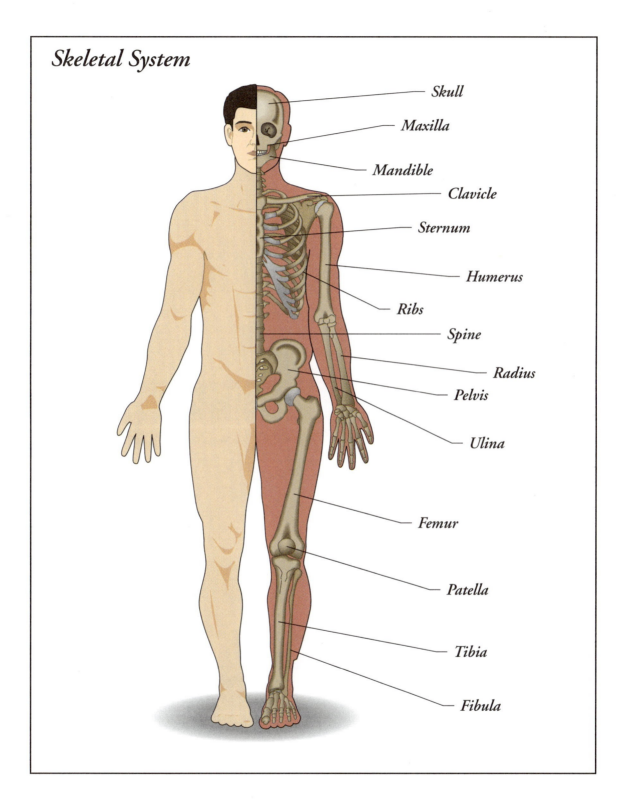

- Skull
- Maxilla
- Mandible
- Clavicle
- Sternum
- Humerus
- Ribs
- Spine
- Radius
- Pelvis
- Ulina
- Femur
- Patella
- Tibia
- Fibula

has been replaced, usually by the time an individual reaches the end of puberty (cartilage remains at the ends of bones to prevent wear and tear).

Bones may be classified according to their various traits, such as shape and texture. Four types are recognized based on shape. These are long bones, short bones, flat bones, and irregular bones.

Long bones are found in the extremities: the arms, legs, hands, and feet (but not the wrists or ankles). As their name indicates, long bones have a long central shaft with knobby end portions. The shaft is called the diaphysis and each end is called the epiphysis. Short bones, which are cube-shaped, are found in confined spaces such as the wrist and ankle. Flat bones are thin and wide, providing surfaces for muscle attachment and protection for underlying organs. The ribs, shoulder blades, sternum (breastbone), pelvis (hips), and most of the bones of the skull are consider flat bones. Irregular bones are those that do not fit into the first three categories. Vertebrae (bones of the spinal column) and facial bones are types of irregular bones.

A thin white membrane, called the periosteum, covers the surface of bones except at the joints (areas where bones articulate or connect). Made of

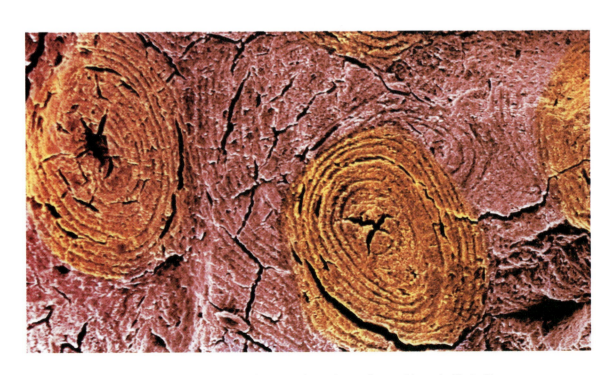

A false-color scan of compact bone tissue. Compact bone is filled with numerous microscopic passageways carrying nerves, blood vessels, and other structures that provide living bone cells with nutrients. (Copyright 1992 CNRI. Reproduced by permission of Custom Medical Stock Photo.)

connective tissue, the periosteum contains nerves and blood vessels. Underneath the periosteum lie two different types of bone tissue: compact bone and spongy (or cancellous) bone. Although dense and smooth, compact bone is filled with numerous microscopic passageways carrying nerves, blood vessels, and other structures that provide living bone cells with nutrients. Spongy bone has a lacy network of bone tissue with many cavities, making it look like a sponge. Although lighter in weight than compact bone, spongy bone is nearly as strong.

The diaphyses of long bones are made of compact bone with a hollow center that forms a canal. That canal is filled with yellow bone marrow, which is mostly adipose or fatty tissue. The epiphyses of long bones consist of spongy bone covered with a thin layer of compact bone. Yellow bone marrow also fills the cavities of spongy bone in long bones.

Short, flat, and irregular bones are all made of spongy bone covered by a thin layer of compact bone. The cavities of the spongy bone in these bones are filled with red bone marrow, which is the loose connective tissue that produces blood cells in certain bones. In adults, red blood cells, five types of white blood cells, and platelets are formed in the red bone marrow of portions of the ribs, vertebrae, sternum, and pelvis.

The bones forming the human skeletal system are divided into two divisions: the axial skeleton and the appendicular skeleton. The axial skeleton includes bones associated with the body's main axis—the spine. This includes the skull, the spine or vertebral column, and the rib cage. The appendicular skeleton is attached to the axial skeleton and consists of the bones associated with the body's appendages—the arms and legs. This includes the bones of the pectoral girdle (shoulder area), the arms, the pelvic girdle (hip area), and the legs.

Please note: in the naming of the major bones of the body on the following pages, pronunciations are provided in parenthesis when necessary.

Axial skeleton

THE SKULL. The skull consists of two sets of bones: cranial bones and facial bones. In addition to protecting the brain, these bones protect and support the organs responsible for sight, hearing, smell, and taste.

the skeletal system

THE BARE BONE FACTS

Over half of the bones in the body are located in the arms and legs—120 bones.

The hyoid bone in the throat is the only bone that does not touch another bone. It is usually broken when a person is hanged or strangled, and therefore will often figure in trials concerning such crimes.

The longest and strongest bone in the body is the femur.

The clavicle (collar bone) is one of the most frequently fractured bones in the body. Fractured clavicles are caused either by a direct blow or a transmitted force resulting from a fall on an outstretched arm.

The smallest bones in the body are the three bones found in each middle ear, collectively known as the ossicles (OS-si-kuls).

The skeleton of an average person accounts for about 20 percent of total body weight.

The eight bones of the cranium (the part of the skull that encloses the brain) are thin and flat. Interlocking at their joints, they are immovable. The frontal bone forms the forehead and the upper part of the eye sockets. The two parietal (pah-RYE-ah-tul) bones form the sides and upper portion of the cranium. Lying underneath the parietal bones are the two temporal bones. The occipital (ok-SIP-i-tal) bone forms the back of the cranium.

In infants, fibrous connective tissue fills the spaces between the cranial bones. Known as fontanels or soft spots, these spaces allow the skull bones to move slightly during birth. This makes birth easier and helps prevent skull fractures. Eventually, the fontanels are replaced by bone by the age of eighteen to twenty-four months.

Fourteen bones compose the face. Of these bones, only the mandible (MAN-di-buhl) or lower jaw is movable. It houses the lower set of teeth. The upper jaw, the maxilla (MAK-sill-lah), is formed by the fusion of two bones. The maxilla also forms the inner lower portion of the eye sockets and houses the upper set of teeth. The two zygomatic (zie-go-MA-tik) bones are commonly called the cheekbones. They also form the outer lower portion of the eye sockets.

Certain facial bones contain hollow, air-filled spaces known as sinuses. The main functions of the sinuses are to lighten the skull and to provide resonance (sound quality) for the voice. The sinuses in the bones that surround the nasal cavity are called the paranasal sinuses. They are lined with mucous membrane. The mucus produced in the sinuses drains into the nasal cavity to help moisturize and warm air as it flows into the respiratory tract. Infections occurring in the nasal sinuses tend to move into the paranasal sinuses, causing a condition known as sinusitis.

A few bones are not considered a part of the bones of the skull, but are associated with them. These include the bones of the middle ear and the hyoid (HI-oid) bone. Within each middle ear cavity are three auditory bones. They aid the hearing process by transmitting vibrations from the ear drum to receptors in the inner ear (for a further discussion of this process, see chapter 12). The hyoid bone is the only bone in the body that does not attach directly to any other bone. Horseshoe-shaped, it is suspended by ligaments (cords of fibrous tissue that connects bones) from the lower portions of the temporal bones. It lies in the neck about 1 inch (2.5 centimeters) above the larynx (voice box). The hyoid plays a major role in swallowing, supporting the tongue and larynx.

ARE SOME PEOPLE ACTUALLY DOUBLE-JOINTED?

No. Only one joint can occur at an area where bones come together. People who can move their bones beyond normal range are able to do so because the ligaments attached to those particular bones can stretch farther than normal. Contortionists have "stretchy" ligaments, not "double joints."

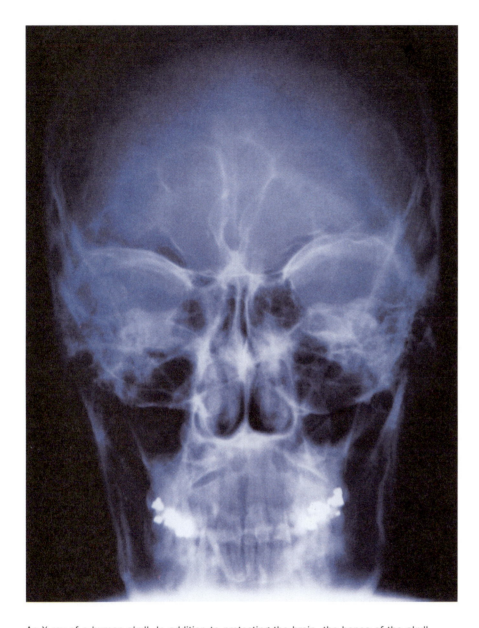

An X ray of a human skull. In addition to protecting the brain, the bones of the skull protect and support the organs responsible for sight, hearing, smell, and taste. (Photograph by Jim Cummings. Reproduced by permission of FPG International.)

VERTEBRAL COLUMN. The skull rests atop the vertebral column, which encloses the spinal cord. Also called the spine or backbone, the vertebral column protects the spinal cord and helps to support the weight of the body, transmitting that weight to the lower limbs. It also provides attachment sites for the ribs as well as the muscles that move the trunk (main part of the body). The individual bones making up the column are collectively called vertebrae (VER-te-bray). A single bone is called a vertebra (VER-te-brah).

Before birth, thirty-three vertebrae compose the vertebral column. The nine lower vertebrae eventually fuse, forming the sacrum (SAY-krum) and the coccyx (KOK-siks). The sacrum is formed by the fusing of the first five of those nine vertebrae; the coccyx is formed by the fusing of the last four. The coccyx, or tailbone, is a remnant of the tail other vertebrate animals have.

The remaining twenty-four vertebrae are divided into regions based on their structure. The initial seven bones under the skull are referred to as cervical (SIR-vi-kul) vertebrae. They form the neck region of the spine. The first cervical vertebra is called the atlas (in Greek mythology, Atlas was a Titan who was forced by the gods to support the sky on his shoulders for eternity). Its special shape supports the skull and allows the head to nod "yes". The second cervical vertebra is called the axis. It acts as a pivot for the atlas (and skull) above. The twelve vertebrae below the cervical vertebrae are called the thoracic (thuh-RA-sik) vertebrae. The next five vertebrae are the lumbar vertebrae. The sacrum and coccyx then form the end of the vertebral column.

The vertebrae sit on top of each other to form the vertebral column. Although vertebrae in each region differ from each other, all vertebrae have the same basic structure. Each has a round body that bears the weight of the column. Discs of flexible cartilage lie between the bodies of vertebrae to provide cushioning, like shock absorbers. In a young person, the discs are about 90 percent water and are spongy and compressible. As a person ages, the water content decreases, and the discs become harder and less compressible. Processes or projections extending out from the bodies toward the back of the human body form a canal through which the spinal cord passes. The processes also allow the vertebrae to interlock with each other and serve as sites for muscle and ligament attachment.

The vertebral column is not rigid, but is capable of limited movement such as bending and some twisting. It is also not a straight structure. It has four major curves, forming a long S. This adds strength to the column, increasing the skeleton's balance and ability to hold the body upright. The outward curves (toward the back of the body) of the thoracic and sacral regions are known as primary curves because they are present at birth. The inward curves (toward the front of the body) of the cervical and lumbar regions develop when a baby begins to raise his or her head (cervical) and when the baby begins to walk (lumbar). By the time a child is ten years old, all four spinal curves are fully developed.

THE RIB CAGE. Twelve pairs of ribs (a total of twenty-four bones) extend forward from the thoracic vertebrae. Most of the ribs (the first seven pairs) attach in the front of the body by cartilage called costal cartilage to the long, flat sternum (STIR-num) or breastbone. These ribs are called true ribs. The next five pair of ribs are called false ribs. The first three pair of false ribs do not attach directly to the sternum, but to the costal cartilage of the seventh pair of ribs. The lower two pair of ribs of false ribs, also called floating ribs, do not attach to the sternum at all.

Ribs give shape to the chest and support and protect the body's major organs, such as the heart and lungs. The rib cage, formed by the ribs and sternum, also provides attachment points for connective tissue, to help hold organs in place.

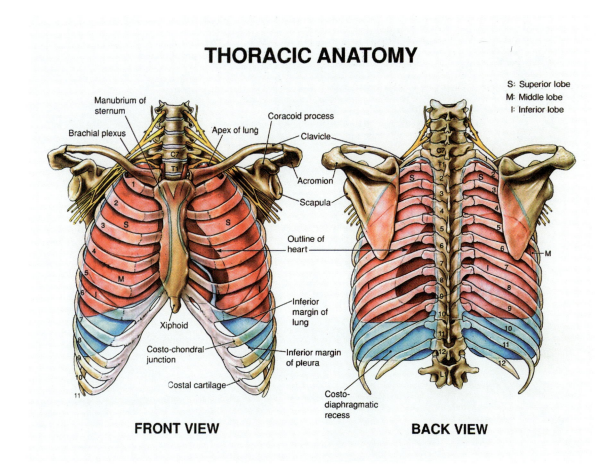

Chest cavity anatomy and its relationship to underlying structures such as the heart and lungs. (Reproduced by permission of Photo Researchers, Inc.)

Appendicular skeleton

THE PECTORAL GIRDLE. Forming a loose attachment with the sternum is the pectoral girdle, or shoulder. Each shoulder is formed by two bones: the scapula (SKAP-yoo-lah) or shoulder blade and the clavicle (KLAV-i-kul) or collar bone. The large triangular-shaped scapula anchors some of the muscles that move the upper arm. The S-shaped clavicle is small and light and relatively fragile. Each clavicle acts as a brace for its corresponding scapula, preventing the shoulder from coming too far forward.

The major advantage to the loose attachment of the pectoral girdle is that it allows for a wide range of shoulder motions and greater overall freedom of movement.

THE ARMS. Each arm or upper limb (composed of the upper arm, forearm, wrist, and hand) contains thirty bones. The upper arm contains only one bone, the humerus (HYOO-mer-us), which extends from the shoulder joint to the elbow joint. At the elbow joint, the humerus articulates or connects with the two bones of the forearm, the radius (RAY-dee-us) and the ulna (UL-na). When the arm is held out and palm faces upward, the radius and ulna are parallel to each other; the radius is on the thumb side and the ulna is on the little finger side. When the arm is turned over and the palm faces downward, the radius crosses on top of the ulna to form an X.

Each wrist is composed of eight bones known as carpal (CAR-pal) bones. They are arranged in two irregular rows of four bones each. Ligaments bind the carpals together, restricting their movement.

Nineteen bones form each hand. The bones forming the framework of the palm, which articulate with the carpals, are the five metacarpals (meh-tah-CAR-pals). In turn, the metacarpals articulate with the fourteen finger bones or phalanges (fah-LAN-jees). The thumb has two phalanges, while the four fingers each have three.

THE PELVIC GIRDLE. Unlike the pectoral girdle, the pelvic girdle is strong and dense. It consists of two large coxal (KOK-sal) or hip bones. Each coxal bone, left and right, consists of three fused bones—the ilium (ILL-ee-yum), the ischium (ISH-ee-um), and the pubis (PEW-bis). The ilium is the flared, upper portion of a hip. Each ilium attaches at the rear to the sacrum, connecting the pelvic girdle to the vertebral column. The ischium is the ring-shaped lower part on which a person sits, and the pubis is the most forward portion at the bottom of a hip. These three bones generally have fused together by the time an individual reaches adolescence.

WHAT HAPPENS WHEN YOU "CRACK" YOUR KNUCKLES?

When a person pulls quickly on his or her finger, a vacuum is created in the joint cavity between the phalanges, displacing the synovial fluid normally found in the cavity. The popping sound occurs when the fluid rushes back into the cavity.

The bones in the human hand include the metacarpals and phalanges. (Reproduced by permission of Custom Medical Stock.)

The pelvic girdle is bowl-shaped, with an opening at the bottom (*pelvis* is the Latin word meaning "basin"). In a pregnant woman, this bony opening is a passageway through which her baby must pass during birth. The pelvic girdle of women is generally wider than that of men, which helps to ease birth. The pelvic girdle protects the lower abdominal organs, such as the intestines, and helps support the weight of the body above it.

THE LEGS. Each leg or lower limb is similar in form to an arm or upper limb. Each leg (composed of the thigh, lower leg, and foot) also contains thirty bones. The thigh contains only one bone, the femur (FEE-mur), which extends from the hip joint to the knee joint. The bones of the lower limbs are thicker and stronger than the bones of the upper limbs. In fact, the femur is the longest, strongest, and heaviest bone in the body. As it runs down the upper part of the leg, the femur slants inward. This helps bring the knees in line with the body's center of gravity.

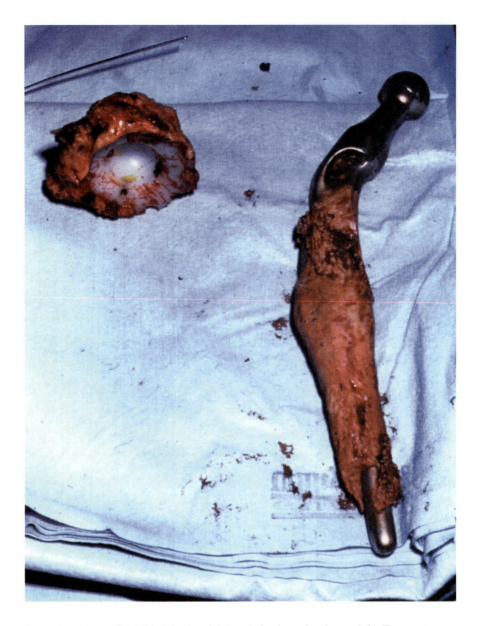

A prosthetic, or artificial, hip joint (on right) and plastic socket (upper left). The most common joints to be replaced are hips and knees. (Reproduced by permission of Custom Medical Stock.)

The patella (pah-TELL-ah) or kneecap is a thick, flat, triangular-shaped bone that lies above and protects the knee joint. At that joint, the femur articulates with the larger of the two bones of the lower leg, the tibia (TI-bee-ah) or shinbone. The fibula (FI-byoo-lah), which lies along the outer side of the tibia, is slender and sticklike. It has no part in forming the knee joint, but provides a surface for muscle attachment and helps keep the ankle bones from sliding laterally (side to side). The inner and outer bulges at the ankle are formed by the ends of the tibia (the inner bulge) and fibula (the outer bulge).

At the ankle joint, the tibia and fibula articulate with the seven tarsal (TAR-sal) bones forming the ankle and heel. The weight of the body is mostly carried by the two largest tarsals: the calcaneus (kal-KAY-nee-us) or heel bone and the talus (TAL-us), which lies between the tibia and fibula.

As in each hand, nineteen bones form each foot. The bones forming the framework of the sole, which articulate with the tarsals, are the five metatarsals (meh-tah-TAR-sals). In turn, the metatarsals articulate with the fourteen toe bones or phalanges (fah-LAN-jees). There are two phalanges in the big toe and three in each of the other toes.

Ligaments and tendons

Two types of dense connective or fibrous tissue are attached to bones— ligaments and tendons. Ligaments fasten bone to bone at joints, wrapping around the joints to hold the bones together. By doing so, they make joints more stable. Depending on their location in the body, they can be shaped like a thick strap, a rope, or a flat ribbon or bandage. Because they are bundles containing elastic fibers as well as collagen fibers, ligaments can stretch to a certain degree.

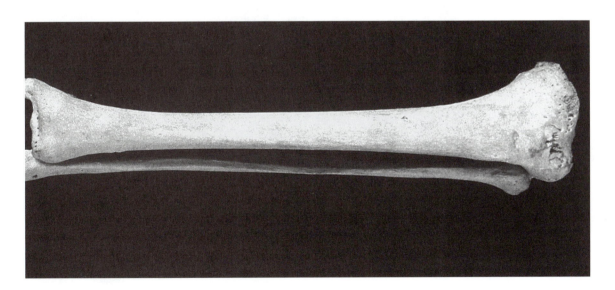

A tibia bone. Found in the lower leg, the tibia (or shinbone) articulates with the femur.
(Reproduced by permission of Custom Medical Stock Photo.)

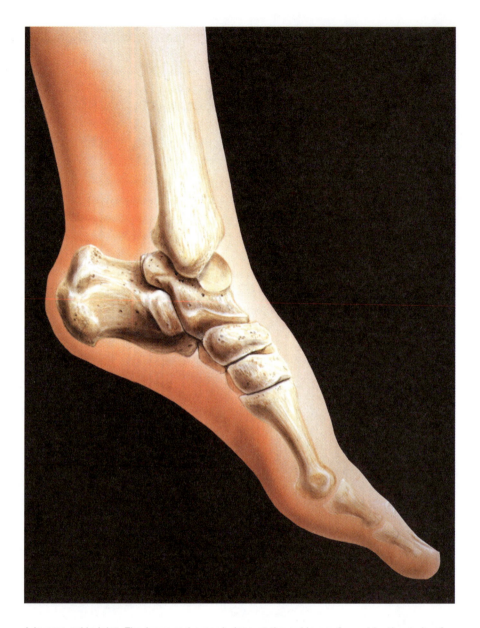

A human ankle joint. The inner and outer bulges at the ankle are formed by the ends of the tibia (the inner bulge) and fibula (the outer bulge). (Reproduced by permission of Photo Researchers, Inc.)

OPPOSITE: The structure of the foot. As in each hand, nineteen bones form each foot (see image at bottom right for details). (Reproduced by permission of Photo Researchers, Inc.)

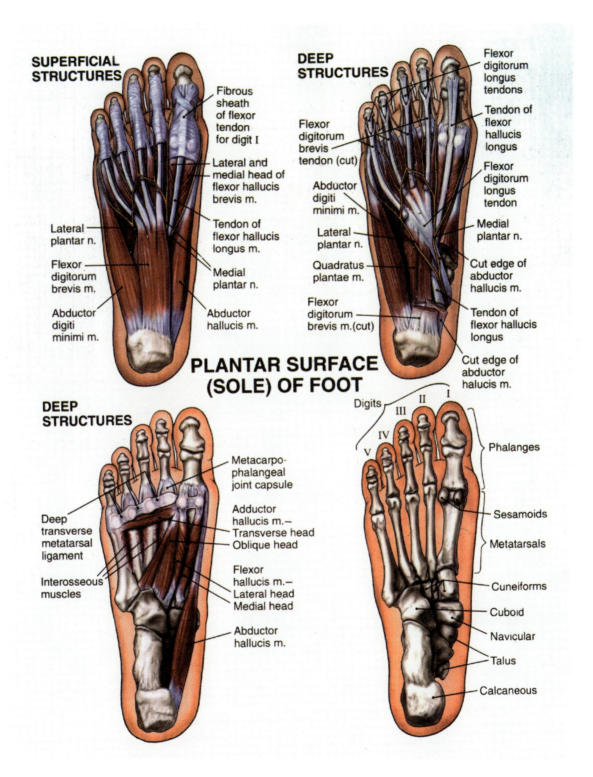

SUPERFICIAL STRUCTURES

Fibrous sheath of flexor tendon for digit I

Lateral and medial head of flexor hallucis brevis m.

Tendon of flexor hallucis longus m.

Medial plantar n.

Abductor hallucis m.

Lateral plantar n.

Flexor digitorum brevis m.

Abductor digiti minimi m.

DEEP STRUCTURES

Flexor digitorum longus tendons

Tendon of flexor hallucis longus

Flexor digitorum longus tendon

Medial plantar n.

Cut edge of abductor hallucis m.

Tendon of flexor hallucis longus

Cut edge of abductor halucis m.

Flexor digitorum brevis tendon (cut)

Abductor digiti minimi m.

Lateral plantar n.

Quadratus plantae m.

Flexor digitorum brevis m.(cut)

PLANTAR SURFACE (SOLE) OF FOOT

DEEP STRUCTURES

Deep transverse metatarsal ligament

Interosseous muscles

Metacarpo-phalangeal joint capsule

Adductor hallucis m.—
Transverse head
Oblique head

Flexor hallucis m.—
Lateral head
Medial head

Abductor hallucis m.

Digits

II
I
III
IV
V

Phalanges

Sesamoids

Metatarsals

Cuneiforms

Cuboid

Navicular

Talus

Calcaneous

Tendons attach skeletal muscles to bone. A tendon is the tough, white, cordlike tissue that is formed when the layers of connective tissue that bundle the various parts of a muscle converge or come together at the end of the muscle. Tendons contain fibers of the tough protein collagen, but they cannot stretch as much as ligaments. Tendons are much stronger than muscle tissue. As muscles are used, the tendons are able to withstand the constant pulling and tugging of the muscles on the bones.

WORKINGS: HOW THE SKELETAL SYSTEM FUNCTIONS

The most obvious function of the skeletal system is to provide shape and form to the body. Like the steel girders of a building, the bones provide a framework around which the body is built. Delicate tissues and organs are attached to and protected by this bony framework. For example, the skull encloses the brain, the ribs protect the heart and lungs, and the vertebrae shield the spinal cord.

Bones are also storehouses for minerals, the most important of which are calcium and phosphorus. Both are used to build and maintain bones and teeth. Calcium serves other vital functions, too. Muscles need it in order to contract and blood needs it in order to clot. For these two bodily processes to occur, calcium must be present in the bloodstream at all times. When blood calcium levels drop below normal, hormones trigger osteoclasts to break down bone matrix, releasing calcium. When blood calcium levels rise above normal, hormones cause excess calcium to be deposited in the bones in the form of calcium salts.

BONES ARE STOREHOUSES FOR MINERALS, THE MOST IMPORTANT OF WHICH ARE CALCIUM AND PHOSPHORUS.

As stated earlier, some bones serve as production sites for blood cells. Red blood cells and other blood elements are formed in the red bone marrow of certain flat and irregular bones.

Perhaps the most dramatic function of the skeletal system is to allow the human body to move through space. Walking, running, jumping, dancing, and even breathing are all possible because of the combined actions of the muscles and the bones. Skeletal muscles are attached to bones, and when a muscle contracts, it pulls on its attached bone and movement occurs at a specific joint.

Joints

Joints, also called articulations, are the places where two or more bones meet or articulate. Every bone in the body (with the exception of the hyoid bone in the neck) forms a joint with at least one other bone.

Joints allow a great variety of motion, and the function of each joint is closely related to its structure. When movement is not required, such as between the bones of the cranium, the joint is immobile and strong. The bones are locked together as if they were a single bone. Other joints, such as those between the vertebrae, allow limited movement while still maintaining a certain amount of strength. Finally, in areas where movement is more important than strength, joints can be freely movable. The shoulder joint, for example, allows the arm to move in a variety of ways. Because it allows such a range of motion, the shoulder joint is relatively weak and prone to injury.

As stated, ligaments fasten bone to bone at joints. To prevent friction, the ends of bones at joints are covered in smooth cartilage. In freely movable joints, extra protection is afforded by a joint capsule under the ligaments that surrounds the joint. Made of fibrous connective tissue, the capsule encloses the joint like a sleeve. Lining the capsule is the synovial membrane, which secretes a thick and slippery fluid into the joint cavity. This fluid, called synovial fluid, helps prevent further friction as the bones move.

In areas where tendons cross bone, small sacs filled with synovial fluid lie between the tendon and the joint. These sacs, called bursae (singular: bursa), help cushion the tendon as it slides across the bone.

Freely movable joints are the largest category of joints in the body, especially in the appendicular skeleton where mobility or movement is important. The five main types of freely movable joints are the ball-and-socket, saddle, hinge, pivot, and gliding.

WHEN DID HUMANS BEGIN WALKING UPRIGHT?

The human species, or *Homo sapiens,* belongs to the hominid family tree. Hominid means "human types," and describes early creatures who split off from the apes and took to walking upright or on their hind legs.

The reasons that human ancestors started to walk upright are not known. Scientists believe it may have been a response to environmental changes: as tropical forests were beginning to shrink, walking might have been a better way to cross the grasslands to get to nearby patches of forest for food. Standing upright also may have been a means of defense that slowly evolved. By standing upright, animals appear bigger and more impressive in size than they normally are. In addition, the ability to stand up and get a wider view of the surroundings gives an animal an advantage in the tall grasses. Walking upright also frees up the hands to carry objects, such as tools.

The oldest known humanlike animals to have walked upright are believed to be *Australopithecus afarensis,* meaning the southern ape of the Afar region in Ethiopia, Africa, where the fossils were found. The most famous of these fossils, nicknamed Lucy, was found in 1974 near Hadar, Ethiopia, by a team of anthropologists led by American Donald Johanson (1943–). Lucy lived about 3.18 million years ago. Her skull, knees, and pelvis were more similar to humans than to apes. Her brain size was about one-third that of modern humans, yet larger than any apelike ancestor to have come before. She would have stood about 3.5 feet (1 meter) tall, with long arms, a V-shaped jaw, and a large projecting face.

BALL-AND-SOCKET JOINT. A ball-and-socket joint provides the most freedom of movement of any joint. In this type of joint, the round head of one bone (the ball) fits into a cup-shaped depression in another bone (the socket). The joint allows movement in all directions, including rotation. The shoulder and hip joints are examples of ball-and-socket joints.

SADDLE JOINT. A saddle joint allows the next greatest amount of movement. In a saddle joint, the bones are shaped like a horseback rider sitting in a saddle. All movement except rotation is possible with this type of joint. The joint at the base of the thumb is an example of a saddle joint.

HINGE JOINT. A hinge joint allows backward and forward movement in only one direction, much like a door opening and closing. In this type of joint, the convex surface of one bone fits in the concave surface of the other. The joints at the knees, elbows, and knuckles are hinge joints.

PIVOT JOINT. A pivot joint consists of a cylinder of one bone rotating within a ring formed by another bone. Movement occurs only around a single axis. The pivot joint between the atlas and the axis (first and second cervical vertebrae) allows the head to be turned from side to side.

GLIDING JOINT. A gliding or plane joint allows only a small amount of movement as the flattened or slightly curved surfaces of bones slide or glide over each other in various directions. The joints between the carpal bones in the wrist, the tarsal bones in the ankle, and the vertebrae in the spine are examples of gliding joints.

AILMENTS: WHAT CAN GO WRONG WITH THE SKELETAL SYSTEM

The skeletal system is constructed to withstand the pressures and stresses of daily activities, protecting the body's delicate inner organs in the process. Sometimes, however, the system can be stressed beyond its capacity and injuries can result.

A common but serious skeletal injury is a fracture, a complete or incomplete break in a bone. A fracture usually occurs when excessive force is applied in some manner to the bone. Sports activities such as football, skiing, and

SKELETAL SYSTEM DISORDERS

Arthritis (ar-THRIGH-tis): Inflammation of the joints.

Dislocation (dis-low-KAY-shun): Condition in which a bone is forced out of its normal position in the joint cavity.

Fracture (FRAK-cher): Broken bone.

Osteoarthritis (os-tee-oh-ar-THRIGH-tis): Arthritis marked by the deterioration of the cartilage covering the bones in the joints.

Osteoporosis (os-tee-oh-po-ROW-sis): Condition in which bone matrix is lost and not replaced, resulting in an increased softening and weakening of the bones.

Rheumatoid arthritis (RUE-ma-toyd ar-THRIGH-tis): Arthritis characterized by the chronic inflammation of the lining of the joints.

Rickets (RI-kets): Disease in young children due to a deficiency in vitamin D that results in soft and deformed bones.

Scoliosis (sko-lee-OH-sis): Sideways curvature of the spine.

Spina bifida (SPY-na BI-fi-da): Birth defect in which a portion of the spinal cord protrudes through an opening in the vertebral column.

Sprain: Damage or tear in a ligament.

skating often jeopardize the bones, putting them at risk for fractures. Car accidents and falls also take their toll on bones. As an individual ages, the bones become thin and weak, and fractures occur more easily.

When excessive force is applied to a joint, the ligaments that hold the bones together in the area may be torn or damaged. This results in a sprain. Its seriousness depends on how badly the ligaments are torn. Any joint can be sprained, but the most frequently injured joints are the ankle, knee, and finger.

A violent movement at a joint may also cause a dislocation, a condition in which a bone is forced out of its normal position in the joint cavity. When a bone is dislocated, its ligaments are often torn or overstretched in the process. Nerves in the area may also be pinched, causing pain. In a severe dislocation, small chips of bone may be torn away.

A herniated or "slipped" disc occurs when any direct and forceful pressure is applied to a vertebral disc (such as when lifting a heavy object), causing it to rupture. This most often occurs to a disc in the lumbar region of the vertebral column. When the disc is ruptured, pressure is placed on the spinal cord, causing considerable pain and damage to the nerve.

The following are just a few of the more serious disorders and diseases that can impair the functioning of the skeletal system or its parts.

Arthritis

Arthritis is a general term meaning an inflammation of a bone joint. More than 100 diseases have symptoms of joint inflammation or injury. This condition—the body's response to tissue damage—can cause pain, swelling, stiffness, and fatigue. Since the areas most commonly involved are the hands, arms, shoulders, hips, and legs, any action requiring movement of these parts becomes difficult. Arthritis is usually a chronic condition, meaning it persists throughout a person's life. In all its forms, arthritis is the most widespread, crippling disease in the United States.

COMMON FRACTURES

Comminuted: Bone has been broken into many fragments.

Compound: Bone has been broken and an end or ends of the bone protrude through the skin. Now often referred to as an open fracture.

Compression: Bone has been crushed.

Greenstick: Bone has not been broken completely, but only partly across its shaft, similar to the way a green stick or twig breaks. Now often referred to an incomplete fracture.

Impacted: Bone has been broken and a fragment of the bone has been firmly driven into another fragment.

Simple: Bone has been broken cleanly and does not penetrate or break the skin. Now often referred to as a closed fracture.

Spiral: Bone has been twisted apart.

Osteoarthritis and rheumatoid arthritis are the two most common forms of the disease. Osteoarthritis occurs as a result of aging or injury. Rheumatoid arthritis is an autoimmune disease, meaning that the body produces antibodies (proteins normally produced by the body to fight against foreign substances in the body) that act against its own tissues.

Osteoarthritis is the deterioration of the cartilage covering the bones in the joints of the body. It is most often seen in people who are forty years of age or older. Causes of osteoarthritis include wear and tear due to aging or overuse, injury, hereditary factors, and obesity. The wearing away of the cartilage results in the bones scraping against each other, causing the development of bony spurs and the deep joint pain characteristic of this disease.

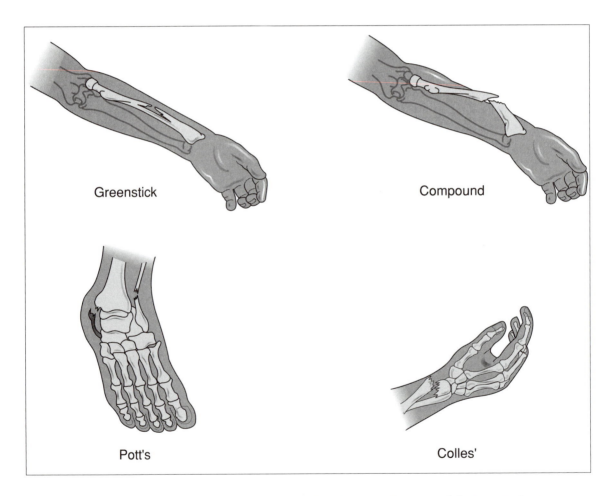

Greenstick

Compound

Pott's

Colles'

Common types of fractures and the sites where they occur. A fracture usually occurs when excessive force is applied in some manner to the bone. (Illustration by Electronic Illustrators Group.)

The joints most commonly affected by osteoarthritis are those of the knees, hips, and fingers. Other areas can be affected by injury or overuse. The condition can cause minor stiffness and pain, or it can result in severe disability. Treatment of osteoarthritis includes the use of anti-inflammatory drugs such as aspirin to reduce pain and swelling; supportive devices such as a brace, walker, or crutches; massage; moist heat; and rest.

Rheumatoid arthritis is one of the most crippling forms of arthritis. It is characterized by chronic inflammation of the lining of joints. It also affects the muscles, tendons, ligaments, and blood vessels surrounding these joints. Deformities can result from the deterioration of bone, muscle, and tissue, impairing function and affecting mobility. Rheumatoid arthritis can occur at any age but usually appears between the ages of thirty and sixty. Three times more women than men are stricken with this disease.

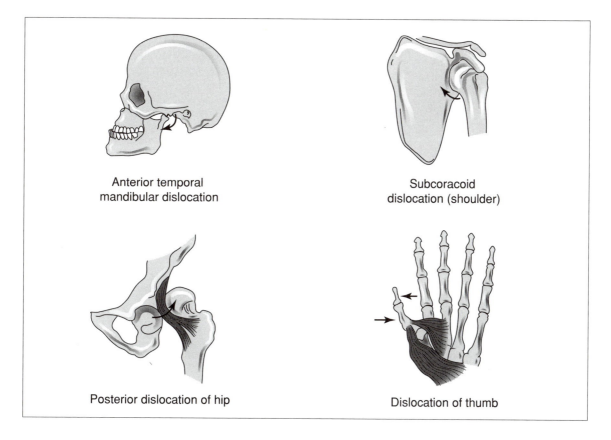

Anterior temporal
mandibular dislocation

Subcoracoid
dislocation (shoulder)

Posterior dislocation of hip

Dislocation of thumb

Four common dislocation sites. A violent movement at a joint may cause a dislocation—a condition in which a bone is forced out of its normal position in the joint cavity. (Illustration by Electronic Illustrators Group.)

The cause of the chronic inflammation of rheumatoid arthritis is not known. Scientists believe that a bacterial or viral infection may trigger an autoimmune response in genetically predisposed people. People with rheumatoid arthritis produce antibodies that attack their own body tissues. This sets off an immune response that results in the body's release of chemicals that produce inflammation.

Treatment of rheumatoid arthritis includes aspirin therapy to reduce inflammation and relieve pain, application of heat to joints and muscles, rest, and physical therapy. In some cases, surgery may be required to reconstruct joints that have been destroyed.

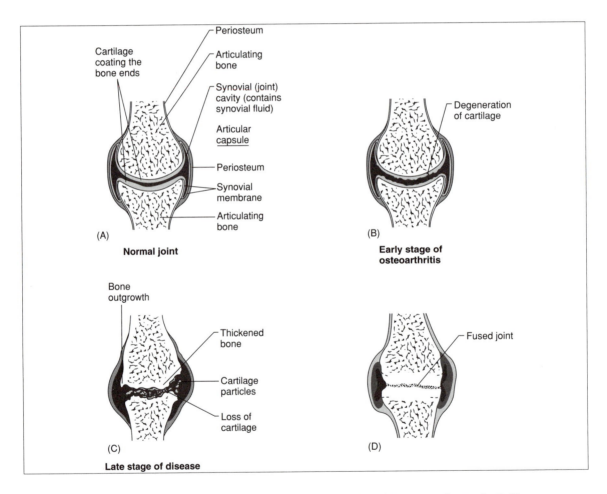

The progression of osteoarthritis. One of the most common forms of arthritis, osteoarthritis is the deterioration of the cartilage covering the bones in the joints of the body. (Illustration by Hans & Cassady.)

Osteoporosis

Osteoporosis (which literally means "porous bones") occurs when a body's blood calcium level is low and calcium from bones is dissolved into the blood to maintain a proper balance. Over time, bone mass and bone strength decrease. As a result, bones become dotted with pits and pores. Weak and fragile, they break easily. Even a sneeze or a sudden movement can cause a fracture in someone with severe osteoporosis.

About 28 million people in the United States are affected by this disease, which causes about 1.5 million fractures each year. Any bone can be affected, but common locations include the hip, spine, and wrist. Osteoporosis occurs in nearly half of all people over the age of seventy-five. However, women are five times more likely than men to develop the disease. After a woman goes through menopause (period in a woman's life when menstrual activity ceases), her body stops producing estrogen, a hormone that helps maintain the health and density of a woman's skeleton.

Other factors besides age can lead to osteoporosis. These include a diet low in calcium and protein, a lack of vitamin D, smoking, excessive alcohol drinking, and insufficient weight-bearing exercises to stress the bones.

Rheumatoid arthritis is one of the most crippling forms of arthritis. It is characterized by chronic inflammation of the lining of joints. (Reproduced by permission of Science Photo Library/Photo Researchers, Inc.)

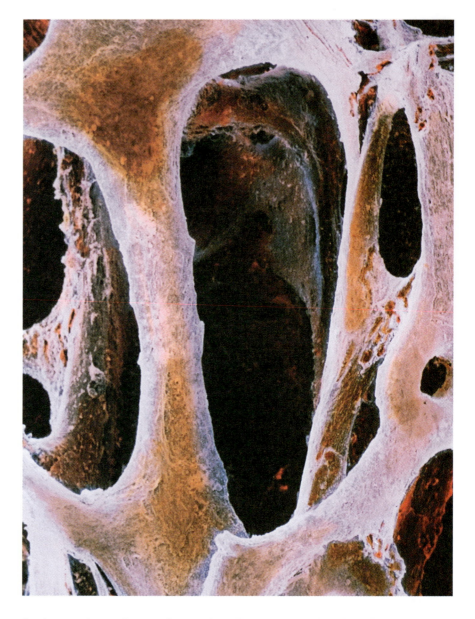

An electron micrograph scan of spongy bone in an osteoporosis patient. Osteoporosis occurs when a body's blood calcium level is low and calcium from bones is dissolved into the blood to maintain a proper balance. (Photograph by P. Motta. Reproduced by permission of Photo Researchers, Inc.)

There is no cure for osteoporosis, but drugs are available that stop further bone loss and even help build new bone. For some people, though, these drugs may not help build enough bone to replace that already lost in the body. The best way to prevent osteoporosis is to maintain a healthy lifestyle

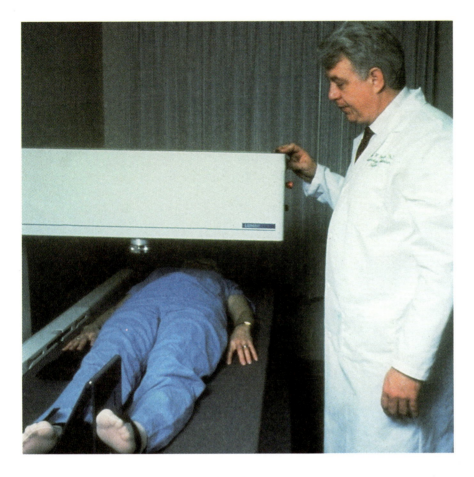

A physician administers a bone density test. The test, which measures the strength of an individual's bones, is used to check for osteoporosis. (Reproduced by permission of Custom Medical Stock.)

throughout one's life: adhering to a diet with the proper amounts of calcium and vitamin D, avoiding smoking and heavy alcohol drinking, and exercising regularly.

Rickets

Rickets is a disease in young children that is brought about by a deficiency of vitamin D (the disease is also called vitamin D deficiency). When the deficiency occurs for a period of many months in children whose bones are still developing, softened bones and other bone defects occur.

While some vitamin D is supplied by the diet, most of it is made in the body from the Sun's rays. In the lower layers of the epidermis (thin, outer layer of the skin), cells contain a form of cholesterol or a fatlike substance produced by the liver that is an essential part of cell membranes and body chemicals. When exposed to UV radiation from the Sun, that cholesterol changes into vitamin D. The body then alters vitamin D to produce a hormone that keeps the concentration of calcium at a constant level in the bloodstream by stimulating the absorption of calcium from digested food in the intestines.

When there is a vitamin D deficiency, though, the calcium level in the blood is too low to help create hardened bone. The result is soft bone.

The symptoms of rickets include bowed legs and arms. The bowed appearance is due to the softening of the bones and their bending if the bones are weight-bearing (such as the legs). Other symptoms include a distorted sternum (which produces a protruding pigeon breast), bony bumps on the ribs, and knock-knees. Seizures may also occur because of reduced levels of dissolved calcium in the bloodstream.

Rickets is almost always treated with oral supplements of vitamin D. Children suffering from the disease are also encouraged to play outside with their faces exposed to sunlight for at least twenty minutes a day. This type of treatment heals rickets promptly. Bone abnormalities generally disappear gradually over a period of three to nine months.

Foods that are good sources of vitamin D include cod liver oil, egg yolks, butter, and oily fish. Some food, including milk and breakfast cereals, are also fortified with synthetic vitamin D. Food fortification (the adding of vitamin to food by the manufacturer) has almost completely eliminated rickets in the United States.

Scoliosis

Scoliosis is a sideways curvature of the spine or vertebral column. Normally, the spine has a set of front-to-back curves. When viewed from rear, a normal spine usually appears straight.

A small degree of lateral (sideways) curvature in the spine does not cause any medical problems, but larger lateral curves can cause imbalance and lead to muscle fatigue and pain. More severe scoliosis can interfere with breathing and lead to arthritis of the spine.

APPROXIMATELY 10 PERCENT OF ALL ADOLESCENTS HAVE SOME DEGREE OF SCOLIOSIS.

Approximately 10 percent of all adolescents have some degree of scoliosis. Fewer than 1 percent, however, have curves that require medical attention. Scoliosis is found in both boys and girls, but a girl's spinal curve is much more likely to progress. The cause behind 80 percent of scoliosis cases is unknown. Some cases can be linked to birth defects, while others are caused by a loss of control of the nerves or muscles that support the spine. Scientists do know that scoliosis is not caused by poor posture, diet, or carrying a heavy bag exclusively on one shoulder. There is no known way to prevent scoliosis.

Treatment for scoliosis depends on the degree of curvature. If the curvature is moderate, a brace may be worn. Bracing cannot correct curvature, but may be effective in halting or slowing the progression of the curve. Surgery is often required if the curvature is severe, if the curve has progressed despite bracing, or if there is significant pain. During surgery, the spine is straightened as much as possible, then vertebrae are fused together to prevent further curvature. Spinal fusion leaves the involved area of the vertebral column permanently stiff.

Spina bifida

Spina bifida is the common name for a range of birth defects caused by problems with the early development of the vertebral column or spine. The main defect of spina bifida is an abnormal opening somewhere along the vertebral column due to a failure of the vertebrae to wrap completely around the spinal cord. This leaves the spinal cord unprotected and vulnerable to either injury or infection.

In North America, spina bifida is much more common among whites than African Americans. It occurs in 1 of every 700 births to whites, but only in 1 in every 3,000 births to African Americans. Scientists are unsure of the reasons for this difference.

Different levels of the spinal cord control different functions in the body. Therefore, the location and size of the defect in spina bifida will determine what kind of disabilities an individual will experience. Most will have some degree of weakness in the legs. Depending on the condition of the spinal cord, that weakness may lead to paralysis. The higher up in the spine the defect occurs, the more severe the disabilities. These may include problems with bladder and bowel function, abnormal curves in the spine (scoliosis), clubfeet, hip dislocations, and water on the brain (a condition called hydrocephalus).

Treatment for spinal bifida is aimed first at surgically closing the spinal defect to prevent infection. Further operations are often necessary to repair the hip dislocations, clubfeet, scoliosis, or other conditions that accompany spina bifida. The success of treatments is still dependent on the severity of the original spinal defect. Current care for children with spina bifida usually enables them to live into adulthood.

TAKING CARE: KEEPING THE SKELETAL SYSTEM HEALTHY

Like every other system in the body, the skeletal system is affected by age. As people grow older, bone tissue tends to lose more calcium than is replaced. This is especially true for women who have gone through menopause (period in a woman's life when menstrual activity ceases).

An individual can lessen the effects of aging on the skeletal system (like every other system in the body) by following a healthy lifestyle. This includes getting adequate rest, reducing stress, drinking healthy amounts of good-quality drinking water, not smoking, drinking moderate amounts of alcohol (or not drinking at all), following a proper diet, and exercising regularly.

A proper diet and exercise are key factors in maintaining the health of the skeletal system. To help slow the rate of bone loss later in life, it is important to build as much bone mass as possible early in life. Without calcium, phosphorus, protein, certain vitamins (A, C, and D), and other nutrients, bones cannot grow properly.

A PROPER DIET AND EXERCISE ARE KEY FACTORS IN MAINTAINING THE HEALTH OF THE SKELETAL SYSTEM.

Bones are specialized to bear or carry weight. Without this stress, they lose calcium. It cannot be emphasized too strongly that bones have to be physically stressed to remain healthy. The more they are used, the stronger they become. Exercising regularly builds and strengthens bones. Weight-bearing exercises—where bones and muscles are used against gravity—are best. These include aerobics, dancing, jogging, stair climbing, walking, tennis, and lifting weights. The exercise need not be too strenuous, but it should be engaged in regularly.

FOR MORE INFORMATION

Books

Arnau, Eduard. *The Skeletal System.* New York: Chelsea House, 1995.

Ballard, Carol. *The Skeleton and Muscular System.* Austin, TX: Raintree/ Steck-Vaughn, 1997.

Parker, Steve. *Skeleton.* New York: Random Library, 1990.

Silverstein, Alvin, Virginia Silverstein, and Robert Silverstein. *The Skeletal System.* New York: Twenty-First Century Books, 1994.

Walker, Richard. *The Visual Dictionary of the Skeleton.* London, England: DK Publishing, 1995.

WWW Sites

The Bones of the Body
http://www.msms.doe.k12.ms.us/biology/anatomy/skeletal /skeletal.html
Site provides links to a list of all the bones in the body, a discussion of the physiology of bones, and a short look at the gross anatomy of the skeletal system.

Cyber Anatomy: Skeletal System
http://tqd.advanced.org/11965/html/cyber-anatomy _skeletal.html

Geared for students in grades 6 through 12, site provides an broad
discussion of the skeletal system. Also includes a diagram of the
skeleton with the major bones identified.

Muscular and Skeletal Systems
http://gened.emc.maricopa.edu/bio/BIO181/BIOBK/
BioBookMUSSKEL.html
Site presents a detailed chapter (with extensive images) on the
muscular and skeletal systems from the On-Line Biology textbook.

Skeletal System
http://hyperion.advanced.org/2935/Natures_Best/Nat_Best_Low_Level/
skeletal_page.L.html
Site offers an extensive discussion of the skeletal system and its various
parts, including a discussion of the composition of bone.

Skeletal System
http://www.lasallehs.org/courses/science/anatomy/html/
skeletal_system.html
Site provides an image of the human skeleton; all major bones in that
image may be clicked on, leading to a larger, more detailed image of
the bone or bones in that area with all parts identified.

Your Gross and Cool Body—Skeletal System
http://www.yucky.com/body/index.ssf?/systems/skeletal
Site presents facts and answers questions about the skeletal system and
its various parts.

11

The Urinary System

When cells in the body break down proteins into forms they can utilize, they produce ammonia wastes that the liver turns into urea (a chemical compound of carbon, hydrogen, nitrogen, and oxygen). When cells break down carbohydrates, they produce water and carbon dioxide as waste products. If these useless waste products were allowed to accumulate in the body, they would become dangerous to the body's health. The body eliminates these wastes (and solid wastes, also) in a process known as excretion. The body system most responsible for waste excretion is the urinary system, which eliminates water, urea, and other waste products from the body in the form of urine. Because of this main function, it is often referred to as the excretory system.

DESIGN: PARTS OF THE URINARY SYSTEM

The main organs of the urinary system are the kidneys, which form urine. The other parts of the system—the ureters, the urinary bladder, and the urethra—neither form urine nor change its composition. They are merely structures that transport urine from the kidneys to the outside of the body.

The kidneys

The kidneys are kidney bean-shaped organs located on either side of the vertebral column or spine near the small of the back (the beans were so named because they resembled small kidneys). The left kidney usually sits slightly higher than the right one. The size of an adult kidney is approximately 4 inches (10 centimeters) long, 2.5 inches (6 centimeters) wide, and 1 inch (2.5 centimeters) thick. The upper portions of the purplish-brown kidneys rest on the lower surface of the diaphragm, a membrane of muscle separating the thoracic or chest cavity from the abdominal cavity. The lower portion of the rib cage encloses and protects the kidneys. The kidneys are held in place by the abdominal lining and supporting connective tissue.

On the side of each kidney facing the vertebral column is an indentation called the hilus. Through the hilus the renal artery enters and the renal vein and ureter exit (the adjective renal comes from the Latin word *renes*, meaning "kidneys"). The renal artery brings blood to the kidneys from the ab-

WORDS TO KNOW

Aldosterone (al-DOS-te-rone): Hormone secreted by the adrenal cortex that controls the salt and water balance in the body.

Antidiuretic hormone (an-tee-die-yu-REH-tik HOR-mone): Hormone produced by the hypothalamus and stored in the posterior pituitary that increases the absorption of water by the kidneys.

Bowman's capsule (BOW-manz KAP-sul): Cup-shaped end of a nephron that encloses a glomerulus.

Calyces (KAY-li-seez): Cup-shaped extensions of the renal pelvis that enclose the tips of the renal pyramids and collect urine.

Creatinine (kree-AT-i-neen): Waste product in urine produced by the breakdown of creatine.

Filtration (fill-TRAY-shun): Movement of water and dissolved materials through a membrane from an area of higher pressure to an area of lower pressure.

Glomerulus (glow-MER-yoo-lus): Network of capillaries enclosed by a Bowman's capsule.

Henle's loop (HEN-leez LOOP): Looped portion of a renal tubule.

Hilus (HIGH-lus): Indentation or depression on the surface of an organ such as a kidney.

Micturition (mik-tu-RISH-un): Urination, or the elimination or voiding of urine from the urinary bladder.

Nephrons (NEFF-ronz): Urine-forming structures in the kidneys.

Peristalsis (per-i-STALL-sis): Series of wavelike muscular contractions that move material in one direction through a hollow organ.

Renal corpuscle (REE-nul KOR-pus-el): Part of a nephron that consists of a glomerulus enclosed by a Bowman's capsule.

Renal cortex (REE-nul KOR-tex): Outermost layer of the kidney.

Renal medulla (REE-nul muh-DUH-luh): Middle layer of a kidney.

Renal filtrate (REE-nul FILL-trait): Fluid formed in a Bowman's capsule from blood plasma by the process of filtration in the renal corpuscle.

Renal pelvis (REE-nul PELL-vis): A cavity at the innermost area of a kidney that connects to the ureter.

Renal pyramids (REE-nul PEER-ah-mids): Triangular or pie-shaped segments of the renal medulla in which urine production occurs.

Renal tubule (REE-nal TOO-byool): Twisting, narrow tube leading from the Bowman's capsule in a nephron.

Renin (REE-nin): Enzyme secreted by the cells of renal tubules that helps to raise blood pressure.

Urea (yoo-REE-ah): Main nitrogen-containing waste excreted in the urine, produced when the liver combines ammonia and carbon dioxide.

Ureter (you-REE-ter): Muscular tube that carries urine from the renal pelvis in a kidney to the urinary bladder.

Urethra (yoo-REE-thrah): Thin-walled tube that carries urine from the urinary bladder to the outside of the body.

Uric acid (YUR-ik AS-id): Waste product in urine formed by the breakdown of nucleic acids.

Urinary bladder (YER-i-nair-ee BLA-der) Hollow, collapsible, muscular sac that stores urine temporarily.

Urine (YUR-in): Fluid formed by the kidneys from blood plasma.

dominal aorta. The renal vein returns blood to the inferior vena cava. Both the renal artery and renal vein have a right and left branch, each connected to a corresponding kidney.

Each kidney is covered with a thin yet tough capsule of fibrous connective tissue. The transparent capsule gives a kidney a glistening appearance. Inside, a kidney can be divided into three layers. The outer layer, light in color, is called the renal cortex. The next layer, a darker reddish-brown, is called the renal medulla. It contains six to eighteen pie-shaped structures called renal pyramids, the tips of which face toward the center of a kidney.

Attached to the tips of the renal pyramids are cup-shaped tubes called calyces (singular: calyx), which collect urine from structures in the renal pyramids. The smaller calyces unite to form larger calyces, which in turn unite to form the renal pelvis, a cavity at the innermost part of a kidney. The renal pelvis collects urine from the calyces and funnels it to the ureter, to which it is attached.

NEPHRONS. The urine-forming structures in the kidneys are called nephrons. There are approximately 1.25 million nephrons in each kidney. Almost 0.5 inch (1.2 centimeters) in length, each nephron begins in the lower portion of the renal cortex, then twists and coils down into a renal pyramid in the renal medulla. A nephron has two major portions: a renal corpuscle and a renal tubule.

The renal corpuscle is a knotted network of fine capillaries surrounded by a cup-shaped chamber. The knot of capillaries is called a glomerulus (plural: glomeruli). The cup-shaped chamber is called the Bowman's capsule, and it is filled with fluid and has an inner and outer wall. The inner wall encloses the glomerulus and has many pores that make it permeable or able to allow fluids or material to pass easily through it. Its outer wall has no pores and is, thus, not permeable.

The renal tubule is a long passageway that continues from the Bowman's capsule. It twists and turns down through a renal pyramid before forming a loop (called Henle's loop) and ascending back through the renal pyramid. As it ascends, it becomes slightly larger. This larger section of the renal tubule twists and coils across the top of the renal pyramid before descending once again. It then empties into a collecting duct that serves several renal tubules. Several collecting ducts then unite to form larger ducts that empty urine into a calyx at the tip of the renal pyramid.

GETTING BY ON ONE KIDNEY

It is not necessary for an individual to have two kidneys in order to live. In fact, one kidney can easily perform the job of two, filtering wastes from the body and creating urine. People who have only one kidney because of an illness or because they donated a kidney for transplantation can and do lead healthy lives. When only one kidney is functioning in the body, it usually increases in size by 50 percent in order to perform well.

Urinary System

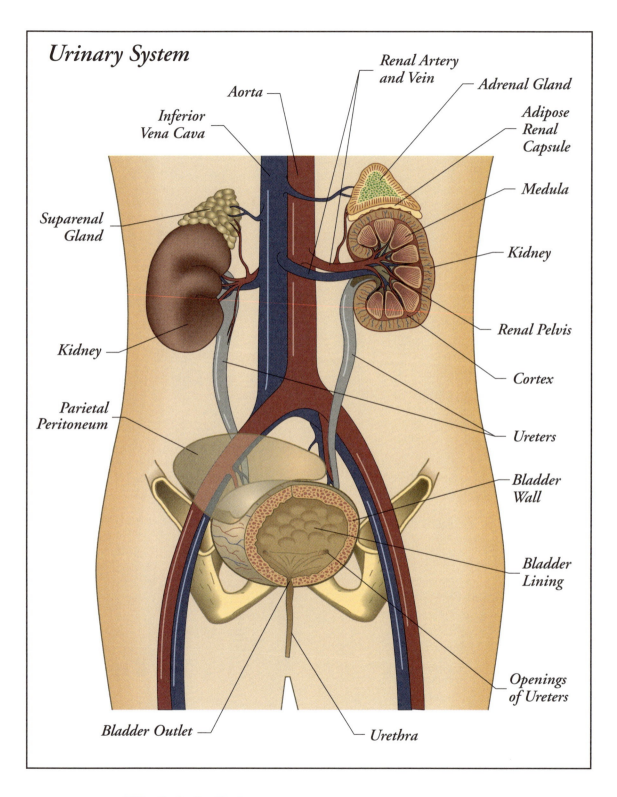

Renal Artery and Vein

Aorta

Adrenal Gland

Adipose Renal Capsule

Inferior Vena Cava

Medula

Suparenal Gland

Kidney

Renal Pelvis

Kidney

Cortex

Parietal Peritoneum

Ureters

Bladder Wall

Bladder Lining

Openings of Ureters

Bladder Outlet

Urethra

The ureters

The ureters are muscular tubes that carry urine from the renal pelvis in each kidney to the urinary bladder. Each ureter measures about 10 to 12 inches (25 to 30 centimeters) in length, extending from the hilus of a kidney to the rear wall of the urinary bladder, where it enters at an angle. The extremely thin ureters only measure about 0.25 inch (0.64 centimeter) in diameter.

Urine drains through the ureters to the urinary bladder by gravity, but the smooth muscular walls of the ureters also help propel urine along. They compress in a series of wavelike contractions (an action known as peristalsis) that move the urine through the ureters in only one direction. When urine has entered the urinary bladder, it is prevented from flowing back into the ureters by small, valvelike folds of membrane that flap over the ureter openings.

The urinary bladder

The urinary bladder is a hollow, collapsible, muscular sac that stores urine temporarily. It is located in the pelvis behind the pelvic bones, and is held in place by ligaments. In women, the bladder is behind the uterus; in men, it is above the prostate gland.

The size of the urinary bladder varies depending on the amount of urine it contains. When empty, it is normally no longer than 2 to 3 inches (5 to 7.6 centimeters). During this state, its walls are thick and heavily folded. As it begins collecting urine, the urinary bladder's muscular walls stretch and expand, and it rises in the abdominal cavity. A urinary bladder that is moderately full measures about 5 inches (12.7 centimeters) in length and holds just over 1 pint (500 millimeters) of urine. When completely full, the urinary bladder can contain over 2 pints (1 liter) of urine.

The muscular walls of the urinary bladder contract to expel urine out of the bladder into the urethra. A sphincter or ring of muscle surrounding the opening to the urethra, called the internal urethral sphincter, controls the flow of urine. This is an involuntary sphincter, meaning a person cannot consciously control its workings.

The urethra

The urethra is a thin-walled tube that carries urine from the urinary bladder to the outside of the body. Its length and function differ in females and males.

OPPOSITE: The main components of the urinary system. This system—often referred to as the excretory system—is responsible for eliminating water, urea, and other waste products from the body in the form of urine. (Illustration by Kopp Illustration, Inc.)

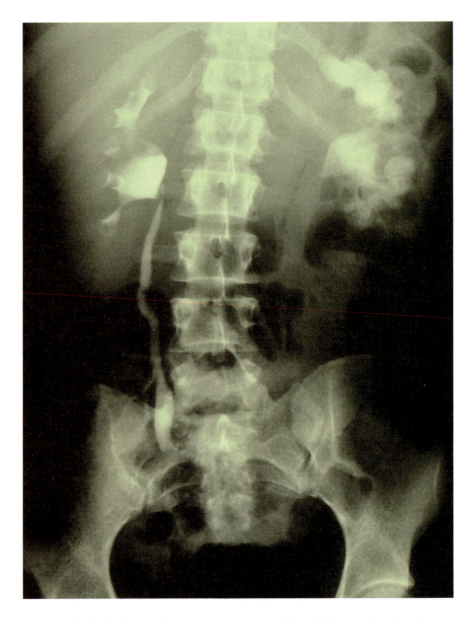

An X ray of a blocked ureter. The ureters are muscular tubes that carry urine from the renal pelvis in each kidney to the urinary bladder. (Reproduced by permission of Custom Medical Stock Photo.)

In females, the urethra measures about 1 to 1.5 inches (2.5 to 3.8 centimeters) in length. Its external opening lies in front of the vaginal opening. The only purpose of the urethra in females is to conduct urine to the outside of the body.

In males, the urethra serves a dual purpose. It transports semen and urine to the body exterior, but never at the same time. Thus, it serves both the reproductive and urinary systems. In men, the urethra extends from the urinary bladder through the prostate gland to the tip of the penis, a distance of 6 to 8 inches (15 to 20 centimeters).

In both sexes, the urethra contains a ring of skeletal muscle that forms the external urethral sphincter as the urethra passes through the floor of the pelvis. A person is normally able to control the opening and closing of this sphincter. When the sphincter is voluntarily relaxed, urine flows into the urethra, emptying the urinary bladder. However, when the bladder fills with urine and becomes stretched beyond normal, voluntary control of the sphincter becomes no longer possible.

WORKINGS: HOW THE URINARY SYSTEM FUNCTIONS

The urinary system is not the sole system in the body concerned with excretion. Other systems and organs also play a part. The respiratory system eliminates water vapor and carbon dioxide through exhalation (the process of breathing out). The digestive system removes feces, the solid undigested wastes of digestion, by a process called defecation or elimination. The skin (the integumentary system; see chapter 4) also acts as an organ of excretion by removing water and small amounts of urea and salts (as sweat).

Through its primary role of forming and eliminating urine, the urinary system also helps regulate blood volume and pressure. In addition, it regulates the concentrations of sodium, potassium, calcium, chloride, and other mineral ions (an ion is an atom or group of atoms that has an electrical charge) in the blood. These combined actions by the urinary system help the body maintain homeostasis or the balanced state of its internal functions.

Formation of urine

Urine is the fluid waste excreted by the kidneys. It can range in color from pale straw to amber (the deeper the color, the more concentrated the urine). Fresh urine is sterile (meaning it contains no bacteria) and has very little odor. Some drugs, vegetables (such as asparagus), and various diseases alter the normal smell of urine. Water forms approximately 95 percent of urine; the remaining 5 percent is made up of urea, creatinine, uric acid, and various salts.

Urea, creatinine, and uric acid are nitrogen-containing compounds produced as wastes during cellular activity. When cells break down amino acids, they produce ammonia as a waste product. Ammonia is very toxic to the body's cells, so the liver combines ammonia with carbon dioxide to create the less toxic urea, the most abundant of the nitrogen-containing wastes. Creatinine is produced when skeletal muscle cells break down the compound creatine to generate energy for muscle contraction. Uric acid, which forms only a small portion of the urine, is a normal waste product of the breakdown of nucleic acids (complex organic molecules found in living cells).

Urine is formed in the kidneys as a result of three processes: filtration, reabsorption, and secretion. Filtration takes place in the renal corpuscles; reabsorption and secretion take place in the renal tubules.

FILTRATION. Filtration is the movement of water and dissolved materials through a membrane from an area of higher pressure to an area of lower

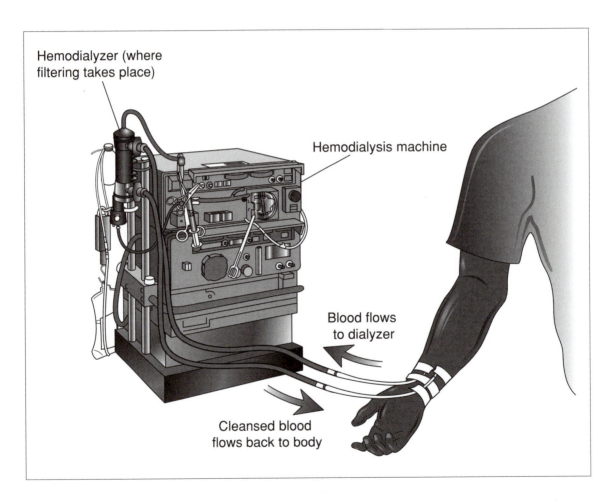

Dialysis treatment replaces the functions of the kidneys, which normally serve as the body's natural filtration system. Hemodialysis is the most frequently prescribed dialysis treatment. (Illustration by Electronic Illustrators Group.)

pressure. In the body, the pressure of blood in the capillaries is higher than the pressure of the interstitial fluid, or the fluid surrounding the body's cells. Thus, through filtration, blood plasma (fluid portion of blood) and nutrients such as amino acids, glucose, and vitamins are forced through the capillary walls into the surrounding interstitial fluid to be used by the cells.

The pressure of the blood in the glomeruli is higher than in other types of capillaries in the body. This high pressure forces plasma, dissolved waste substances, and small proteins out of the glomeruli and into the Bowman's capsules. The process is called glomerular filtration. Blood cells and larger proteins are too large to be forced out of the glomeruli, so they remain in the blood. The pressure in a Bowman's capsule is low and its inner membrane is permeable, so the material that filters out of a glomerulus passes into the capsule. The fluid and material in a Bowman's capsule is referred to as renal filtrate, which is very much like blood plasma, except it contains very little protein and no blood cells.

REABSORPTION. In an average twenty-four-hour period, the kidneys form 160 to 190 quarts (150 to 180 liters) of renal filtrate. Normal urinary output in that same time frame is only about 1.1 to 2.1 quarts (1 to 2 liters). Many factors (such as increased water intake or increased sweating) can significantly alter that output amount. Nonetheless, it is quite obvious that most of the renal filtrate does not become urine, but is reabsorbed or taken back into the blood. This is important because renal filtrate contains many useful substances—water, glucose, amino acids, and mineral ions—that are needed by the body.

Reabsorption is the return of water and other substances from the filtrate to the blood. The process begins as soon as the filtrate enters the renal tubule. Cells lining the tubule actively take up useful materials (such as glucose, amino acids, vitamins, proteins, and certain ions), move them through their cell bodies, then release them into the interstitial fluid outside the tubule.

As these materials collect in the interstitial fluid, water in the tubules is drawn out through the process of osmosis. Osmosis is the diffusion of water through a semipermeable membrane from an area where it is abundant to an area where it is scarce or less abundant. Once in the interstitial fluid, the materials and water then diffuse into or enter nearby capillaries, which empty into the renal vein.

The reabsorption process is selective. The cells of the renal tubules have been "programmed" to retain substances that are useful to the body, not those substances that are of no use (such as urea and uric acid). Also, the amount of a substance that is reabsorbed is dependent on its concentration in the blood. If it exists in a low concentration in the blood, a large amount of it will be reabsorbed from the renal tubules. Conversely, if it already exists in a high concentration, very little of it will be reabsorbed into the blood.

SECRETION. Secretion is the transport of materials from the interstitial fluid into the renal filtrate. It is essentially reabsorption in reverse. The process is important for getting rid of substances not already in the filtrate. Waste products such as ammonia, some creatinine, and the end products of medications move from the blood in the capillaries around the renal tubules into the interstitial fluid. They are then taken in by the cells of the tubules and deposited into the renal filtrate to be eliminated in the urine.

Hormones and the composition of urine

Hormones are chemical "messengers" secreted by endocrine glands that control or coordinate the activities of other tissues, organs, and organ systems in the body. Each type of hormone affects only specific tissue cells or organs, called target cells or target organs. Most hormones are composed of amino acids, the building blocks of proteins. The smaller class of hormones are steroids, which are built from molecules of cholesterol (fatlike substance produced by the liver).

The hormones that affect the urinary system help it regulate the amount of water and mineral ions in urine. By extension, this action also regulates the pressure in the bloodstream and the concentration of mineral ions in the blood.

Excessive water loss in the urine is controlled by the antidiuretic hormone (ADH), which is released by the pituitary gland (a small gland lying at the base of the skull). If an individual perspires a lot, fails to drink enough water, or loses water through diarrhea, special nerve cells in the hypothalamus (a region of the brain controlling body temperature, hunger, and thirst) detect the low water concentration in the blood. They then signal the pituitary gland to release ADH into the blood, where it travels to the kidneys. With ADH present, the renal tubules are stimulated to reabsorb more water from the renal filtrate and return it to the blood. The volume of water in the urine is thus reduced, and the urine becomes more concentrated. Harmful substances are still eliminated from the body, but necessary water is not.

The action of ADH also controls blood volume and pressure. As more water is removed from the urine and transported into the bloodstream, blood volume and pressure increase. This is an important safeguard against low blood volume and pressure, which might be brought about by an injury.

THE FIRST SUCCESSFUL ORGAN TRANSPLANT

In 1950, Ruth Tucker, a forty-nine-year-old American woman, was dying from chronic kidney failure. American surgeon Richard Lawler of Loyola University in Chicago transplanted a kidney from a cadaver (dead body) into Tucker. Although her body rejected the new kidney after only a short time, Tucker became the first human to survive an organ transplantation.

With the development of immunosuppressant drugs (those that hinder the body's immune response to "foreign" tissue), the success of kidney transplants has risen. Today, individuals who receive a kidney transplant from a living donor (who is often a close relative) have a survival rate of 80 percent.

On the other hand, if an individual takes in too much water, production of ADH decreases. The renal tubules do not reabsorb as much water, and the volume of water in the urine is increased. Alcohol and liquids containing caffeine (coffee, tea, and cola drinks) inhibit ADH production (these substances are called diuretics). Large amounts of urine are consequently excreted from the body and blood pressure decreases. If that fluid is not replaced, an individual may feel dizzy due to low blood pressure.

Another hormone that helps to control blood volume by acting on the kidneys is aldosterone. Aldosterone is a steroid hormone secreted by the adrenal cortex (the outer layer of an adrenal gland, which sits like a cap on top of a kidney). A decrease in blood pressure or volume, a decrease in the sodium ion level in blood, and an increase in the potassium ion level in blood all stimulate the secretion of aldosterone. Once released, aldosterone spurs the cells of the renal tubules to reabsorb sodium from the urine and to excrete potassium instead. Sodium is then returned to the bloodstream. When sodium is reabsorbed into the blood, water in the body follows it, thus increasing blood volume and pressure.

The kidneys themselves play a role in regulating blood pressure. When blood pressure around the kidneys decreases below normal, the cells of the renal tubules react by secreting the enzyme renin (an enzyme is a protein that speeds up the rate of chemical reactions). Renin, in turn, stimulates an inactive blood protein to change into a hormone that causes blood vessels to constrict or narrow, which immediately raises blood pressure.

THE KIDNEYS PLAY A ROLE IN REGULATING BLOOD PRESSURE.

Elimination of urine

The process of eliminating urine from the urinary bladder is known as urination. It is also called micturition or voiding. The sensation of having to urinate usually occurs after the urinary bladder has filled with about 7 ounces (200 milliliters) of urine. The bladder has stretched enough at this point to activate receptors within its walls. Once activated, these receptors send impulses to the spinal cord, which sends impulses back to the bladder, causing it to contract. The internal urethral sphincter (surrounding the opening of the urethra) relaxes and urine is forced into the upper portion of the urethra. This initiates the "feeling" of having to urinate.

Urination occurs when an individual voluntarily relaxes his or her external urethral sphincter. Urine flows through the urethra and the bladder is emptied. Babies do not exert control over their external urethral sphincter and urine is automatically forced out of the body when it reaches a certain level. As children mature, they learn to control their external urethral sphincter, retaining their urine until it is appropriate to urinate.

If the external urethral sphincter is not relaxed, urine will continue to accumulate in the bladder. When it reaches a volume over 1 pint (475 milliliters), the pressure created will cause pain and the external urethral sphincter eventually will be forced open, regardless of an individual's desire.

AILMENTS: WHAT CAN GO WRONG WITH THE URINARY SYSTEM

Most urinary system problems are associated with age. As individuals grow older, the functioning of their kidneys declines. An average seventy-five-year-old person has half the original number of nephrons in their kidneys. Because of this, the kidneys lose some of their ability to concentrate urine. The urinary bladder also shrinks with age, leading to a need to urinate more frequently. In some older people, the ability to control urination is lost, a condition known as urinary incontinence (see discussion below).

Disorders and diseases of the urinary system do not affect only the elderly, however. The systems in children and adults through late middle age can also be affected, mainly by bacterial infections that cause inflammation. If not treated properly, many of these infections can lead to serious, even life-threatening, conditions.

KIDNEY DIALYSIS

Dialysis is a process by which small molecules in a solution are separated from large molecules. The process has come to play a crucial role in the health of humans. For some people, the term dialysis refers to a specific kind of medical treatment in which a machine (the dialysis machine) takes on the functions of a human kidney. Dialysis machines have made possible the survival of thousands of people who would otherwise have died as a result of kidney failure.

The kidney dialysis machine was invented by Dutch-American surgeon Willem Johan Kolff in 1945. Since that time, many improvements have been made to the machine and to the procedure of removing wastes from the blood of people whose kidneys have ceased to function.

The most common dialysis treatment prescribed in the United States is known as hemodialysis (he-moe-die-AL-i-sis). In short, during this procedure, two needles atached to tubes are inserted into veins in an individual's arm. Blood is drawn out of the person's body through one tube and pumped through the dialysis machine.

Inside the machine, the blood is circulated on one side of a semipermeable membrane. This means that the membrane allows the passage of certain sized molecules (such as waste products) across it, but prevents the passage of other, larger molecules (such as blood cells). A special dialysis fluid containing mineral ions and other substances necessary to the body circulates on the other side of the membrane.

As blood circulates in the machine, wastes and other unneeded substances in the blood are drawn out through the membrane. At the same time, the mineral ions and other chemicals in the dialysis fluid cross the membrane into the blood. The "cleansed" and chemically-balanced blood is then returned to the person's body through the second tube.

Most hemodialysis patients require treatment two to three times a week, and each treatment can last several hours.

Infections and diseases that strike elsewhere in the body can eventually impair the functioning of the kidneys. Acute (short-term) kidney failure appears most frequently as a complication of a serious illness such as heart failure, liver failure, dehydration, severe burns, and excessive bleeding. Acute kidney failure is a temporary condition that can be reversed with proper and timely treatment. Chronic kidney failure, which is long-term and irreversible, can be triggered by diabetes, hypertension, glomerulonephritis (see below), and sickle cell anemia, among other conditions. Without proper treatment to remove wastes from the bloodstream, chronic kidney failure is fatal.

The following are just a few of the many diseases and disorders that can affect the urinary system or its parts.

Bladder cancer

Bladder cancer develops when cells lining the urinary bladder become abnormal and grow uncontrollably, forming tumors. It is the fifth most common cancer in the United States. The disease is three times more common in men than woman. Most cases of bladder cancer are found in people who are fifty to seventy years old.

ONE OF THE FIRST SIGNS OF BLADDER CANCER IS BLOOD IN THE URINE.

The exact cause of bladder cancer is unknown. However, smokers are twice as likely as nonsmokers to get the disease. Workers who are exposed to certain chemicals in the dye, rubber, leather, textile, and paint industries are also believed to be at a higher risk for developing bladder cancer.

One of the first warning signs of bladder cancer is blood in the urine. Painful urination, increased frequency of urination, and a feeling of having to urinate but not being able to are additional signs of bladder cancer.

If bladder cancer is diagnosed, the three standard methods of treatment are surgery, radiation therapy, and chemotherapy. During surgery, surgeons may remove the tumor, part of the bladder containing the tumor, or the entire bladder and adjoining organs (the prostate gland in men; the uterus, ovaries, and fallopian tubes in women). Radiation therapy (using X rays or other high-energy rays to kill any remaining cancer cells and shrink any tumors) is generally used after surgery. Chemotherapy (using a combination

URINARY SYSTEM DISORDERS

Cystitis (sis-TIE-tis): Inflammation of the urinary bladder caused by a bacterial infection.

Glomerulonephritis (glah-mer-u-lo-ne-FRY-tis): Inflammation of the glomeruli in the renal corpuscles of the kidneys.

Kidney stones: Large accumulations of calcium salt crystals from urine that may form in the kidneys.

Pyelonephritis (pie-e-low-ne-FRY-tis): Inflammation of the kidneys caused by a bacterial infection.

Urethritis (yer-i-THRY-tis): Inflammation of the urethra caused by a bacterial infection.

Urinary incontinence (YER-i-nair-ee in-KON-tinence): Involuntary and unintentional passage or urine.

of drugs to kill any remaining cancer cells and shrink any tumors) may also be given after surgery.

When detected early and treated appropriately, bladder cancer can be cured. In those people who have sought early treatment, at least 94 percent survive five years or more. However, when the disease has spread to nearby tissues, the survival rate drops below 50 percent.

Glomerulonephritis

Glomerulonephritis is the inflammation of the glomeruli in the renal corpuscles. It is generally caused by a bacterial infection elsewhere in the body, mostly in the throat or skin. In children, it is mostly associated with an upper respiratory infection, tonsillitis, or scarlet fever.

During a bacterial infection, the body produces antibodies or substances that help protect the body against foreign invaders. Glomerulonephritis develops when antibodies and the bacteria they attach to accumulate in the glomeruli, producing inflammation. If left untreated, the glomeruli are soon replaced by fibrous tissue and waste products cannot be effectively filtered from the blood. The kidneys become enlarged, fatty, and congested.

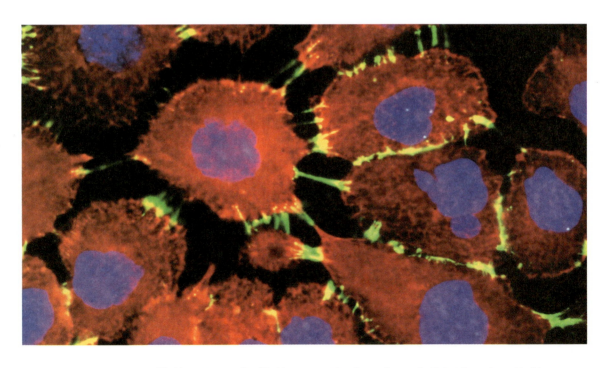

Bladder cancer cells. Bladder cancer develops when cells lining the urinary bladder become abnormal and grow uncontrollably, forming tumors. (Photograph by Nancy Kedersha. Reproduced by permission of Photo Researchers, Inc.)

Symptoms of severe cases of glomerulonephritis include fatigue, nausea, vomiting, shortness of breath, high blood pressure, blood in the urine, and swelling in the face, hands, feet, and ankles.

Treatment for glomerulonephritis includes bed rest to maintain adequate blood flow to the kidneys and antibiotics to rid the body of the infection. If too much fluid has accumulated in the body, diuretics may be given to increase urine output. Sodium and protein intake may also be decreased to help rest the kidneys. Symptoms of glomerulonephritis usually disappear in two weeks to several months. Ninety percent of children recover without complications. Adults often recover more slowly.

Kidney cancer

Kidney cancer develops when cells in certain tissues in the kidneys become abnormal and grow uncontrollably, forming tumors. Kidney cancer accounts for 3 percent of cancer cases in the United States. The disease occurs most often in men over the age of forty. Men are twice as likely as women to suffer from this type of cancer.

The exact causes of kidney cancer are unknown. However, there is a strong connection between cigarette smoking and kidney cancer; smokers are twice as likely as nonsmokers to get the disease. Obesity may be another risk for kidney cancer.

The most common symptom of kidney cancer is blood in the urine. Other symptoms include painful urination, pain in the lower back or sides, abdominal pain, a lump or hard mass that can be felt in the kidney area, unexplained weight loss, fever, weakness, and high blood pressure.

The primary treatment for kidney cancer that has not spread to other parts of the body is surgical removal of the diseased kidney. Because most cancers affect only one kidney, an individual can function well on the one remaining. Radiation therapy (using X rays or other high-energy rays to kill cancer cells and shrink any tumors) may be used when the cancer is inoperable, but it is has not proven to be of much use in destroying kidney cancer cells. Chemotherapy (using a combination of drugs to kill any cancer cells and shrink any tumors) has also not produced good results.

Because kidney cancer is often caught early and sometimes progresses slowly, the chances of a surgical cure are good.

Kidney stones

Kidney stones are solid accumulations or material that form in the tubal system of the kidneys. Kidney stones cause problems when they block the flow of urine through or out of the kidneys. When the stones move along the ureter, they cause severe pain.

Kidney stones are most common among white males over the age of thirty. The stones can be composed of a variety of substances, but the majority (about 80 percent) are formed from calcium salts that have separated from the urine to form crystals that combine to form larger stones. Some may grow as big as golf balls.

Increased blood levels of calcium caused by a diet heavy in meat, fish, and poultry can lead to the formation of kidney stones. Certain diseases—hyperthyroidism and some types of cancer—can also increased blood calcium levels.

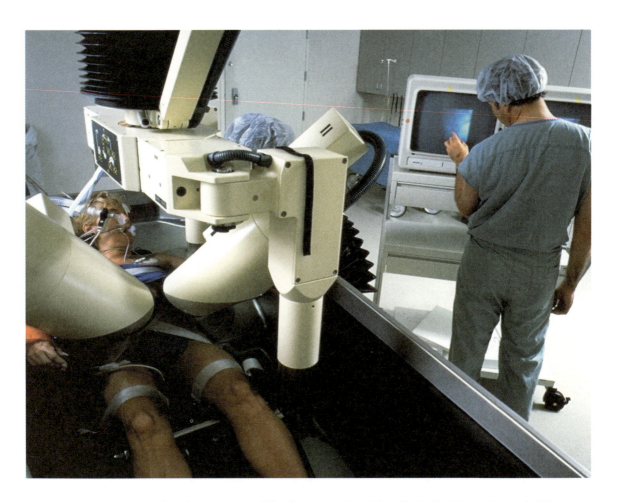

A patient undergoes lithotripsy, a treatment for eliminating kidney stones. In this process, physicians use a machine called a lithotriptor to generate sound waves through the body and shatter the stones. (Reproduced by permission of Photo Researchers, Inc.)

Individuals who have kidneys stones usually do not have symptoms until the stones pass into the ureter. Prior to this, some people may notice blood in their urine. Once the stone is in the ureter, however, most people will experience severe bouts of crampy pain that usually begins in the area between the lower ribs and the hip bone. Nausea, vomiting, and extremely frequent and painful urination may then occur.

Although most kidney stones will pass out of the body on their own, some will not. If a stone is too large to pass or is causing a serious obstruction, surgical removal of the stone may be necessary. In the past, open surgery to remove the stone was common. Now, however, physicians may use a machine to aim shock waves at the stone, either from outside or inside the body. The shock waves often crush the stone into smaller fragments, which may then pass on their own or may be removed surgically. In most cases, individuals with uncomplicated kidney stones will recover very well.

Urinary incontinence

Urinary incontinence is the involuntary and unintentional passage of urine. Approximately 13 million Americans suffer from this disorder. Women are affected more frequently than men; approximately one out of every ten women under the age of sixty-five are affected. Older people, too, are more prone to the condition. Twenty percent of Americans over the age of sixty-five are incontinent.

The inability to control urination can be caused by a wide variety of physical conditions. Any blockage at the bladder outlet that permits only small amounts of urine to pass; irritation of the bladder due to an infection; undue pressure placed on the bladder (such as in obese individuals); and the loss of muscle tone in the pelvic muscles, the bladder, or the urethral sphincter muscles—these are all just a few of the many causes of urinary incontinence.

Left untreated, incontinence can cause physical and emotional harm. Those people with long-term incontinence suffer from urinary tract infections and skin rashes. Incontinence can also affect their self-esteem, causing depression and social withdrawal.

LEFT UNTREATED, INCONTINENCE CAN CAUSE PHYSICAL AND EMOTIONAL HARM.

There are numerous treatment options for urinary incontinence, depending on the cause. The condition may not be stopped, but it can at least be improved. If weakened pelvic muscles are to blame, exercises to tone them can be performed. In certain people, especially older women, medications may help tighten pelvic muscle tone or the urethral sphincters. A balloonlike device may be inserted into a woman's urethra and inflated to prevent urine leakage. Surgery to raise and support the bladder neck and urethra may also be undertaken.

Urinary tract infections

Urinary tract infections (UTIs) are inflammations of the urinary tract caused by a bacterial infection. UTIs have specific names, depending on the location of the inflammation. Inflammation of the urethra is known as urethritis. Inflammation of the urinary bladder is known as cystitis. When the bacterial infection spreads to the kidneys, the condition is known as pyelonephritis.

UTIs are much more common in women than in men, probably due to anatomy. In women, bacteria from fecal matter and vaginal discharges can enter the urethra because its opening is very close to the vaginal opening and the anus. Once an infection occurs in the urethra of a woman, the relative shortness of the urethra makes it easy for bacteria to gain entry to the bladder and multiply. In men who are not circumcised, the foreskin can harbor bacteria that can enter the urethra and cause UTIs. UTIs can also be sexually transmitted.

Sometimes, a UTI has no symptoms. When symptoms appear, they include pain or a burning sensation when urinating, frequent urination, or blood in the urine. In pyelonephritis, additional symptoms include fever and chills, aching pain on one or both sides of the lower back or abdomen, fatigue, nausea, vomiting, and diarrhea. If left untreated, pyelonephritis can last for months or years. Scarring of the kidneys and the possible loss of kidney function may result.

Typical treatment for all three types of UTIs is a course of antibiotics. An individual suffering from pyelonephritis may also require hospitalization if the disorder is severe. Given the appropriate antibiotic, UTIs usually go away quickly. Drinking plenty of fluids at the first sign of a UTI may help ward it off by diluting the bacteria present and flushing the urinary system. Drinking unsweetened cranberry juice may also help. The juice seems to contain a compound that can prevent bacteria from sticking to and thus growing in the urinary tract.

TAKING CARE: KEEPING THE URINARY SYSTEM HEALTHY

It is well known that aging taxes the urinary system. However, the many problems than can arise are not the inevitable consequence of aging and can be prevented or at least minimized. A person can lessen the effects of aging on the urinary system (like every other system in the body) by following a healthy lifestyle. This includes getting adequate rest, reducing stress, drinking healthy amounts of good-quality drinking water, not smoking, drinking moderate amounts of alcohol (or not drinking at all), following a proper diet, and exercising regularly.

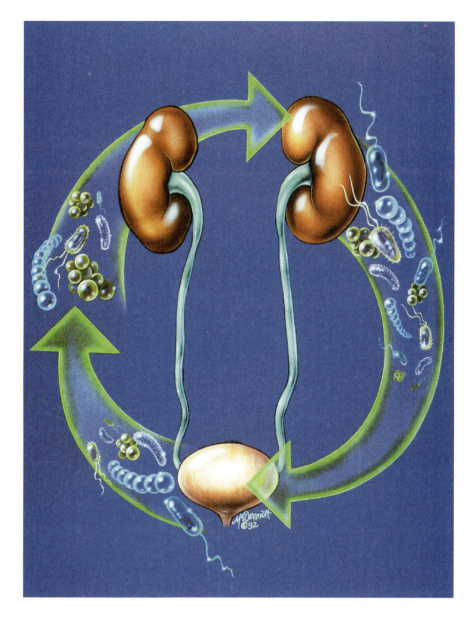

Urinary tract infections, or UTIs, are inflammations of the urinary tract caused by a
bacterial infection. This illustration depicts the cycle of infection between the kidneys (at
top of page) and the bladder and the urethra (bottom center). (Reproduced by permission
of Custom Medical Stock Photo.)

A healthy diet is important in maintaining the health of the urinary system. A poor diet—one high in fats and meats—can cause kidney stones to develop. People who are obese or overweight place undue pressure on the organs of the urinary system, which can lead to further medical problems.

Drinking plenty of water is a necessity in keeping the urinary system healthy. The amount of water in the body helps the urinary system determine how many mineral ions, such as sodium, should be eliminated. The urinary bladder should be emptied every few hours during the day, and drinking enough water should allow an individual to produce a large enough amount of urine to accomplish this. Producing large amounts of urine also helps to flush the urinary system, washing bacteria out of the normally sterile urinary tract.

DRINKING PLENTY OF WATER IS A NECESSITY IN KEEPING THE URINARY SYSTEM HEALTHY.

To further prevent infection of the urinary system by bacteria, it is important to practice good hygiene by keeping the genital area clean. This is vital in both sexes, but is of special concern to women because of the structure of their anatomy. In women, the urethral opening is very close to the vaginal opening and the anus. After urinating or defecating, women should wipe their genital area from the front to the back to avoid introducing fecal matter into the urethral opening.

Good hygiene after sexual intercourse is also important. During intercourse, bacteria from the vagina or from a man's penis may be introduced into a woman's urethra. If left unchecked, the bacteria may spread and create conditions such as urethritis and cystitis. Washing the genital area and urinating after intercourse can help flush out any bacteria from the urethra.

FOR MORE INFORMATION

Books

Silverstein, Alvin, Virginia Silverstein, and Robert Silverstein. *The Urinary System.* New York: Twenty-First Century Books, 1994.

WWW Sites

Cyber Anatomy: Excretory System
http://tqd.advanced.org/11965/html/cyber-anatomy_excboth.html
Geared for students in grades 6 through 12, site provides a broad discussion of the urinary system. Also includes a diagram of the system with the major parts identified.

Excretory System
http://gened.emc.maricopa.edu/bio/BIO181/BIOBK/
BioBookEXCRET.html
Site presents a detailed chapter (with extensive images) on the excretory (urinary) system from the On-Line Biology textbook.

Nephron Information Center
http://www.nephron.com

Site provides information about the kidneys and links for further information.

The Urinary System http://www.msms.doe.k12.ms.us/biology/anatomy/ urinary/urinary.html Site provides a diagram of the urinary system and links that give information on the four main parts of the system, including larger diagrams of each organ.

What Kids Need to Know About Kidneys http://kidshealth.org/kid/normal/ kidneys.html Site presents information explaining how kidneys clean wastes out of the body and how they maintain a balance of fluids and minerals in the body.

Your Urinary System and How It Works http://www.niddk.nih.gov/health/ urolog/pubs/yrurinar /index.htm The site, a service of the National Institute of Diabetes and Digestive and Kidney Diseases (part of the National Institutes of Health), provides information on how the urinary system works, what can cause problems with the system, and what are some disorders of the system, among other items.

12

The Special Senses

The senses connect humans to the real world, allowing them to interpret what is happening around them and respond accordingly. The color of the sky at dusk, the sound of laughter at a party, the scent of eucalyptus and pine, the taste of freshly baked bread—all would be meaningless without the senses. They not only provide pleasure, but warn of danger. Traditionally, sight, hearing, smell, taste, and touch have been considered the five main senses of the body. However, touch (along with the senses of pressure, temperature, and pain) is one of the general senses that has small sensory receptors scattered throughout the body in the skin (for a further discussion, see chapter 4). The other four "traditional" senses—sight, hearing, smell, and taste—are the special senses.

DESIGN: PARTS OF THE SPECIAL SENSES

The abilities to see, to hear, to smell, and to taste are all possible because of sensory receptors, or special nerve cells or endings of the peripheral nervous system (part of the nervous system consisting mainly of nerves that extend from the brain and spinal cord to areas in the rest of the body). Sensory receptors respond to a stimulus by converting that stimulus into a nerve impulse. The impulse is then carried by sensory nerves to a specific part of the brain, where the sensation of sight, sound, smell, or taste is perceived or "felt."

Sensory receptors are classified according to the type of stimulus that arouses or excites them. The receptors for the sense of sight are photoreceptors that are sensitive to light. The receptors for the sense of hearing are mechanoreceptors that are sensitive to sound waves or vibrations. The receptors for the senses of smell and taste are chemoreceptors that are sensitive to various chemicals.

The special sensory receptors for sight and hearing are located in large, complex sensory organs—the eyes and the ears. Those for smell and taste are located in organs that function in other systems—the nose in the respiratory system and the mouth in the digestive system.

Anatomy of the eye

The eye is the organ of sight or vision. Each eye works with the brain to transform light waves into visual images. Eighty percent of all information received by the human brain comes from the eyes.

The human eyeball is about 0.9 inch (2.3 centimeters) in diameter and is not perfectly round, being slightly flattened in the front and back. Only about one-sixth of an eye's front surface can normally be seen. The rest of the eye is enclosed and protected by a cushion of fat and the walls of the orbit, a cavity in the skull formed by facial and cranial bones. The eye wall consists of three covering layers: the sclera, the choroid, and the retina.

WORDS TO KNOW

Accommodation (ah-kah-mah-DAY-shun): Process of changing the shape of the lens of the eye to keep an image focused on the retina.

Aqueous humor (AYE-kwee-us HYOO-mer): Tissue fluid filling the cavity of the eye between the cornea and the lens.

Binocular vision (by-NOK-yoo-lur VI-zhun): Ability of the brain to create one image from the slightly different images received from each eye.

Ceruminous glands (suh-ROO-mi-nus GLANDZ): Exocrine glands in the skin of the auditory canal of the ear that secrete earwax or cerumen.

Chemoreceptors (kee-moe-re-SEP-terz): Receptors sensitive to various chemicals substances.

Choroid (KOR-oid): Middle, pigmented layer of the eye.

Ciliary body (SIL-ee-air-ee BAH-dee): Circular muscle that surrounds the edge of the lens of the eye and changes the shape of the lens.

Cochlea (KOK-lee-ah): Spiral-shaped cavity in the inner ear that contains the receptors for hearing in the organ of Corti.

Cones: Photoreceptors in the retina of the eye that detect colors.

Cornea (KOR-nee-ah): Transparent front portion of the sclera of the eye.

Conjunctiva (kon-junk-TIE-vah): Mucous membrane lining the eyelids and covering the front surface of the eyeball.

Eardrum (EER-drum): Thin membrane at the end of the outer ear that vibrates when sound waves strike it.

Eustachian tube (yoo-STAY-she-an TOOB): Slender air passage between the middle ear cavity and the pharynx, which equalizes air pressure on the two sides of the eardrum.

External auditory canal (ex-TER-nal AW-di-tor-ee ka-NAL): Also called the ear canal, the tunnel in the ear between the pinna and eardrum.

Gustation (gus-TAY-shun): The sense of taste.

Gustatory cells (GUS-ta-tor-ee CELLS): Chemoreceptors located within taste buds.

Iris (EYE-ris): Pigmented (colored) part of the eye between the cornea and lens made of two sets of smooth muscle fibers.

Lacrimal gland (LAK-ri-muhl GLAND): Gland located at the upper, outer corner of each eyeball that secretes tears.

Lens: Clear, oval, flexible structure behind the pupil in the eye that changes shape for the focusing of light rays.

THE SCLERA. The sclera, the outer layer made of fibrous connective tissue, encases and protects the eyeball. The visible portion of the sclera is seen as the "white" of the eye. When that portion is irritated, the small blood vessels contained in the layer enlarge, producing a "bloodshot eye." In the center of the visible portion of the sclera is the cornea, which projects slightly forward. The cornea is transparent and has no capillaries. It is the "window" or the first part of the eye through which light enters. A delicate mucous membrane, the conjunctiva, covers the cornea and visible portion of the sclera. It secretes mucus to lubricate the eyeball and keep it moist.

THE CHOROID. The choroid is a thin membrane lying underneath the sclera. It is composed of a dark pigment that absorbs light within the eye (preventing glare) and numerous blood vessels that nourish the internal tissues of the eye. At the front end of the choroid is the ciliary body. Running

---

Mechanoreceptors (mek-ah-no-re-SEP-terz): Receptors sensitive to mechanical or physical pressures such as sound and touch.

Olfaction (ol-FAK-shun): The sense of smell.

Olfactory epithelium (ol-FAK-ter-ee ep-e-THEE-lee-um): Section of mucous membrane in the roof of the nasal cavity that contains odor-sensitive olfactory nerve cells.

Organ of Corti (OR-gan of KOR-tee): Structure in the cochlea of the inner ear that contains the receptors for hearing.

Ossicles (OS-si-kuls): Three bones of the middle ear: hammer, anvil, and stirrup.

Papillae (pah-PILL-ee): Projections on the tongue that contain taste buds.

Photoreceptors (fo-to-re-SEP-terz): Receptors sensitive to light.

Pinna (PIN-nah): Commonly referred to as the ear, the outer, flaplike portion of the ear.

Pupil (PYOO-pil): Opening in the center of the iris though which light passes.

Receptors (re-SEP-terz): Specialized peripheral nerve endings or nerve cells that respond to a particular stimulus such as light, sound, heat, touch, or pressure.

Retina (RET-i-nah): Innermost layer of the eyeball that contains the photoreceptors—the rods and cones.

Rods: Photoreceptors in the retina of the eye that detect the presence of light.

Saccule (SAC-yool): Membranous sac in the vestibule of the inner ear that contains receptors for the sense of balance.

Sclera (SKLER-ah): Outermost layer of the eyeball, made of connective tissue.

Semicircular canals (sem-eye-SIR-cue-lar ka-NALZ): Three oval canals in the inner ear that help to maintain balance.

Taste buds: Structures on the papillae of the tongue that contain chemoreceptors that respond to chemicals dissolved in saliva.

Utricle (YOO-tri-kuhl): Membranous sac in the vestibule of the inner ear that contains receptors for the sense of balance.

Vestibule (VES-ti-byool): Bony chamber of the inner ear that contains the utricle and the saccule.

Vitreous humor (VIT-ree-us HYOO-mer): Transparent, gellike substance that fills the cavity of the eye behind the lens.

like a ring around the visible portion of the eye, the ciliary body connects the choroid with the iris. The ciliary body contains muscles that are connected by ligaments to the lens behind the iris.

The iris is the visible portion of the choroid. It gives the eye its color, which varies depending on the amount of pigment present in the iris. Dense pigment makes the iris brown, while little pigment makes the iris blue. If there is no pigment the iris is pink, as in the eye of a white rabbit. The rounded opening in the center of the iris is the pupil, through which light passes. In bright light, muscles in the iris constrict the pupil, reducing the

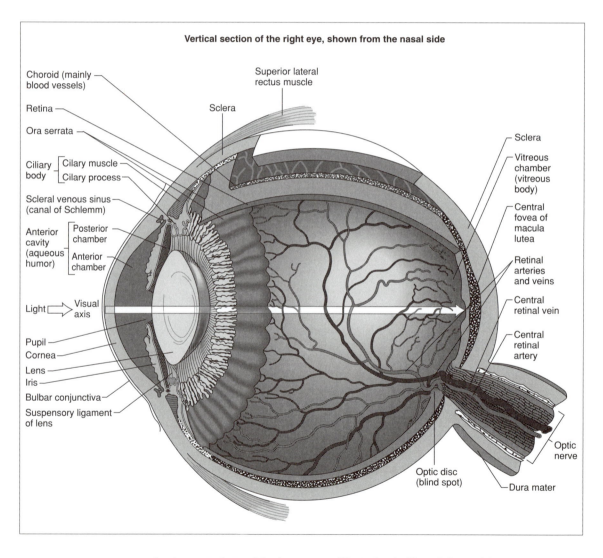

Vertical section of the right eye, shown from the nasal side

Choroid (mainly blood vessels)
Retina
Ora serrata
Ciliary body — Cilary muscle
Ciliary body — Cilary process
Scleral venous sinus (canal of Schlemm)
Anterior cavity (aqueous humor) — Posterior chamber
Anterior cavity (aqueous humor) — Anterior chamber
Light — Visual axis
Pupil
Cornea
Lens
Iris
Bulbar conjunctiva
Suspensory ligament of lens

Sclera
Superior lateral rectus muscle

Sclera
Vitreous chamber (vitreous body)
Central fovea of macula lutea
Retinal arteries and veins
Central retinal vein
Central retinal artery
Optic nerve
Optic disc (blind spot)
Dura mater

A cutaway anatomy of the human eye. (Illustration by Hans & Cassady.)

amount of light entering the eye. Conversely, the pupil dilates (enlarges) in dim light, increasing the amount of light entering. Extreme fear, head injuries, and certain drugs can also dilate the pupil.

THE LENS. The lens is a crystal-clear, oval, flexible body that is biconvex (curving outward on both surfaces). It is made up of approximately 35 percent protein and 65 percent water. The entire surface of the lens is smooth and shiny, contains no blood vessels, and is encased in an elastic membrane. The lens sits behind the iris and focuses light on the retina. In addition to holding the lens in place, the muscles of the ciliary body contract and relax, causing the lens to either fatten or become thin. As the shape of the lens changes, so does its focus.

THE RETINA. The retina, the innermost layer of the eye, is thin, delicate, sensory tissue composed of layers of light-sensitive nerve cells. The retina begins at the ciliary body (not at the front of the eye) and encircles the entire interior portion of the eye. Rods and cones are the photoreceptors of the retina. In each eye there are about 126 million rods and 6 million cones.

Rods function chiefly in dim light, allowing limited night vision: it is with rods that a person sees the stars. Rods cannot detect color (that is why objects in dim light appear in shades of gray), but they are the first cells to detect movement. They are most abundant toward the edge of the retina and provide people with peripheral (or side) vision. Cones function best in bright light and are sensitive to color. They are most abundant in the center of the retina. Scientists believe three types of cones—red, blue, and green—exist in the eye. The perception of different colors is the result of the stimulation of various combinations of these three types.

CAVITIES AND FLUIDS OF THE EYE. Between the cornea and the lens is a small cavity. This cavity is filled with a clear watery fluid known as aqueous humor, formed by capillaries in the ciliary body. This fluid aids good vision by helping maintain eye shape, providing support for the internal structures, supplying nutrients to the lens and cornea, and disposing of cellular wastes produced by the eye.

The large cavity in back of the lens (the center of the eyeball) is filled with a transparent, gel-like substance called vitreous humor. Light passing through the lens on its way to the retina passes through the vitreous humor. The vitreous humor is 99 percent water and contains no cells. It helps to maintain the shape of the eye and support its internal components.

ACCESSORY STRUCTURES OF THE EYE. The lacrimal gland, which lies immediately above each eyeball at the outer corner of the eye socket,

WHY DO ALL NEWBORN BABIES HAVE BLUE EYES?

The amount of pigment in the iris is what determines its color.

In newborns, most of the pigment is concentrated in the folds of the iris. Since only a little bit of pigment exists on the visible portion of the iris, it appears blue. When a baby is a few months old, the rest of the pigment begins moving to the surface of the iris, giving the baby his or her permanent eye color.

produces tears. Tears are mostly water, but also contain antibodies and an enzyme that prevents the growth of most bacteria on the wet, warm surface of the eye. Tears flow through numerous ducts from the lacrimal gland to the area beneath the upper eyelid. Blinking spreads the tears across the cornea's outside surface, keeping it moist and clean. Tear fluid then either evaporates or drains into two small pores in the inner corner of the eye that connect to a larger duct, which eventually drains tears into the nasal cavity.

Eyelids and eyelashes help to protect the eye. The blinking movement of eyelids keeps the front surface of the eye lubricated and free from dust and dirt. The rate of blinking varies. On average, the eye blinks once every five seconds (or 17,280 times a day or 6.3 million times a year). The eyelids can also close firmly to protect the eye. Eyelashes, hairs that project from the border of each eyelid, help to keep dust, dirt, and insects out of the eye.

Extending from the bony surface of the orbit to the outside of the eyeball are six small muscles that contract and relax, allowing the eye to move in various directions. Four of the muscles move the eyeball up and down and side to side. The other two muscles rotate the eye.

Anatomy of the ear

The human ear is the organ responsible for hearing and for equilibrium or balance. The ear consists of three regions or areas: the outer (external) ear, the middle ear, and inner (internal) ear. The mechanoreceptors for hearing and balance are all found in the inner ear.

THE OUTER EAR. The outer ear collects external sounds and funnels them through the auditory system to the eardrum. The outer ear is composed of three parts—the pinna (or auricle), the external auditory canal, and the eardrum (tympanic membrane).

What are commonly called ears—the two flaplike structures on either side of the head—are actually the pinnas of the outer ear. Pinnas are skin-covered cartilage, not bone, and are therefore flexible. In many species of animals, the pinnas act to collect and funnel sound waves into the external auditory canal. In humans, however, the pinnas do not serve this purpose. In fact, humans could lose their pinnas and hearing would not be adversely affected.

The external auditory canal or ear canal is a passageway that begins at the pinna and extends inward and slightly upwards, ending at the

WHAT ARE "FLOATERS" IN THE EYE?

Floaters are semi-transparent or dark little specks that float across the field of vision and can be mistaken for flies in the room. Some floaters originate with red blood cells that have leaked out of the retina. The blood cells swell into spheres—some forming strings—and float around the areas of the retina. Others are shadows cast by microscopic structures in the vitreous humor.

A sudden appearance of dark floaters, if accompanied by bright little flashes, could indicate that the retina has detached, a serious problem that requires medical treatment.

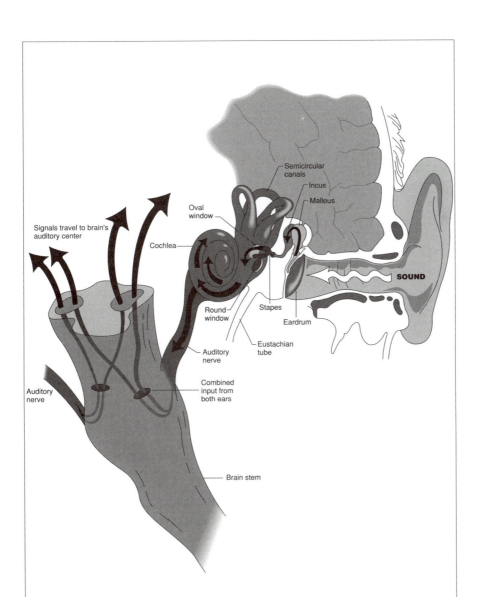

The hearing process. The outer ear collects external sounds and funnels them through the auditory system to the eardrum (far right of illustration). (Illustration by Hans & Cassady.)

eardrum. In the adult human it is lined with skin and hairs and is approximately 1 inch (2.5 centimeters) long. The outer one-third of the canal is lined with wax-producing ceruminous glands and fine hairs. The purpose of the earwax and hairs is to protect the eardrum by trapping dirt and foreign bodies and keeping the canal moist.

The eardrum or tympanic membrane is a thin, concave membrane stretched across the inner end of the auditory canal much like the skin covering the top of a drum. The eardrum marks the border between the outer ear and middle ear. In the adult human, the eardrum has a total area of approximately 0.1 square inch (0.6 square centimeter). The middle point of the eardrum—called the umbo—is attached to the stirrup, the first of three bones contained within the middle ear.

THE MIDDLE EAR. The middle ear transmits sound from the outer ear to the inner ear. The middle ear consists of an oval, air-filled space approximately 0.1 cubic inch (2 cubic centimeters) in volume. Contained in this space are three tiny bones called ossicles. Because of their shapes, the three ossicles are known as the hammer (malleus), the anvil (incus), and the stirrup (stapes).

Connecting the middle ear to the throat is the eustachian tube. This tube is normally closed, opening only as a result of muscle movement during yawning, sneezing, or swallowing. The eustachian tube causes air pressure in the middle ear to match the air pressure in the outer ear.

The most noticeable example of eustachian tube function occurs when there is a quick change in altitude, such as when a plane takes off. Prior to takeoff, the pressure in the outer ear is equal to the pressure in the middle ear. When the plane gains altitude, the air pressure in the outer ear decreases, while the pressure in the middle ear remains the same, causing the ear to feel "plugged." In response to this the ear may "pop." The popping sensation is actually the quick opening and closing of the eustachian tube and the equalization of pressure between the outer and middle ear.

HOW HEARING AIDS WORK

Hearing aids are tools that amplify sound for people who have a hard time hearing. Millions of hearing aids are sold annually, especially to people over the age of sixty-five. More than 1,000 different models are available in the United States.

A typical hearing aid contains a microphone that picks up sounds and changes them into electric signals. The hearing aid's amplifier increases the strength of the electric signals. Then the receiver converts the signals back into sound waves that can be heard by the wearer.

The entire mechanism is housed in an ear mold that fits snugly in the ear canal. The power to run the electronic parts is provided by a small battery. There are a variety of designs to fit the needs of the wearer, some small enough to be completely concealed by the ear canal.

Many modern hearing aids have miniature computer chips that allow the aid to selectively boost certain frequencies. This means that a person could wear such a hearing aid to a loud party and screen out unwanted background noise while tuning in to a private conversation. The hearing aid can also be programmed to conform to a person's specific hearing loss. Some models can be further programmed to allow the wearer to choose different settings depending on the noise of the surroundings.

THE INNER EAR. The inner ear is responsible for interpreting and transmitting sound and balance sensations to the brain. The inner ear, located just behind the eye socket, is small (about the size of a pea) and complex in shape. With its series of winding interconnected chambers, it has been called a labyrinth. The main components of the inner ear are the vestibule, semicircular canals, and the cochlea.

The vestibule, a round open space, is the central structure within the inner ear. The vestibule contains two membranous sacs—the utricle and the saccule (the saccule is the smaller of the two). These sacs, lined with tiny hairs and attached to nerve fibers, function as an individual's chief organs of balance.

Attached to the vestibule are three loop-shaped, fluid-filled tubes called the semicircular canals. These canals, arranged perpendicular to each other, are a key part of the vestibular system. Two of the canals help the body maintain balance when it is moving vertically, such as in falling and jumping. The third maintains horizontal balance, as when the head or body rotates.

The cochlea is the organ of hearing. The cochlea consists of a bony, snail-like shell that contains three separate fluid-filled ducts or canals. The middle canal contains the basilar membrane, which holds or supports the organ of Corti, named after Italian anatomist Alfonso Giacomo Gaspare Corti (1822–1876) who discovered it. The organ contains over 20,000 hair cells (mechanoreceptors) connected at their base to the auditory nerve. The organ is the site where sound waves are converted into nerve impulses, which are then sent to the brain along the auditory nerve.

Anatomy of the sense of smell

Smell, called olfaction, is the ability of an organism to sense and identify a substance by detecting tiny amounts of the substance that evaporate and produce an odor. Smell is the most important sense for most organisms.

In humans, the sense of smell differs from the other senses (sight, hearing, and taste) in its directness. People actually smell microscopic bits or chemicals of a substance that have evaporated and made their way through the nostrils into the nasal cavity. In the roof of the nasal cavity is a section of mucous membrane called the olfactory epithelium. It covers an area of roughly 0.75 square inch (4.8 square centimeters), or about the size of a postage stamp.

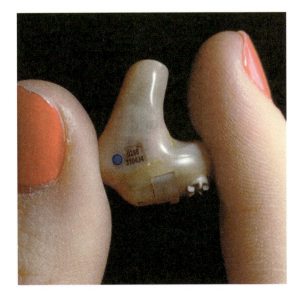

A cochlear implant. The implant works like an artificial human cochlea by helping to send sound from the ear to the brain. (Photograph by L. Steinmark. Reproduced by permission of Custom Medical Stock Photo.)

HEARING COLORS AND SEEING SOUNDS

Normally, when people experience the world through their senses, they do so in an orderly fashion. They see with their eyes, hear with their ears, and taste and smell with the chemoreceptors in their mouths and noses.

For some people, however, the basic rules of sensory perception do not apply. They tend to perceive stimuli not only with the sense for which it was intended, but with others as well—sight mingles with sound, taste with touch. They may see musical notes as color hues or feel flavors as different textures on the skin.

This rare condition is known as synesthesia (sin-es-THE-zee-ah), and the people who have it as synesthetes. Women are about six times as likely as men to be synesthetes.

Some scientists believe that the condition is the result of associations learned at an early age. Other scientists disagree, believing that a unique physical condition exists in the brains of synesthetes. Some brain studies have shown that during synesthetic experiences, blood flow to some parts of the brain decreases. Normally, that blood flow would have been increased by sensory stimuli. Synesthesia also appears to run in families, leading some scientists to theorize that it has a genetic basis.

The olfactory epithelium contains millions of odor-sensitive olfactory receptor cells (chemoreceptors) that are connected to the olfactory nerves. The

SMELL IS THE MOST IMPORTANT SENSE FOR MOST ORGANISMS.

olfactory receptors have long olfactory hairs that protrude outward from the epithelium. Beneath the olfactory epithelium lie olfactory glands that produce mucus that covers the epithelium and bathes the olfactory hairs. The mucus keeps the area moist and clean and prevents the buildup of potentially harmful or overpowering chemicals.

Anatomy of the sense of taste

Taste, called gustation, is the sense for determining the flavor of food and other substances (taste comes from the Latin word *taxare*, meaning "to touch" or "to feel"). It is one of the two chemical senses (the other being smell) and it is stimulated when taste buds on the tongue come in contact with certain chemicals. The sense of taste is also influenced by the smell and texture of substances, hereditary factors, culture, and familiarity with specific taste sensations.

Clusters of small organs called taste buds are located in the mouth. Of the almost 10,000 taste buds, most are located on the upper surface of the tongue (a few are located on the soft palate and on the inner surface of the cheeks). Taste buds (named so because under the microscope they look similar to plant buds) lie in small projections on the tongue called papillae. Within the taste buds are taste receptors known as gustatory cells. Each gustatory cell projects slender taste hairs into the surrounding fluids through a narrow taste pore. As food is broken down in the mouth, these receptors come into contact with chemicals dissolved in the saliva. They then send messages along nerves to the brain, which interprets the flavor as sweet, sour, salty, or bitter.

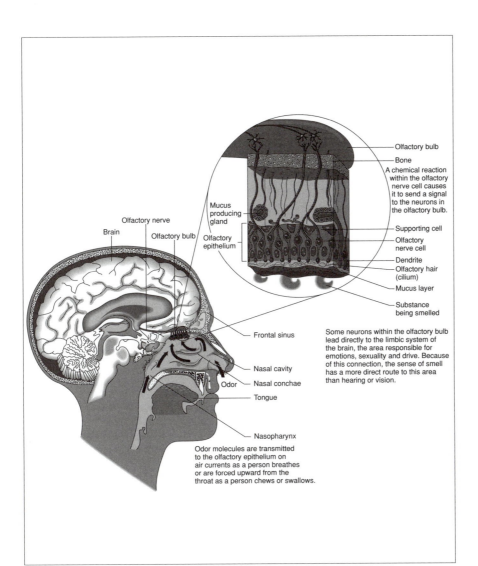

The olfactory transmission process. (Illustration by Hans & Cassady.)

Taste buds for all four taste groups can be found throughout the mouth, but specific kinds of buds are concentrated in certain areas (the areas tend to overlap each other). Sweetness is detected by taste buds on the tip of the tongue. The buds for sour tastes are on the sides of the tongue. Those for salty are toward the front. Bitter taste buds are located on the back of the tongue. Bitterness can make many people gag, which is a defense mechanism. Since many natural poisons and spoiled foods are bitter, gagging helps prevent poisoning.

NEW TASTE BUDS ARE PRODUCED EVERY THREE TO TEN DAYS TO REPLACE THE ONES WORN OUT BY SCALDING OR FROZEN FOODS.

New taste buds are produced every three to ten days to replace the ones worn out by scalding or frozen foods. As people grow older, their taste buds are replaced at a slower rate, and more of a substance is needed to experience its full flavor.

WORKINGS: HOW THE SPECIAL SENSES FUNCTION

An individual's total experience of the external world—what he or she "feels"—is a blending of all the senses. The senses take in information about the world in the form of light waves, sound waves, and dissolved chemicals.

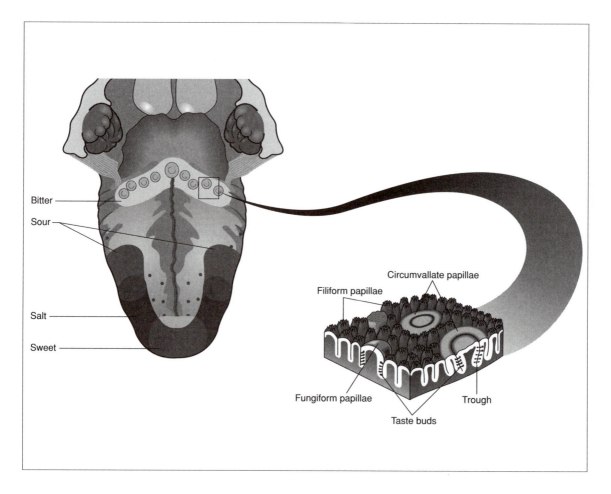

Taste bud anatomy (right) and the taste regions of the tongue (left). Taste buds for all four taste groups can be found throughout the mouth, but specific kinds of buds are concentrated in certain areas. (Illustration by Hans & Cassady.)

They convert those various forms into nerve impulses that are sent to the brain, which then interprets the impulses and gives them meaning in such a way that an individual sees, hears, smells, and tastes.

Sight

Light is a form of electromagnetic radiation—a form of energy carried by waves. The term electromagnetic radiation refers to a vast range of energy waves, including gamma rays, X rays, ultraviolet rays, visible light, infrared radiation, microwaves, radar, and radio waves. Of all these forms, only one can be detected by the human eye: visible light.

The human eye detects two types of visible light: direct light and indirect light. Direct light is light coming directly from a source such as the Sun or a lightbulb. Indirect light is light that has bounced off an object. People see trees, buildings, cars, and even the Moon through indirect light. Regardless of the type of light, an individual can see only if light rays are focused on the retina and the resulting nerve impulses are transmitted to the brain.

In short, sight occurs when light waves enter the eye by passing through the conjunctiva, cornea, aqueous humor, pupil, then the lens behind the iris. The lens focuses the light waves through the vitreous humor onto the retina. The rods and cones in the retina convert the light energy into electrical impulses. These impulses are then carried via the optic nerves to the brain, where they are interpreted as images.

When light passes from one substance to another of greater or lesser density, its waves or rays are refracted or bent. This is what happens when light waves pass from the surrounding air through the cornea and lens. The function of the lens is to focus the waves precisely on the retina. When the lens fails to do so, visual problems occur (see "Ailments" section below).

The lens changes shape depending on whether an object being viewed is far or near. The light waves from distant objects, generally over 20 feet (6 meters) away, approach the eye as parallel rays. In order to focus those rays on the retina, the lens does not change its normal, relatively flat shape, and the muscles of the ciliary body are relaxed. On the other hand, light waves from close objects tend to scatter and diverge or spread out. In order to focus those rays

SEEING INTO THE FUTURE

Researchers at Harvard University have found that everyone, not just fortune tellers, can see into the future. Tennis players routinely react to balls travelling over 100 miles (160 kilometers) per hour. The researchers conducted studies to determine how an individual could respond to an object that was moving faster than the eye had time to transmit its image to the brain.

The researchers found that the retina of the eye contains cells, called ganglion cells, that can calculate the future position of a moving object. The cells send nerve messages to the brain about the position of an object thousandths of a second before it actually arrives in that place in space.

This finding contradicts the notion that the eye acts like a simple camera, recording an image placed directly before it.

on the retina, the lens must bulge or become more spherical. To achieve this, the muscles in the ciliary body contract and the body forms a smaller circle. The elastic lens recoils and bulges in the middle (becoming convex). This process of changing the shape of the lens to keep an image focused on the retina is called accommodation.

When light rays strike the retina, they stimulate chemical reactions in the rods and cones. Different wavelengths of visible light (which result in different colors) bring about different types of chemical reactions. The reactions generate electrical impulses that are transmitted from the rods and cones by neurons. These neurons come together to form the optic nerve, which passes out through the rear wall of the eyeball.

The optic nerves from the two eyes then converge and nerve fibers from the inside portion of each optic nerve cross over to the other side. The nerves then separate again and travel to the occipital lobes of the cerebral cortex, the outermost layer of the cerebrum (largest part of the brain). The visual area in the right occipital lobe (on the right side or right hemisphere of the brain) receives nerve fibers from the right side of each eye. The visual area in the left occipital lobe receives nerve fibers from the left side of each eye.

When an image is formed on the retina by the light-bending action of a lens, it is an upside-down likeness of the object the light rays bounced off of. The image is also smaller than the original object (the farther away an object, the smaller its image on the retina) and reversed left to right. When the brain receives impulses containing information about these small, upside-down, reversed images from the eyes, it corrects the images to produce normal vision. Scientists still do not know how the brain does this.

Another ability of the brain is to bring together the two separate images (one from each eye) to form a single image. Each eye forms its own flat, two-dimensional (with height and width) image from a slightly different angle. The brain compares and combines the two images to create a single image that is three-dimensional (one that also has depth). This ability of the brain, producing normal vision using both eyes, is known as binocular vision.

Hearing

Sound is produced by a vibrating object or body. As an object vibrates or moves back and forth, it causes molecules in the surrounding air to be pushed together or stretched apart. This disturbance in the air radiates outward in the form of waves that can travel through air, water, and solids. When these waves enter the ear, the effect is perceived as sound.

Frequency is the number of back-and-forth motions (called oscillations) a wave makes in a unit of time. Frequency is usually measured in cycles (vibrations) per second, and the unit used to measure frequency is the hertz (abbreviation: Hz). For example, 1,000 Hz is equal to 1,000 cycles per second.

An infant tests his depth perception. Depth perception—including how the mind sees in three dimensions though the retina on which the image is registered is flat—appears to be related to binocular vision. (Photograph by Gabe Palmer. Reproduced by permission of The Stock Market.)

Objects can vibrate with a great range of frequencies, from only a few cycles (or vibrations) per second to millions of times per second. However, the human ear is able to detect only a limited range of those vibrations, generally those between 20 to 20,000 Hz. When the rate of vibration is less than

20 Hz, the sound is said to be infrasonic; when the rate is above 20,000 Hz, it is said to be ultrasonic.

When sound waves reach the outer ear, the pinna funnels the waves into the external auditory canal and toward the eardrum. As the waves strike the eardrum, it vibrates in response to the pressure or force of the sound waves. The initial vibration causes the eardrum to be pushed inward by an amount equal to the intensity of the sound. Once the eardrum is pushed inward, the pressure within the middle ear causes the eardrum to be pulled outward, setting up a back-and-forth motion.

The movement of the eardrum sets all three ossicles in motion. The vibrating pressure of the stirrup (the last ossicle) on the small opening leading to the inner ear sets the fluid in the cochlea in motion. The fluid motion causes a corresponding, but not equal, wavelike motion of the basilar membrane.

When the basilar membrane moves, it causes the small hairlike fibers on the top of the hair cells of the organ of Corti to bend. The bending of the hair cells causes chemical reactions within the cells themselves, creating electrical impulses in the nerve fibers attached to the bottom of the hair cells. The nerve impulses travel up the auditory nerves to auditory areas in the temporal lobes of the cerebral cortex of the brain, which interpret those nerve impulses as "sounds."

Sound waves usually reach the two ears at different times, allowing an individual to hear "in stereo." The brain uses this difference to determine from where in the surrounding environment the sound waves are coming. Scientists are not quite sure how the brain determines whether a sound is high-pitched or low-pitched, but they believe the sensation of pitch is dependent on which area of the basilar membrane vibrates (causing certain hair cells of the cochlea to bend). They also believe that the amount of vibration of the basilar membrane determines whether the brain will interpret a sound as loud or soft.

SOUND WAVES USUALLY REACH THE TWO EARS AT DIFFERENT TIMES, ALLOWING AN INDIVIDUAL TO HEAR "IN STEREO."

BALANCE. Besides hearing, the inner ear is also concerned with balance. The utricle and saccule (the membranous sacs in the vestibule of the inner ear) provide the brain with information about the body at rest. The tiny hair cells within these sacs project into a jellylike material that contains tiny mineral crystals. As the position of the head changes (while the body stays at rest), gravity causes the crystals to shift, pulling on the jellylike material. This movement bends the hair cells, and they are stimulated to generate nerve impulses that are sent to the cerebellum of the brain, informing it of the position of the head. The brain then uses this information to maintain equilibrium or balance.

Helping to maintain balance while the body moves through space are the fluid-filled semicircular canals. They provide the brain with information concerning rotational movements of the head. The three semicircular canals are arranged at right angles to each other, oriented in the three planes of space (up and down, right and left, forward and back). An area at the base of each semicircular canal contains sensory hair cells. Depending on the direction in which the body moves, the thick fluid in one or more of the semicircular canals moves in the opposite direction and the hair cells are bent. This stimulates the hair cells to generate nerve impulses that are sent to the cerebellum. The brain then uses the information to maintain balance (by coordinating muscle movements) while the body is moving.

Smell

Scientists believe there are only a few basic odors or scents that combine to form all other odors. However, they have found it hard to agree on the number of basic odors. Estimates range from seven to fifty or more. Although many animals have a sense of smell far superior to that of humans, the human nose is capable of detecting over 10,000 different odors, even some that occur in extremely minute amounts in the air.

For smelling to occur, chemicals in the air must enter the nostrils into the nasal cavity. There, they must be dissolved in the mucus covering the olfactory epithelium. Once dissolved, the chemicals bind to the olfactory hairs, stimulating the olfactory receptors to send nerve impulses along the olfactory nerves to the olfactory areas in the temporal lobes of the cerebral cortex. The brain interprets the impulses as a specific odor or odors.

Olfactory information is also sent to the limbic system, a horseshoe-shaped area of the brain concerned with emotional states and memory. Thus, the impressions formed by odors or smells are long-lasting and very much a part of an individual's memories and emotions.

Taste

Although there are only four general types of taste receptors—sweet, sour, salty, and bitter—people experience many different tastes because the chemicals in foods stimulate different combinations of the four receptors.

The mechanism for tasting is similar to that for smelling. Chemicals from foods and liquids that are dissolved in the saliva come in contact

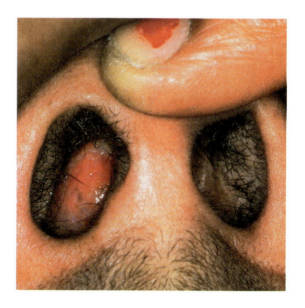

A nasal polyp (in nostril on the left). Polyps are overgrowths of tissue that can block the nasal cavity and inhibit a person's ability to smell. (Reproduced by permission of Custom Medical Stock Photo.)

with the taste hairs of the gustatory cells. The cells are then stimulated to generate nerve impulses that are carried by three cranial nerves to the parietal and temporal lobes of the cerebral cortex. The brain then interprets those impulses as taste sensations.

Scientists have discovered that individual tasting abilities and preferences for specific foods are partially hereditary. Some people are genetically programmed to have more taste buds than others and, as a result, taste more flavors in a particular food. Additionally, culture and familiarity with foods greatly influence taste preferences. Foods that are a tradition in certain cultures may be unappealing to those who are unfamiliar with them. A taste for a particular food usually develops as a person consumes it more frequently.

SCIENTISTS HAVE DISCOVERED THAT INDIVIDUAL TASTING ABILITIES AND PREFERENCES FOR SPECIFIC FOODS ARE PARTIALLY HEREDITARY.

The smell, texture, and temperature of foods also affect taste. People often first experience the flavor of a food by its odor. When an individual's sense of smell is decreased due to congestion from a cold or flu, that person frequently experiences a reduced ability to taste. Some people will not eat pears because of the fruit's gritty texture, while others would not think of drinking cold coffee.

AILMENTS: WHAT CAN GO WRONG WITH THE SPECIAL SENSES

Most problems that afflict the special senses are the result of normal aging. As people grow older, their lacrimal glands become less active. The eyes become dry and are more prone to infection and irritation. The muscles of the iris also become less efficient, and the lens tends to lose its crystal clarity. Both of these conditions cause less light to reach the retina, thereby reducing vision.

The ears are affected by few problems during childhood and adult life (except for ear inflammations or infections). However, after the age of sixty, the organ of Corti begins gradually to deteriorate and the ability to hear high tones and human speech decreases.

Smell and taste, the chemical senses, usually stay sharp throughout childhood and adult life. They gradually begin to decrease when a person reaches middle age because of a loss in the number of chemoreceptor cells. During life, impairment of smell and taste are usually the result of a nasal cavity inflammation (due to a cold, an allergy, or smoking) or a head injury. More serious infections in the nasal or oral cavity, such as oral candidiasis (yeast infection of the mucous membranes of the oral cavity), can obviously impair smell and taste.

SPECIAL SENSE DISORDERS

Astigmatism (ah-STIG-mah-tiz-um): Incorrect shaping of the cornea that results in an incorrect focusing of light on the retina.

Cataract (KAT-ah-rakt): Condition in which the lens of the eye turns cloudy, causing partial or total blindness.

Conjunctivitis (kon-junk-ti-VIE-tis): Inflammation of the conjunctiva of the eye.

Farsightedness: Known formally as hyperopia, the condition of the eye where incoming rays of light reach the retina before they converge to form a focused image.

Glaucoma (glaw-KOE-mah): Eye disorder caused by a buildup of aqueous humor that results in high pressure in the eyeball, often damaging the optic nerve and eventually leading to blindness.

Meniere's disease (men-ee-AIRZ): Ear disorder characterized by recurring dizziness, hearing loss, and a buzzing or ringing sound in the ears.

Nearsightedness: Known formally as myopia, the condition of the eye where incoming rays of light are bent too much and converge to form a focused image in front of the retina.

Otitis media (oh-TIE-tis ME-dee-ah): Infection of the middle ear.

The following are just a few of the disorders or diseases that can afflict some of the special senses.

Astigmatism

Astigmatism is a condition brought about by an uneven curvature of the cornea. As a consequence, some light rays entering the eye focus on the retina while others focus in front or behind it. The result is an indistinct or slightly out-of-focus image. Some cases of astigmatism are caused by problems in the lens. Minor variations in the curvature of the lens can result in minor degrees of astigmatism. In these cases, the cornea is usually normal in shape.

Astigmatism is a condition that may be present at birth. It may also be acquired if something is distorting the cornea. The upper eyelid resting on the eyeball, trauma or scarring to the cornea, tumors in the eyelid, or a developing condition in which the cornea thins and becomes cone shaped can all cause distortion. Diabetes can also play a role. High blood sugar levels can cause changes in the shape of the lens, resulting in astigmatism.

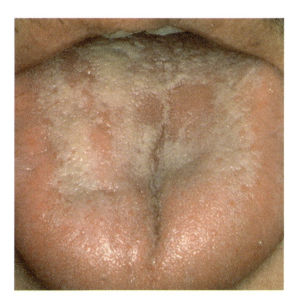

A tongue infected with candidiasis, a yeast infection of the mucous membranes in the oral cavity. Serious infections such as oral candidiasis can impair the ability to taste. (Photograph by Edward H. Gill. Reproduced by permission of Custom Medical Stock Photo.)

Body By Design   **333**

The main symptom of astigmatism is blurring. People with the condition can also experience headaches and eyestrain.

Astigmatism can generally be corrected by the use of cylindrical lenses, which can be in eyeglasses or contact lenses. The lenses are shaped to counteract the shape of the sections of the cornea that are causing the difficulty. In 1997, the U.S. Food and Drug Administration (FDA) approved laser treatment of astigmatism.

ASTIGMATISM IS A CONDITION THAT MAY BE PRESENT AT BIRTH.

Cataracts

A cataract is a cloudiness in the normally transparent crystalline lens of the eye. This cloudiness can cause a decrease in vision and may lead to eventual blindness. Because cataracts are so common in the elderly, they are thought to be a normal part of the aging process. Of those people who are seventy years of age or older, at least 70 percent are affected by cataracts.

As people age, the lens hardens and changes shape less easily. The materials making up the lens also tend to degenerate. Changes in the proteins, water content, enzymes, and other chemicals of the lens are some of the reasons for the formation of a cataract. Some medical studies have determined that smoking, high alcohol intake, and a diet high in fat all increase the likelihood of cataract formation.

Common symptoms of cataracts include poor central vision, changes in color perception, increased glare from lights, poor vision in sunlight, and the painless onset of blurry or fuzzy vision. If the cataract forms in the area of the lens directly behind the pupil, vision may be significantly impaired. If it occurs on the outer edge or edges of a lens, vision loss is less of a problem.

When a cataract causes only minor visual changes, no treatment may be necessary. When it causes severe vision problems, surgery is the only treatment option. Cataract surgery, in which the lens is removed and a replacement or artificial lens is inserted, is the most frequently performed surgery in the United States. It generally improves vision in over 90 percent of those who undergo the procedure.

Conjunctivitis

Conjunctivitis, commonly known as pinkeye, is an inflammation of the conjunctiva that is usually the result of an infection (viral or bacterial) or an allergic reaction. It is an extremely common eye problem because the conjunctiva is continually exposed to microorganisms and environmental agents that can cause infections or allergic reactions. If caused by an infection, conjunctivitis is extremely contagious and can be easily transmitted to others during close physical contact.

Conjunctivitis caused by a viral infection (such as a cold) is marked by mild to severe discomfort in one or both eyes; redness in the eye or eyes; swelling of the eyelids; and a watery, yellow, or green discharge. Symptoms of bacterial conjunctivitis include redness, swelling, a puslike discharge, and crusty eyelids upon awakening. Conjunctivitis caused by wind, smoke, dust, pollen, or grass has symptoms ranging from itching and redness to a mucus discharge.

In most cases, warm compresses applied to the affected eye several times a day may help to reduce discomfort. In cases caused by a bacterial infection, an antibiotic eye ointment or eye drops may be prescribed. For conjunctivitis caused by an allergic reaction, cool compresses may be applied to the affected eye. Antihistamine drugs and eye drops may also be prescribed.

If treated properly, viral or bacterial conjunctivitis usually clears in ten to fourteen days. Conjunctivitis caused by an allergic reaction should clear up once the allergen (substance causing the allergic reaction) is removed.

Farsightedness

Farsightedness, known formally as hyperopia, is a condition of the eye where incoming rays of light reach the retina before they converge to form a focused image. While objects far away may be seen clearly, objects close up cannot. Babies are generally born farsighted, but this normally decreases with age as the eye grows.

Light waves from close objects tend to scatter. In order to focus those light waves precisely on the retina, the lens must bulge or become convex. In farsightedness, the lens is flatter than needed for the length of the eyeball. In other words, the eyeball is too short for the curvature of the lens, and the image of a nearby object is focused behind the retina.

People who are farsighted can see far objects clearly because light waves from distant objects approach the eye as parallel rays. The lens does not change its relatively flat shape in order to focus those rays on the retina.

There is no way to prevent farsightedness. Individuals with low to moderate farsightedness can achieve full vision by wearing corrective convex lenses (either eyeglasses or contact lenses). At the beginning of the twenty-first century, surgery to correct farsightedness had not yet been perfected or approved.

Glaucoma

Glaucoma is a serious vision disorder caused by a buildup of aqueous humor, which is prevented for some reason from properly draining. The excessive amount of fluid causes pressure to build up. The high pressure distorts the shape of the optic nerve and destroys the nerve. Destroyed nerve cells result in blind spots in places where the image from the retina is not being transmitted to the brain.

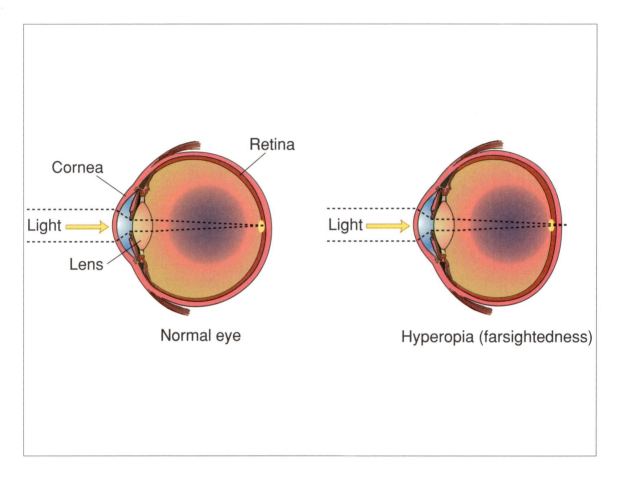

Farsightedness, known formally as hyperopia, is a condition of the eye where incoming rays of light reach the retina before they converge to form a focused image. (Illustration by Electronic Illustrators Group.)

Following cataracts, glaucoma is the second leading cause of blindness in the United States. Over 2 million people in the country have glaucoma. Some 80,000 of those are legally blind as a result. Glaucoma is the most frequent cause of blindness in African Americans. There are many underlying causes and forms of glaucoma, but most causes of the disorder are not known.

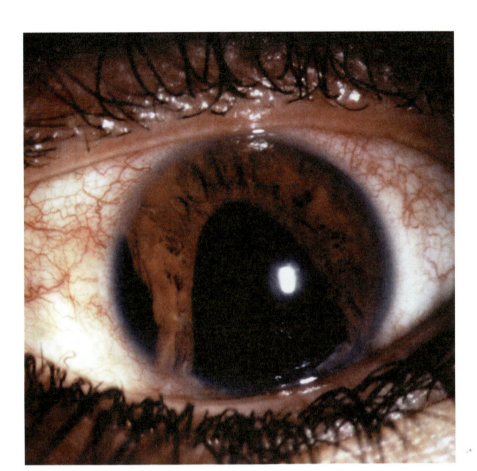

An eye under pressure from glaucoma. This serious vision disorder is caused by a buildup of aqueous humor, which is prevented for some reason from properly draining. (Photograph by SPL. Reproduced by permission of Custom Medical Stock Photo.)

In the most common form of glaucoma, the field of vision is lost over time. Usually the condition starts with a loss of the peripheral (side) vision so that the person does not realize he or she is losing sight until it is too late for treatment.

IN THE MOST COMMON FORM OF GLAUCOMA, THE FIELD OF VISION IS LOST OVER TIME.

If treated early, the condition can be controlled with drugs (typically given as eye drops) that either increase the outflow of aqueous humor or decrease its production. Laser surgery or microsurgery to open up drainage canals can be effective in increasing the outflow of aqueous humor. Although the surgeries are successful, the effects often last less than a year.

There is some evidence that marijuana lowers the pressure caused by excess aqueous humor. However, marijuana has serious side effects and contains carcinogens (cancer-causing substances). The U.S. Food and Drug

Administration and the National Institutes of Health are currently supporting medical research into marijuana and its possible use as a treatment for glaucoma.

Meniere's disease

Meniere's disease is a condition characterized by recurring vertigo or dizziness, hearing loss, and tinnitus (a buzzing or ringing sound in the ears). The disease is named for French physician Prosper Meniere, who first described the illness in 1861. An estimated 3 to 5 million people in the United States are afflicted with the condition. Meniere's disease usually starts between the ages of twenty and fifty, and it affects men and women equally. In about 85 percent of the cases, only one ear is affected.

The disease is an abnormality in the inner ear, specifically within the fluid-filled semicircular canals. A change in the fluid volume within the canals or a swelling of the canals is thought to result in symptoms characteristic of the disease. The cause of Meniere's disease is unknown.

In addition to the symptoms listed above, a person suffering from the disease may feel pain or pressure in the affected ear. Symptoms can appear suddenly and last up to several hours. They can occur as often as daily or as infrequently as once a year. Attacks of severe vertigo can force the sufferer to have to sit or lie down. Headache, nausea, vomiting, or diarrhea may accompany the attack.

There is no cure for Meniere's disease. Certain symptoms of the disease, such as vertigo, nausea, and vomiting, can be controlled with a variety of medications that are either taken orally or injected by needle. If the vertigo attacks are frequent and severe, surgery may be required.

The most common surgical procedure is the insertion of a shunt or small tube to drain some of the fluid from the canal. Unfortunately, this is not a permanent cure in all cases. In another surgical procedure, the nerves responsible for transmitting nerve impulses related to balance are cut. The distorted impulses causing dizziness then no longer reach the brain. This procedure permanently cures the majority of cases, but there is a slight risk that hearing or facial muscle control will be affected.

Nearsightedness

Nearsightedness, known formally as myopia, is the condition of the eye where incoming rays of light are bent too much and converge to form a focused image in front of the retina. While objects close to the eye may be seen clearly, distant objects appear blurred or fuzzy. Nearsightedness affects about 30 percent of the population in the United States.

Light waves from distant objects approach the eye as parallel rays. Normally, the lens does not change its relatively flat shape in order to focus those rays on the retina. In nearsightedness, the lens is thicker and more convex than needed for the length of the eyeball. In other words, the eyeball is too long (oblong instead of the normal almost spherical shape) for the curvature of the lens, and the image of a distant object is focused in front of the retina.

People who are nearsighted can see close objects clearly because light waves from those objects tend to scatter or spread out. The already convex shape of the lens helps to focus those rays on the retina.

NEARSIGHTEDNESS IS CONSIDERED TO BE PRIMARILY A HEREDITARY DISORDER, MEANING THAT IT RUNS IN FAMILIES.

Nearsightedness is considered to be primarily a hereditary disorder, meaning that it runs in families. However, some medical researchers believe that it results from a combination of genetic and environmental factors. The tendency toward being nearsighted may be inherited, but it may actually be brought about by factors such as close work, stress, and eye strain.

People who are nearsighted can (but not always) achieve full vision by wearing corrective concave lenses (either eyeglasses or contact lenses). Another possible treatment for nearsightedness is refractive eye surgery. In most surgical procedures, either a laser is used to vaporize small amounts of tissue from the cornea's surface (thereby flattening it) or a knife is used to cut a circular flap on the cornea, then a laser is used to change the shape of the inner layers of the cornea underneath. Depending on a person's degree of nearsightedness and other factors, refractive surgery can make permanent improvements.

Otitis media

Otitis media is an infection of the middle ear space behind the eardrum. By the age of three, almost 85 percent of all children will have had otitis media at least once. Babies and children between the ages of six months and six years are most likely to develop this type of infection. The most usual times of the year for otitis media to strike are in winter and early spring.

Otitis media is an important problem because it often results in fluid accumulation within the middle ear. The fluid can last for weeks or months, and it can cause significant hearing impairment. When hearing impairment occurs in a young child, it may interfere with the development of normal speech.

Because the middle ear is connected to the throat by the eustachian tube, an infection in the throat may easily reach the middle ear. In fact, most cases of otitis media occur during a bacterial infection of the upper respiratory tract.

Symptoms of otitis media include fever, ear pain, and problems with hearing. When significant fluid is present in the middle ear, pain may increase when a person lies down. Pressure from increased fluid buildup may also perforate or rupture the eardrum, causing bloody fluid or greenish-yellow pus to drip from the ear.

Antibiotics are the treatment of choice for ear infections. The type of drug depends on the type of bacteria causing the infection. Special nose drops, decongestants, or antihistamines may also be prescribed to improve the functioning of the eustachian tube. In rare cases, a procedure to drain the middle ear of pus may be performed.

TAKING CARE: KEEPING THE SPECIAL SENSES HEALTHY

As stated earlier, aging brings about a decline in the functioning of the special senses. Older people often do not see, hear, smell, and taste as well as they once did. This decline is often gradual and, for the most part, affects the quality of an individual's life to a modest degree.

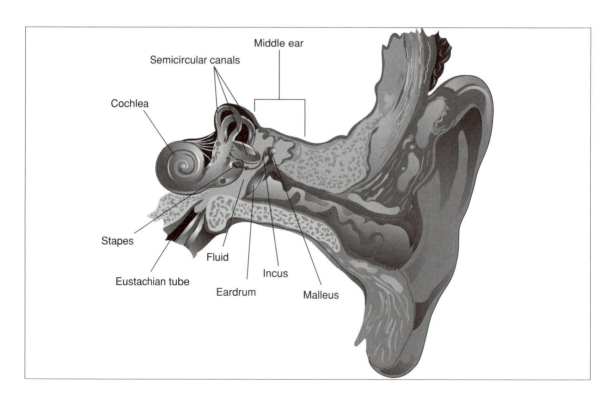

Otitis media is an infection of the middle ear space behind the eardrum. The infection poses a special problem because it often results in fluid accumulation within the middle ear. (Illustration by Electronic Illustrators Group.)

However, neglect of the senses during life can cause a premature decline in their ability to function. Excessive exposure to loud sounds can damage hair cells in the ears that cannot be replaced. Operating modern machinery without wearing protective ear devices or listening to loud music for long periods of time both contribute to hearing loss.

Wearing protective devices over the eyes in most work situations is equally important to prevent injury and possible permanent damage. Eye strain brought on by staring at a computer screen for hours is an increasingly common problem in modern life. To minimize the strain placed on the eyes, an individual should regularly take breaks and walk away from the computer or look away from the screen and focus on some distant object for a while.

Since the special senses are often affected by problems in other parts or systems of the body, it is important to take care of the body as a whole. By getting adequate rest, reducing stress, drinking healthy amounts of good-quality drinking water, not smoking, drinking moderate amounts of alcohol (or not drinking at all), following a proper diet, and exercising regularly, a person can help his or her body to operate at peak efficiency.

FOR MORE INFORMATION

Books

Green, Patrick. *Seeing Is Believing*. Englewood Cliffs, NJ: Silver Burdett Press, 1996.

Kittredge, Mary, and Mary Talbot. *The Senses*. New York: Chelsea House, 1990.

Llamas, Andreu. *Taste*. New York: Chelsea House, 1996.

Parker, Steve. *Senses*. Brookfield, CT: Copper Beech Books, 1997.

Ripoll, Jaime. *How Our Senses Work*. New York: Chelsea House, 1994.

Suzuki, David, and Barbara Hehner. *Looking at Senses*. New York: John Wiley, 1991.

WWW Sites

Mystery of the Senses Activity Guide
http://www.weta.org/weta/education/teachers/itv/mos /mos_guide.html
Site provides information on the five traditional senses and an activity/experiment for the student related to each of those senses. Information based on the NOVA special mini-series *Mystery of the Senses*.

Neuroscience for Kids—The Senses
http://faculty.washington.edu/chudler/chsense.html

The special senses

Highly recommended interactive site provides an extensive amount of information about the five traditional senses. A link to each sense provides further information and experiments/activities to learn more about that particular sense.

Seeing, Hearing, and Smelling the World
http://www.hhmi.org/senses/
Site developed by the Howard Hughes Medical Institute is an extensive educational resource with information about brain function and the senses. Also contains a useful glossary of terms relating to sight, hearing, and smell.

The Way the Eye Works
http://www.eyeinfo.com/wayworks.html
Site provides a straightforward discussion of the way the eye works and what happens when it does not.

Your Gross and Cool Body—Sense of Sight
http://www.yucky.com/body/index.ssf?/systems/sight/
Site presents facts and answers questions about the sense of sight.

Your Gross and Cool Body—Sense of Smell
http://www.yucky.com/body/index.ssf?/systems/smell/
Site presents facts and answers questions about the sense of smell.

Bibliography

BOOKS

Arnau, Eduard, and Parramon Editorial Team. *The Human Body*. Hauppauge, NY: Barron's Educational Series, 1998.

Balkwill, Frances R. *The Incredible Human Body: A Book of Discovery and Learning*. New York: Sterling Publications, 1996.

Beckelman, Laurie. *The Human Body*. Pleasantville, NY: Reader's Digest, 1999.

Beres, Samantha. *101 Things Every Kid Should Know About the Human Body*. Los Angeles, CA: Lowell House, 1999.

Burnie, David. *Concise Encyclopedia of the Human Body*. London, England: DK Publishing, 1995.

Clayman, Charles. *Illustrated Guide to the Human Body*. London, England: DK Publishing, 1995.

Incredible Voyage: Exploring the Human Body. Washington, D.C.: National Geographic Society, 1998.

Marieb, Elaine N. *Anatomy and Physiology Coloring Book: A Complete Study Guide*. Fifth edition. Menlo Park, CA: Addison-Wesley, 1996.

Parker, Steve. *Body Atlas*. London, England: DK Publishing, 1993.

Parker, Steve. *How the Body Works*. Pleasantville, NY: Reader's Digest, 1999.

Parsons, Alexandra. *An Amazing Machine*. New York: Franklin Watts, 1997.

Rose, Marie, and Steve Parker. *The Human Body*. Alexandria, VA: Time-Life, 1997.

Rowan, Peter. *Some Body!* New York: Knopf, 1995.

Bibliography

Smith, Anthony. *Intimate Universe: The Human Body*. New York: Random House, 1999.

Suzuki, David. *Looking at the Body*. New York: John Wiley, 1991.

Walker, Richard. *3D: Human Body*. London, England: DK Publishing, 1999.

Walker, Richard. *The Children's Atlas of the Human Body: Actual Size Bones, Muscles, and Organs in Full Color*. Brookfield, CT: Millbrook Press, 1994.

Walker, Richard, ed. *The Visual Dictionary of Human Anatomy*. London, England: DK Publishing, 1996.

Weiner, Esther. *The Incredible Human Body: Great Projects and Activities that Teach about the Major Body Systems*. New York: Scholastic Trade, 1997.

Whitfield, Philip, ed. *The Human Body Explained: A Guide to Understanding the Incredible Living Machine*. New York: Henry Holt, 1995.

WWW SITES

Please note: Readers should be reminded that Internet addresses are subject to change. Some of the following web sites addresses (and those included at the end of each chapter) may have been removed and new ones added.

AMA Health Insights—Specific Conditions
  http://www.ama-assn.org/consumer/specond.htm
  Part of the American Medical Association's web site, this section provides in-depth information on a number of well known health conditions, focusing on what the condition is, symptoms, diagnosis, treatment, frequently asked questions, and support and information groups.

Anatomy and Physiology
  http://www.msms.doe.k12.ms.us/biology/anatomy/apmain.html
  Site provides varied information on nine human body systems. Although aimed at high school students, material also should be accessible to students in grades immediately below.

Atlas of the Human Body
  http://www.ama-assn.org/insight/gen_hlth/atlas/atlas.htm
  From the American Medical Association, an online atlas of the human body, including images and information on all major systems and organs.

BodyQuest
  http://library.advanced.org/10348/home.html
  Award-winning site is an exploration of human anatomy designed for students aged between eleven and sixteen. Information is present on

major body systems and parts. Site also includes experiments related to specific system or parts, a discussion board, and an interactive quiz section.

Explore the Human Body
http://www.eca.com.ve/wtutor/dani/introweb.htm
Site presents information (along with images) on the human body in seven lessons, each one focusing on a different body system.

How the Body Works
http://KidsHealth.org/parent/healthy/bodyworks.html
Information on certain major systems of the body is present on this site, along with information on topics ranging from nutrition to health problems (all with a focus on kids).

Human Anatomy Central
http://nurse-dk.com/anat/
Recommended site has a human anatomy links database that provides sixty-eight links to sites that provide information on certain body systems and on general anatomy and physiology.

Human Anatomy On-Line
http://www.innerbody.com/htm/body.html
Educational, interactive site presents information on the major systems of the human body with over 100 images and animations of the body.

Human Body
http://www.fcasd.edu/schools/dms/HBody.htm
Site, prepared by and geared toward middle school students, presents extensive information on seven major body systems: Circulatory, digestive, excretory, muscular, nervous, respiratory, and skeletal.

Human Body System Resources on the World Wide Web
http://www.stemnet.nf.ca/CITE/body.htm
Sponsored by Gander Academy of Gander, Newfoundland, Canada, this highly recommended, extensive site features links to ten body systems, each containing numerous links to information on that system and its parts. Site also provides links for general and teacher resources.

Mayo Clinic Health Oasis—Medical Reference Library
http://www.mayohealth.org/mayo/common/htm/library.htm
Site run by the renowned Mayo Clinic provides information on diseases and conditions ranging from arthritis to those affecting the skin.

NOAH: Health Topics and Resources
http://www.noah.cuny.edu/qksearch.html
Site run by the New York Online Access to Health (NOAH) presents extensive information on numerous health topics, from aging and Alzheimer's disease to tuberculosis.

Bibliography

Science Fact File: Inside the Human Body
http://www.imcpl.lib.in.us/nov_ind.htm
Images of and information on seven body systems is present on this site prepared by the Indianapolis-Marion County Public Library.

The Virtual Body
http://www.medtropolis.com/vbody/
Site is an interaction presentation of the human body, containing a series of elaborate displays of the various parts and functions of the human body using Shockwave technology.

United States National Library of Medicine
http://www.nlm.nih.gov/
Home page of the U.S. National Library of Medicine, the world's largest medical library.

Index

Italic type indicates volume number; **boldface** type indicates main entries and their page numbers; (ill.) indicates photos and illustrations.

Index